*Japan's Colonization of Korea*

A STUDY OF THE WEATHERHEAD EAST ASIAN INSTITUTE
COLUMBIA UNIVERSITY

# Japan's Colonization of Korea

## DISCOURSE AND POWER

Alexis Dudden

 UNIVERSITY OF HAWAI'I PRESS

HONOLULU

**Library of Congress Cataloging-in-Publication Data**
Dudden, Alexis.
Japan's colonization of Korea : discourse and power / Alexis Dudden.
     p.  cm. — (The studies of the Weatherhead East Asian Institute)
   Includes bibliographical references and index.
   ISBN 0-8248-2829-1 (hardcover : alk. paper)
   1. Korea—History—Japanese occupation, 1910–1945. 2. Japan—Foreign
relations—Korea. 3. Korea—Foreign relations—Japan. 4. Japan—Foreign
relations—1868–1912. 5. Korea—Foreign relations—1864–1910. 6. Korea—
International status. 7. Law—Japan—History. 8. Law—Korea—History. I. Title.
II. Studies of the Weatherhead East Asian Institute, Columbia University.
   DS916.55.D83 2005
   341.26—dc22

                    2004017575

The Weatherhead East Asian Institute is Columbia University's center for research, publication, and teaching on modern East Asia. The Studies of the Weatherhead East Asian Institute were inaugurated in 1962 to bring to a wider public the results of significant new research on modern and contemporary East Asia.

Designed by the University of Hawai'i Press Design & Production Department

*Printed by The Maple-Vail Manufacturing Group*

*To my mother and father*

# Contents

# Acknowledgments

I am grateful to too many teachers, friends, and family members for these few paragraphs to suffice, and many of these people fall into each category anyway, so my attempts are muddled from the start. I simply wish that I could win the lottery and get everyone together for a "Babette's feast" to thank you all.

Tetsuo Najita is a wonderful historian, and I will always be lucky to call him my adviser. Prasenjit Duara and Bruce Cumings challenged and expanded my questions in ways that I still haven't begun to address, and Norma Field demonstrated the importance of examining the world with compassion at all times. Carol Gluck and Jim McClain were my first teachers of Japan, and in many ways they brought this book into being. Bill Sibley showed that without friendship there is no use for any of it, and Igarashi Akio remains too generous with time, space, and sake to thank in words.

Any mistakes are, of course, mine, but Andre Schmid is responsible for this book. As I was blithely heading off to graduate school, he told me that I would never understand modern Japan without studying Korea. He was right, of course, but I didn't know why until Han Suk-Jung became my teacher and friend and explained to me the human dimensions of Japan's empire and the world in its wake. In this regard, I will also always look forward to learning from Melissa Wender.

Geoff Klingsporn, Mark Schmeller, Alexandra Gillen, and Linda Zuckerman were the best friends, critics, and sparring partners that anyone could hope for during the delights of writing a dissertation. Chris Hill, Sarah Thal, Jonathan Field, Billy Hinton, Paul Gilmore, Sarah Rose, Kevin Bogart, Mark Bradley, Lydia Liu, Namhee Lee, David Ambaras, David Leheny, Angus Lockyer, Doug Howland, Tanaka Shinichi, Rob Oppenheim, Amanda Seaman, Sarah Frederick, Kris Troost, Karen Wigen, Mark Lincicome, Andy Gordon, Mark Selden, and especially Mark Caprio and Mike Molasky offered advice, music, and humor throughout this project, and the big Australian cane toad, Hayden Lesbirel, gave strength and friendship as things got a little more exciting than usual toward its end.

Colleagues and students at Connecticut College have been tremendously helpful during a series of tar pits encountered on the road toward this book, and I am especially grateful to Lisa Wilson, Marc Forster, Cathy Stock, Sarah Queen, Tristan Borer, Janet Gezari, Lorraine McKinney, Alex Hybel, Tony Crubaugh, and Jeff Lesser. Support from Connecticut College as well as the Fulbright board, the Mellon Foundation, the University of Chicago, and the NEH made it all possible. My late colleague at Seoul National University, Kim Jangkwon, and the students in our seminar suffered through the manuscript's final stages with me, and I will always be especially thankful to them, as well as to Professor Kim Ki-seok, for inviting me there.

In uncanny ways, Sam Perry has been with me since the conception of these pages, and there will always be a Sam Suite waiting for you, provided, of course, that we can race off at a moment's notice to places of nationalist frenzy wherever we are. Kobayashi Tsuyoshi, Takahashi Jin, Sakamoto Ayumi, the Yoshidas, and Kodama Nobuko made making this book a lot more fun. So did Song Daehon, and I promise that the next one won't make your eyes go round in circles. What he doesn't know, though, is how much better the book is now than it was before Madge Huntington, Joe Parsons, Suzy Kim, Karen Kodner, Ann Ludeman, and my excellent editor, Patricia Crosby, took charge.

My Japanese parents, the Ichinoses, have been a home away from home for years, and my grandmother, Muzzie, was patient throughout. Adrianne and Arthur Dudden have been supportive beyond understanding, and I dedicate the following pages to them.

Finally, there is no way to thank Robert Gay. We'll just have to have dinner together.

*Japan's Colonization of Korea*

# *Introduction*

*T*ranslating international law into Japanese and using its terms in practice were among the most transformative aspects of Japan's Meiji era (1868–1912). Doing so gave Japanese rulers a new method of intercourse with the United States and Europe and enabled them to reorder the vocabulary of power within Asia. Moreover, this discourse inscribed the legitimacy of Japan's empire from the time of its creation.

Although historians of modern Japan have long studied the staggering changes in Japan's social, political, and economic fabric at the turn of the last century, they have paid less attention to the internal discourses that arose as Japan's leaders described the country anew. To neglect these discourses is to ignore a critical element in the making of imperial Japan. The island nation had intentionally isolated itself for centuries, and the Meiji government used new discourses so that Japan would make new international sense, at a time when *not* making sense in this manner rendered a nation ripe for colonization. In the terminology of the day, the world's emerging colonial powers viewed countries that shunned specific forms of international relations—particularly commercial relations—as "backward" or "barbaric."

In the face of new global terms of power, Tokyo policymakers created language to describe Japan's rapid industrialization, mass militarization, and territorial expansion. The challenge for these officials was to craft a vocabulary that was consistent both with traditional Japanese practices and Japan's new aspirations, and that was, furthermore, intelligible to an international audience. The encoders of Japan's new place in the world never defined themselves collectively, but their efforts converged along mutual lines. The resulting discourses captured foreign terms to the fullest extent possible and presented Japan's new policies as legitimate. In the process, the policymakers created perceptions of the justness of imperialist practices around the world at the time. Thus, rather than distinguishing the Japanese empire from others, these efforts confirmed Japan's place in the international history of global empire.

Unlike other diplomatic histories and imperialism studies, this book traces the construction and dispersion of terms that are too often considered transhistorical. Many scholars have ignored Japan's discursive shift in this regard by assuming the naturalness of concepts such as sovereignty and independence, or they have blurred Japan's intellectual history by describing the transition as yet another example of the "copycat Japanese." Writing treaties and conducting diplomacy was by no means a new practice in Meiji Japan, but executing such transactions in the language of international law required new techniques. The scholars and state aggrandizers who translated international terms into Japanese did not create the imperialist nation that Japan would become. Their fluent use of this discourse, however, legitimated Japan's imperialist claims within Japan and abroad.

The Meiji regime's incorporation of Hokkaido (1869), Okinawa (1871), Taiwan (1895), and the southern part of Sakhalin (1905) into the Japanese empire laid the groundwork for later imperialist expansion. Although Japan did not officially annex Korea until 1910, throughout the late nineteenth century, Meiji rulers in Korea vied doggedly with Europe and the United States over strategic privileges, mining and railroad rights, and souls to proselytize. Because it was important for Japan to engage other nations in competition, Meiji officials recognized that the need was more critical for Japan's new policies toward Korea to make sense than for the country's other colonial schemes. Within Japan's expanding empire, therefore, the annexation of Korea significantly established the *perceived* legitimacy of Japan as a modern imperial nation. During the years between Japan's opening of Korea in 1876—an opening that self-consciously mimicked the U.S. opening of Japan in 1853—and Japan's annexation of Korea in 1910, Japan's legal theorists, politicians, and translators defined the country's Korean policy as legitimate under international law. The international arena's quick and formally uncontested sanction of this act in 1910 confirmed the significance of these endeavors to Japan's future empire.

In the chapters that follow, I examine the discursive aspects of Japan's annexation of Korea, with particular attention to the international legality of that moment. The international politics of imperialism taught Meiji state aggrandizers that, if they were to gain full legitimacy for Japan as a colonizing nation, they needed to define their policies in mutually referential terms of law. Colonizing politics were above all a reflexive process; therefore, even before Japan annexed Korea in 1910, its leaders determined to demonstrate that their nation had embarked on a legal and often legislating mission—a *mission législatrice*—to Korea. Japan's endeavor to make its annexation of Korea *legal* in the eyes of the international community brings into relief a forgotten, yet highly significant, component of the process of Japan's development as an imperialist power at the outset of the twentieth century.

History largely recounts the dominator's story at the expense of the dominated. Nevertheless, looking at it here brings to light numerous overlooked presumptions of the so-called international system while describing Japan's engagement with that system, and it is only by following this story that it is possible to imagine writing the script anew for a more balanced world.

Japanese and Korean readers are sufficiently aware of this topic and are not surprised by the question, "Was Japan's annexation of Korea legal?" In fact, they might be tired of it. A reader from a so-called Western narrative tradition, however, might be taken aback to learn that this question not only resonates in daily life in these countries but also periodically explodes into major diplomatic and political incidents. Such a reader might be tempted to dismiss the problem as local or, worse, "Asian," when in fact it entwines with histories of imperialism around the world, raising questions about how related issues linger in contemporary international relations.

Since the collapse of Japan's empire in 1945, Japan's and Korea's respective stances on the question of the 1910 annexation have been, at different moments and on different levels, at the core of national self-definition. To varying degrees, the official Japanese response maintains that the annexation was legal. The "party line" necessitates that Japan simply did what the other imperialist nations of the world were doing at the time. The logic is not wrong per se, but almost sixty years after the end of the empire this line of argument merely perpetuates the "authorized" view of the twentieth century, which continues to present Japan as a victim of the times. Conversely, and almost without exception, the official Korean position is that the annexation in 1910 was illegal. This position, however, is made more complex by the fact that South Korea and North Korea—two governments that remain officially at war today—speak in unison on an issue that arguably contributed to the civil war that divided them. One of the most cogent points of agreement in current Korean reunification talks categorically declares Japan's past colonization of the Korean peninsula as "illegal," thus sidetracking the sticky issue regarding which Koreans benefited from Japan's rule.

Unfortunately, therefore, the debate over annexation follows an endless Möbius strip, but it is vital to consider this seemingly endless question anew because the dispute lies at the heart of many postcolonial and postenslavement claims now heard throughout the world. Simply put, it is necessary to alter the question and examine what constituted *legal* at the time in order to understand what was upheld as legitimate practice.

Several groundbreaking works have analyzed Japan's annexation of Korea and Korea's place in Japan's empire, but the field continues to be ensnared in a logic that measures Japanese imperialism against apparent Western norms.[1] The failure to incorporate Japan's empire into general theories of imperialism remains a fatal flaw of such studies and of international studies in general.[2] Specialists on imperialism and Japan alike stumble by overlooking the Japanese empire or assuming that anyone who is interested can plug the empire's history into European theoretical models, which sustains the idea that Japan's experience is somehow less than that of places where history is presumed to have occurred normally. It is possible, however, to circumvent this problem by analyzing how the terms of international law entered modern Japan's discourse of power. The thinkers and translators who refracted international law into Japanese knew that its original terms were European, but many believed that making these terms Japanese would define Japan as a member of the "civilized world."

By illustrating the fusion of power and words, this book aims to confound the view that only military strength truly prevails in power politics. Within an astonishingly short period of time, the Meiji government wrested the privilege of defining legal concepts away from China and conferred on Japan the status of being Asia's twentieth-century arbiter of power. The international colonial order of knowledge legitimated Japan's annexation of Korea and gave basis to the racially charged assumptions of international exchange at the time. In chapter 1, I describe the global atmosphere that declared Japan the legal ruler of Korea. Chapter 2 frames the significance of the discourse of international law with a brief intellectual history of how its terms became Japanese. In chapter 3, I bring together these discussions by analyzing how Meiji Japan's leaders embedded this discourse into legal precedent for Japan, particularly in the country's relations with Korea. Chapter 4 considers how the Meiji government penalized critics at home and abroad when their understandings challenged state definitions. And, in chapter 5, I analyze the relationship between perceptions of Japan as a legal nation and the government's reordering of the terms of jurisprudence within Japan and Korea, focusing in particular on how such perceptions related to extraterritorial privilege.

In a fulsome concluding section, I square the book's examination of the legality of Japan's imperialist designs by discussing the place of colonial policy studies in Japan at the time. In so doing, I demonstrate how this new discipline further created a common sense that Japan's empire accorded to knowledgeable practice. Although the international arena sanctioned Japan's annexation of Korea in 1910, later on, when Japanese leaders maintained that their empire's extension into parts of north China was similarly legitimate, Japan's former allies began to oppose Japanese imperialism and militarism. In the argument of the day, relations devolved into a devastating but inevitable war to stop Japanese expansion, and the book closes on this point of tension.

Although it is tempting to declare colonial conquest illegal at any time, doing so will not calm the memories of colonial oppression or eradicate the existence of related and ongoing forms of domination. To these ends, we continue to need a more sophisticated understanding of how power works. The pages that follow explore how imperialism's apologists described the legality of their enterprise, attempting to weigh the implications of their actions in the international arena of the early twentieth century and beyond.

# CHAPTER 1

# ILLEGAL KOREA

𝐼n the summer of 1907, the world declared Korea illegal. The previous autumn, Emperor Kojong of Korea sent three representatives on his behalf to the Second International Conference on Peace at The Hague. Their mission was to register the emperor's protest against Japan's 1905 protectorate agreement over Korea. According to the well-known account of their travels overland to Europe, Yi Sangsŏl, Yi Jun, and Yi Ŭijong reached the Netherlands in late June 1907, during the second week of the conference. They carried a letter from their emperor detailing the invalidity of the protectorate and demanding international condemnation of Japan.[1] Although the three young men appealed to diplomats from countries that had long-standing relations with Korea, none except the Russian envoy gave them more than a passing notice. Not coincidentally, of course, Japan's shocking military victory against Russia two years earlier made St. Petersburg eager to support any protest of Japan.

On arriving at The Hague, the Korean emissaries confronted a belief system to which even the Russians had acquiesced. According to the terms of international law—the same ones used to script the conference at The Hague and legitimate the participant states—the Koreans could not legally attend the forum. The Portsmouth Treaty of 1905 secured peace between Japan and Russia, granted Japan the privilege to "protect its interests in Korea," and garnered a Nobel Peace Prize for President Theodore Roosevelt, who orchestrated the negotiations.[2] Shortly thereafter, the Second Japan-Korea Agreement named Korea a Japanese protectorate and gave international legal precedent to Japan's control over Korea's foreign affairs.[3] As a result, the Koreans could not conduct their own foreign relations. Instead, all of Korea's foreign affairs would be con-

*proconate*

ducted by Tokyo. According to international law, without Japan, Korea no longer existed in relation to the rest of the world.

At The Hague, the Koreans' appeal was collectively shunned by the delegates sent from the forty-three countries discussing world peace. The Koreans' attempt to protest—to tell their story—interfered with the world order that the delegates sought to legitimate. According to anthropologist Michel-Rolph Trouillot, some historical moments run so deeply against prevailing ideologies that they are "unthinkable." In these situations, Trouillot notes, "worldview wins over the facts."[4]

Because the Korean envoys demanded rectification in the very terms that oppressed them, they were unable to bring the international community to recognize Korea as an independent country. As a result, their story was "unthinkable" to the organizers of the conference. Conversely, recognition of the Koreans' claims to independence would have dismantled the worldview that not only determined Korea's dependence on Japan but also legitimated the conference's claim to define the meaning of international peace. In practice, of course, this definition of peace meant that certain countries legally controlled and colonized others.

In the early twentieth century, colonization was legal under international law in the way that slavery was once legal. The politics and laws of imperialism resembled the politics and laws of the slave trade and arguably developed from them.[5] In the mid-nineteenth century, many European and American legal theorists viewed slavery as unfortunate. Nonetheless, they maintained that the practice was for the good of the slaves and that the world's emergent colonial powers operated the slave trade in accordance with prevailing international laws. A large body of literature in political economy and social theory supported these claims. Several decades later, the avatars of imperialism framed the central provisions of international law in ways that defended their activities. It is not surprising then that they, too, relied on a substantial literature to support their belief in the moral value of annexations, protectorates, and spheres of influence. Like the environment embracing slavery, the terrain that grounded imperialism reveals how the politically powerful determined what was legal and protected that legality to uphold their power and self-interests.

A discourse I call "enlightened exploitation" informed this historical atmosphere and encompassed the vocabulary of laws and diplomatic agreements, as well as journalistic accounts describing international relations.[6] Various dimensions of this discourse are brought into relief throughout this book, but for now the concept of the "protectorate" can introduce the reach of enlightened exploitation. A diplomatic protocol signed at the Berlin Conference in 1885 defined navigation rights in the Belgian Congo, thus establishing the concept of a "protectorate" as a particular piece of territory governed in part by an alien regime.[7] Of equal importance at the time, race-driven theories of civilization more generally shaped a Euro-American political climate that ordered a taxonomy of the peoples of the world. So-called civilized governments predicated their claims to legitimacy on conquering and ruling so-called barbaric ones; such governments also infused their claims with political and social theories derived in part from nascent evolutionary sciences. A regime was civilized only if it could claim the ability to transform an uncivilized people.[8] The logic of the politics of enlightened exploitation can be described as the practice of legalizing the claim to protect a place inhabited by people who were defined as incapable of becoming civilized on their own. It was understood, of course, that the protecting regime had access to the material and human resources of the place it protected. Ultimately, the ability to control colonial space defined a nation as "sovereign" and "independent." Regimes that sought to dominate others legitimated their actions in terms consistent with this intellectual order. Declaring a territory a protectorate did not merely apply a euphemism to the action of taking over; it established a legal precedent for defining certain people unfit to rule themselves.[9]

Although Japan did not annex Korea until 1910, the fallout from The Hague affair enabled the Japanese colonial regime in Seoul to eviscerate the Korean state by the end of 1907. The judgment at The Hague in the summer of 1907—more specifically, the international turning of a deaf ear to the Koreans—allowed Japanese officials to broaden control of the country on which they and their predecessors had been encroaching for almost fifty years.

In 1876, Japan followed the international pattern of forcibly opening countries to trade by securing the Treaty of Kanghwa with the Chosŏn government of Korea. As a result of this treaty, Japanese merchants and diplomats moved into extraterritorial settlements in Korea that were legally determined. Following another international practice, Tokyo stationed troops to protect these compounds. The same troops later went to war with China (1894–1895) and Russia (1904–1905) in the name of defending Japanese and Korean national interests. When Japan fought and defeated Russia, it did so, Japan claimed, in order to liberate Korea. Thus, because of its apparent beneficence, Japan received Korea as its protectorate from the international community.

The 1907 Korean mission to The Hague to protest this prize, therefore, embarrassed Japanese officials in front of the nations whose policies they were emulating. They demanded the abdication of the Korean emperor on learning of his secret emissaries. The Japanese officials used pliable Korean government ministers such as Yi Wanyong and Sŏng Bongjun—men often known in Korean history books as "traitors for all times"—by assigning them to urge Emperor Kojong to place his son, Sunjong, on the throne.[10] Sunjong, the final sovereign of Korea's Chosŏn era (1392–1910), embodied "puppet sovereignty" as much as if not more than the better known "Last Emperor" of China, Pu Yi, whom the Japanese controlled in Manchuria in the 1930s.[11] In 1907, the "last emperor" of Korea condemned the men who had gone to The Hague on behalf of his father.

Japan's strong response to the Korean mission centered international attention on Seoul. Comments to the press by Japanese leaders in the summer of 1907 revealed an official self-consciousness that Japan's policies were on display. On July 25, Foreign Minister Hayashi Gonosuke told a reporter from the Associated Press that the Korean mission to The Hague was not a consideration in Japan's desiring a new ruler in Korea, or, for that matter, control over Korea's judiciary. He emphasized instead that "the provisions of the new agreement [July 1907] were not anticipated in the protectorate agreement in 1905, and they complete our project. The Korean deputation to The Hague was inherently unimportant."[12] In short, Hayashi's narrative explained Japan's forced abdication of Korea's sovereign and its takeover of domestic laws as standard operating procedures in colonial politics. His detailed explanations were perhaps unnecessary, since the *Times* of London had already given its blessing: "We ourselves have had such long experience of dealing with barbaric or semi-barbaric potentates that we can easily appreciate the position of the Japanese in Korea."[13]

The Meiji government made the most of the momentum behind its actions, displaying Japan's increasingly exploitative relations with Korea as the natural course of events. Despite the broad implications of the new 1907 agreement between Japan and Korea, no official challenge to its legitimacy arose in the international arena.[14] As the world watched and commented on Emperor Kojong's abdication, Japan's Resident General Itō Hirobumi signed papers with Korean Prime Minister Yi Wanyong, transferring all judicial powers in Korea to Japan's command. In the atmosphere that sustained Japan as the legal guardian of Korea, there was only praise for Japan's further means of control: "Under the new Convention, the Marquis Ito's first measure aims at securing life and property in Korea by substituting pure and competent tribunals of justice for the present and unskilled law Courts."[15]

Prior to the 1907 agreement, the Japanese government had not publicized the contents of high-level diplomatic exchanges between Japan and Korea. In contrast, from the moment that Itō and Yi affixed their seals to the new convention, officials distributed copies to Japanese and foreign papers.[16] In 1905, the small portion of the world that bothered to notice Japan's protectorate agreement over Korea upheld that action, and Korea lost its international existence.[17] In 1907, a much larger audience watched what Japan was doing, and it applauded Tokyo's removal of Korea's internal existence. Although a Korean sovereign still sat on the throne, and although the Japanese government demurred that Korea was not *officially* a Japanese colony, Japanese administrators in Seoul gained control of every office that once constituted a functioning Korea.

The international atmosphere that declared Korea an illegal nation and Japan a legal one bred itself on the erasure of certain countries, similar to the political economy of slavery that labeled some humans the owners and traders of other humans. The discourse of enlightened exploitation gave these actions normative support. Literary critic Nishikawa Nagao has explained that Meiji-era politicians understood that the terms of international law generated a world in which "only European-style, civilized countries were seen as sovereign states. Only these states—the subjects *(shutai)* of international law —had the right to intervene in or conquer undeveloped or semi-developed countries."[18]

During the Meiji period, Japanese state aggrandizers worked to embed Japan as a subject in this international formula of power. At the time, international laws justified colonial control over territory and people as a modern form of enslavement. These laws were upheld and practiced as Japan's law over Korea. When the time came for Japanese officials to appear on the world stage, they knew to manipulate unprincipled Korean politicians (such as Yi Wanyong and Sŏng Bongjun) to do the historically damning work of forcing Kojong to abdicate; by these actions, they functioned as imperialist powers everywhere did, relying on local officials for corrupt tasks. These moves by Japanese officials affirmed the smug "appreciation" felt in England and elsewhere concerning the self-justifying morality of enslaving certain places and people. By such logic, certain countries were not fit to rule themselves, and there was little regard for the coercive methods employed to bring about these conditions.

Most important, Japan's erasure of Korea blended into the era's other "thinkable" stories. With odd resonance for today's world, one commentator at the time noted that "the oppressed nationalities of the world [who made their voices heard at The Hague conference] . . . were the Albanians, Armenians, Bosnians, Coreans, Georgians, and Herzegovinians . . . and individual appeals were received from Boers, Egyptians, and Irishmen."[19] The noticeable similarities between the "oppressed nationalities of the world" at the beginning of the twentieth century and also the beginning of the twenty-first century convince me that it remains worthwhile to examine how the international arena of 1907 disqualified certain groups from membership and made them legally dependent on those that did belong. This process is, in a word, the focus of this book.

This historical discourse, defining some nations as legal subjects and others as their objects of control, became entwined with the development of global empire. As discourses do, this one worked recursively to confirm itself. Moreover, this discourse upheld imperialist politics as legitimate practice and, in doing so, advanced the expansion of empire. Although it would be a mistake to say that the international terms of enlightened exploitation made nations imperialist, these terms did legitimate imperialist policies as legal. In the age of empire, the nations that defined the language of international relations—and only those nations—were its legal subjects. All the other nations were relegated to legal obscurity.

By way of introducing the environment surrounding Japan's engagement with this discourse of power, this chapter examines world reaction to the failed Korean protest at The Hague. As this historical moment makes clear, the legal erasure of a country and its people could be made legitimate in a relatively open fashion. Beginning in the 1950s with historian Hilary Conroy, American, Japanese, and Korean scholars have described what is now known as "the Korean incident at The Hague" as it played out in official and unofficial channels.[20] Although discussing some of the same materials Conroy and others have considered, my reading is unlike theirs in highlighting how the terms of enlightened exploitation had become mundane by the time the Koreans sought to enter the international arena. This international discourse effectively prevented the Koreans from registering their nation as a legal subject, and, through the circular nature of these terms, the Koreans' attempt at legitimacy only reinforced the judgment of Korea as illegitimate. Looking at the event this way illustrates how it was legal for the world to declare Korea illegal, thus providing a deeper understanding of what power meant at a given time and place and how it operated.

## JAPAN ON DISPLAY

In August 1898, Russia's Tsar Nicholas II expressed a desire for the "Powers" (as the world's colonizing nations called themselves collectively at the time) to hold large-scale arms-reduction talks. The conference's sponsors chose The Hague as their venue, and the world's first self-proclaimed International Conference on Peace opened on 18 May the following year.[21] The Russian government decided that only countries with diplomatic representatives in St. Petersburg could attend the conference, thus from the outset limiting participation to states classified as independent and sovereign by international law. In his assessment of the conference several years later, William Hull pointed out that from the start the tsar made random exceptions: "This general rule was not observed, however, in some notable instances, both in extending the invitation to some powers not represented at the Russian Court (for example, Luxemburg, Montenegro, and Siam), and in withholding it from some others which were so represented (for example, the South African Republic). The Russian government did not offer any official statement of the reasons for its inclusions and exclusions."[22]

The arbitrary nature of the invitation process is significant. From its founding moments, the organizers of a conference that was a forerunner of today's United Nations made choices that represented de facto the legitimacy and illegitimacy of certain regimes. No other body rivaled The Hague group's powerful claim to decide international policy, and its decisions were legal because no alternate court existed. If any nation lesser than one of the "Powers" tried to call a decision into question, it would only define that regime as illegal or—in today's parlance—as a "rogue" or "outlaw" state.

While the delegates to the 1899 conference congratulated themselves over the state of civilization, issued platitudes about peace, and motioned for another meeting, the Boer War and Japan's war with Russia got in the way of their proceedings and forced the participants to postpone the Second International Conference on Peace until June 1907. The list of delegates attending the second meeting updated the roster of the world's legal nations and set new limits on the international arena. There were twenty parties from Europe and nineteen from the Americas. Persia, Siam, China, and Japan comprised Asia.

Apparently, no legal nation existed in Africa, a decision confirmed by the group's refusal of the envoy from Egypt.

In 1899, representatives had gathered at a small royal palace on the outskirts of the city, but in 1907 organizers felt they needed a larger building, both for the increased number of delegates and the grander expectations of the meeting itself. As the president of the conference, Alexander Nelidoff, proclaimed, "All friends of civilization are following with sympathetic interest," the meeting opened in an austere, thirteenth-century hunting lodge, the aristocratic Ridderzaal (Hall of Knights).[23] Jonkheer van Tets, the Dutch foreign minister, told a reporter that "the hall seemed to us to be worthy to receive the Second Peace Conference," and an editorial in the *Times* of London called the conference "a contemporary Areopagus," referring to the ancient Athenian council.[24] Van Tets also suggested that the building would "acquire a fresh historical fame which will exceed the limits of [its] national history now that within its walls the most completely representative assembly of countries in the world . . . will have been deliberated."[25] The meeting's promoters assumed that the authority of their actions made their endeavors legitimate, and on the conference's opening day, an article in the *Times* described the scene:

> [The Ridderzaal], the meeting place of the Conference, dates from the 13th century and was built by William II, Count of Holland and King of the Romans. It is a long, high-roofed edifice and resembles a church with its two round towers flanking the principal entrance. The interior is imposing by reason of height and simplicity. The massive crossed beams that support the roof are of unpolished wood, and the only decoration of the whitewashed walls consists in the arms of the different States of the Netherlands emblazoned on the stone supports of the roofing. The floor of the hall is fitted throughout with desks and benches covered with green velvet.[26]

Comparing the structure to a church gave a higher moral foundation to the convention. Plush benches dissected the holy space and mapped out the hierarchy of national delegates. As at the first conference, the common language was French, and nations were listed alphabetically by their French names. Hull noted that even "the alphabet favored the large powers by bringing their delegates to the front . . . the Germans, Americans, and British occupied the first row of seats—still in alphabetical order."[27] By July, coal magnate Andrew Carnegie was so pleased with what he was reading in the papers and hearing from friends that he gave the Dutch government one-and-a-quarter million dollars to construct a new and permanent building for future meetings.[28]

Japanese delegates came daily to the Hall of Knights, resplendent in their morning coats and top hats, and participating as subjects in international law. The Korean envoys, on the other hand, even in their suits, could not exist in the same space, and their protest does not appear in the official proceedings.[29] This moment is crucial to understanding how the erasure of Korea took effect. No judge at The Hague sat behind a bench to try a case called "the legality of Korea." But then again, no judge had tried the infamous country-swapping cases two years earlier: the Taft-Katsura meeting (July 1905), in which the United States and Japan traded the Philippines for Korea; and the Second Anglo-Japan Alliance (August 1905), in which Japan and England exchanged Korea for India and Burma.[30] The delegates who determined the survival of Korea officially represented their governments, but the authority they summoned to erase Korea transcended national levels and rested with the presumed power of international law. When the Korean delegates tried to make their appeal in the summer of 1907, the faceless judge of this higher authority no longer recognized the existence of their country. The law's earthly representatives—the "knights" at The Hague—ignored the Korean plea, and they made their decision a legal determination.

Journalists from countries whose delegates sat at the front of the conference sensationalized the Korean mission and in general agreed with their nation's representatives about the nonviability of Korea. Their dispatches worked to further inscribe the legitimacy of The Hague delegates' determination about Korea vis-à-vis Japan for readers around the world. The news generated constant publicity about the conference itself, ensuring the "historic fame" its leaders craved.[31] Both the press coverage of the Korean envoys' attempted entry to the conference and Japan's reaction reveals how commonplace the discourse of enlightened exploitation had become.

The tonal similarity of newspaper articles throughout the so-called civilized world demonstrates that a specific discourse had arisen with the development of knowledge about colonization. David Spurr has described this as a "series of colonial discourses marked by internal repetition, but not by all-encompassing totality."[32] The notion of "internal repetition" usefully explains how, for example, newspapers around the world printed articles that communicated the justness of Japan's control of Korea, a topic that had little concerned them before. A rhetoric of social Darwinism permeated news stories throughout Europe and the United States and sustained the racially driven credo preached by champions of enlightened exploitation: a vigorous people legitimately controlled a stagnant one. Only Russian newspapers condemned the Japanese government's handling of the Korean secret mission; as mentioned above, this was not surprising in light of lingering animosities from the countries' recent war to gain control of Korea.[33]

In newspapers in London, New York, Paris, Frankfurt, and Shanghai, the discourse of enlightened exploitation colored descriptions of the Korean ruler, the Korean people, and how Koreans contrasted with Japanese. In this era of purposeful progress, Emperor Kojong was, for example, "an Oriental despot of the weaker type."[34] Korea was "amongst the most antiquated of Oriental States a by-word for immovable and unreasonable conservatism."[35] In London, the Korean emperor was seen as a "backward Sovereign," "foolish," and "fatuous."[36] In Paris, he was "a sovereign out of an operetta . . . incapable of initiative, energy, [or] will."[37] After the Japanese secured Kojong's abdication, the *New York Times* condescended, "Upon the whole, the poor man is in a less pitiable state now."[38] A report from Frankfurt declared that the new emperor had "a character as tractable as India rubber."[39] A Frenchman confirmed this view: "[Sunjong] used to follow his father about like a dog, never showed the slightest energy or initiative."[40] In the racial typology underpinning the category of "Oriental despot," reporters defined the Korean people as one with their sovereign. An editorial in Paris's *Le Temps* declared that the "passivity of the Korean people" rendered them "incapable of all sustained exertion, of all methodical activity."[41] Even in an article somewhat sympathetic to the plight of the Koreans, their primary defect—according to world opinion—surfaced: "There is, to be sure, much evidence to show that the Koreans, at least the ruling caste, are incapable of carrying on a civilized government."[42] The vocabulary used in the *New York Tribune* was clearest of all: "The Law of survival of the fittest prevails among states as well as among plants and animals. Corea has been conspicuously unfit."[43]

The decision by The Hague delegates to deny the Koreans a voice at the peace conference proved sufficient for the journalists, who described Korea as a nation Japan should control. Reporters at once explained and confirmed the common understanding of this determination. In the logic of the survival of the fittest, Japan's control of Korea was "nothing else than the . . . dominance of a people incredibly clever and strenuous over one which has never stirred out of the sloth of ages."[44] Informed assumptions about colonizer and colonized were manifest in comparisons of the Koreans and the Japanese. These descriptions placed Japan alongside European countries as a colonizing nation. In light of Korea's past, *Le Temps* praised, "All travelers and those knowledgeable about Korea are amazed at what has been accomplished in the country since the Japanese established themselves there."[45] A German newspaper held "a benevolent admiration for the imperturbable decision with which Japan [was] asserting her treaty rights."[46] In a somewhat cynical, yet revealing, comment, the *New York Times* wrote, "Ito may say of Korea what Metternich boasted of Italy, that he has reduced it to a 'geographical expression.'"[47] An English-language paper in Shanghai echoed these sentiments: "In the best interests of the world at large such nations [Korea] had better be wiped off the map, and we do not blame Japan for wiping Korea off the map."[48] Perhaps Britain's extensive treaty connections with the Japanese government encouraged the *Times* to express the fullest esteem for Japan's actions, affirming that Japan's "reputation as a colonizing Power [was] at stake."[49] Popular international approval for Japan's increasing control over Korea demonstrates that, by 1907, Meiji leaders had won support for their policies in Korea, legitimating the ongoing process of "wiping Korea off the map."

The major Japanese newspapers chronicled The Hague affair largely by echoing the international press and government decrees.[50] A few editorials elaborated on Japan's actions as a legal matter, such as Nakamura Shinichi's pedantic explanation of how Japan's Korea policy fit into the international system of protectorate arrangements.[51] And although most of Japan's domestic press followed events such as Kojong's forced abdication with studious understatement, one paper refused to toe the party line and ridiculed the entire affair. In a series of cartoons printed between 18 July and 3 August 1907, the *Yorozu Chōhō* portrayed what it saw as the absurdity of the Japanese government's efforts to control its "reputation as colonizing Power."[52] Kuroiwa Ruikō, the editor of the paper, was known not so much for consistent political views as for being categorically anti-elitist, and the drawings in his paper reflect this by lampooning the self-declared altruism of the international political order and Japan's desire to exist as a subject in that order.[53] The paper's cartoonists depicted Japan's hypocrisy in wanting to be a member of a group that justified the superiority of nations in ways that would—if pushed—exclude Japan from membership.[54]

The first cartoon in the series (Fig. 1) shows Japanese Resident General Itō Hirobumi dressed in a kimono, like an old woman, and chasing after a ragged Korean man. The Korean figure, drawn with the body of a small child and wearing no shoes, might represent either the emperor or one of the envoys sent to The Hague.[55] Itō Hirobumi (1841–1909), the "George Washington of Japan," was one of the chief architects of the Meiji government and arguably the most powerful politician of the era. The cartoonist nonetheless saw him and his pretensions as ridiculous. As the kimono-clad Itō chases the diminutive Korean, the Korean runs to four tall men in suits (Euro-Americans), standing in the background and laughing. The caption chastises, "Grandma isn't too smart letting you out looking so shabby!" In another drawing, Itō and Japanese Foreign Minister Hayashi Gonosuke sit behind the wheel of a roadster and drive over dogs labeled *Kan* and *Min* (the "Korean people"). In yet another cartoon, the former emperor of Korea acts as a puppet-master, manipulating strings attached to his son, the new emperor.

The final drawing in the series features a handsome, young Japanese man dressed in a formal kimono and an imported hat, standing next to a pretty, smiling Korean woman (perhaps his wife) who wears the native Korean *hanbok* and demurely nods toward the man. Their newborn baby (whose gender is not identified) is securely in the man's arms, and the words *Shin Kyōyaku* ("New Agreement") run down its back, referring to the July 1907 accord giving Japan control of Korea's domestic laws. To the side stands a tall Russian naval officer, hands trembling and sweat beading on his face, as he observes the moment. The caption reads, "When this happens, absolutely nothing can be done." The colonizer radiates a stereotypical masculine dominance, while the colonized shows only feminine compliance. The youthful couple and the product of their union contrast sharply with the teetering Russian, pointing

**FIGURE 1.**  A cartoon from *Yorozu Chōhō*, 18 July 1907

to how the times have changed and the dynamics and locus of power have shifted.

Despite the biting satirical nature of this series of cartoons, it is critical to understand that they and their creators—similar to the Korean secret envoys to The Hague—tried to tell a story that was "unthinkable" to most Japanese. In contrast, pictures such as the one featured on this book's cover described the "thinkable" story of the day. By the time the *Yorozu Chōhō* cartoonists criticized the underlying assumptions of Japan's new international relations, many Japanese had come to believe fervently that their country had already become or was about to become a powerful imperialist nation, deserving of its status. Popular woodblock prints, such as Kobayashi Kiyochika's depiction of the Japanese army bombarding the Chinese at Pyongyang in 1894 (featured on this book's jacket), appeared widely in Japanese newspapers around the turn of the century. Often, they were sold separately, sometimes with print runs exceeding 100,000 copies.[56]

Pictures such as these recounted to Japanese throughout the country the enormously popular story of Japan's growing international success, a story that unwittingly fueled moments such as the widespread protests in Japan following the country's victory over Russia. The Hibiya Riots, as they are collectively known, arose first in the fall of 1905 in downtown Tokyo when the terms of Japan's peace settlement with Russia became public. Not satisfied with mere protectorate rights over Korea, tens of thousands took to the streets to clamor for more war prizes for Japan. Many felt they had sacrificed their own lives and the lives of relatives to win what proved to be a terribly costly war in terms of domestic resources and casualties (a belief repeatedly reinforced in woodblock war prints).[57] Protests against what were seen as the paltry spoils spread throughout major cities in Japan. Police arrested more than two thousand demonstrators in Tokyo alone, where at least seventeen died in the rioting. It is important for our discussion to understand that the Hibiya protesters were not angry that Japan wanted to participate as a subject in the international arena, nor were they upset that Japan wanted to control Korea. They were angry because, while the price of rice skyrocketed at home, their government was not winning a larger share of international status, which was to them the "thinkable" outcome.[58] As a result, Japan's increased concessions over Korea during the summer of 1907—the "New Agreement"—seemed to many a matter of course, if not belatedly gained or granted.

In the immediate aftermath of The Hague affair in 1907, the Japanese government formally took charge of defining its Korean policies to the world community in what can only be described as the self-conscious language of colonial power. The Japanese colonial regime in Seoul decided to begin publishing English-language reports detailing its Korean policies. By having printed explanations ready, Japan sought to avoid being unprepared when foreigners asked questions about its policies in Korea. With these reports, Japan set the terms for any discussion of its policies in Korea that might arise, enabling the Japanese government to control some of the uncertainty that attended journalistic inquiry. For example, following quickly on the Korean mission to The Hague, "His Imperial Japanese Majesty's Residency General" (or "H.I.J.M's. R.G."), as Itō called himself in English, published the first copy of the *Annual Report for 1907 on Reforms and Progress in Korea*. The project was so successful from the start that it was pursued annually until the collapse of the Japanese empire in 1945.[59]

Although many scholars have read through these annual reports for statistical information, they have downplayed the historical value of the texts themselves because of what they view as their propagandist nature. The propaganda aspect of the *Report*, however, offers the key to understanding how Japan's official narration of its Korean policies meshed with other nations' colonial discourses, both official and unofficial. For example, the Japanese government relied on formats to describe its policies that the British used in India and that the French used in Algeria, and the *Report*'s authors established a congruence of meaning for Japan's colonial policy in Korea through the use of similar terms.

The *Report* flaunted Japan's efforts in Korea as a wholly civilizing endeavor, a *mission civilisastrice*. One of the compilers of the 1907 *Report* was a young bureaucrat named Hishida Seiji. Hishida began working at the Japanese Foreign Ministry shortly after receiving his doctorate in political science in 1905 from Columbia University, where his advisor, the famous international law scholar John Bassett Moore, recommended his dissertation for publication.[60] Hishida had thus learned the terminology of great-power politics from one of its leading theorists, and he and those who worked with him in compiling the *Report* for Itō detailed Japan's relations with Korea for a like-minded—or at least a similarly educated—audience. The Japanese government sent complimentary copies of these reports to governments whose representatives participated in The Hague conference, as well as to major university libraries in some of those countries.[61] According to the *Report*, the Japanese administrators in Seoul sought only to enlighten the Korean people. The 1907 *Report* (distributed in early 1908), for example, narrated the pains to which Japan had gone to try to make Korea stand on its own in the international arena: "With the hope of making Korea's independence a reality, Japan employed all the resources of friendly suggestion to induce the former to adopt modern civilized methods. . . . In consequence, however, of jealousy between political parties, nothing resulted but plots and counterplots."[62]

The *Report* made clear—to an audience familiar with the Koreans' "unthinkable" behavior at The Hague just months earlier—that the Koreans were unfit to rule themselves and therefore could not participate as subjects in international terms: "[After 1905] Japan had now realized that Korea was not capable of governing herself, and that the policy of maintaining her independence could not be pursued without making certain modifications. . . . Thus Japan took the responsibility of intervention in Korean affairs, after having given the Koreans ample opportunity to prove their fitness for self-government, and after having found them wholly unprepared for the task."[63] It is not difficult to discern the self-aggrandizing aspect of the narrative, but it is crucial to understand that, in applying this aspect, the definers of Japan's enlightened exploitation integrated Japan's relations with Korea into a larger international practice.

Within Japan, the government opted for an even showier display of its increasing control over Korea. Between the winter of 1907 and the summer of 1910—approximately the interval between The Hague affair and the annexation—the Meiji government paraded the young Korean crown prince, Yi Yun, on well-chaperoned tours of Japan.[64] The planning for this visit, as well as the press coverage of his travels, underscores the confidence with which Japan calculated the international and domestic approval of its erasure of Korea.

In early August 1907, only days after the Japanese government forced the Korean emperor to abdicate in favor of his son, Resident General Itō announced that he would take the new emperor's ten-year-old brother, Yi Yun, to Japan to educate him in an "enlightened manner."[65] Itō's plan went forward against the strenuous objection of the boy's mother and various Korean court officials. On 5 December 1907, an entourage including Itō, the prince, two Korean court-appointed teachers, retainers, and guards set sail from Incheon to Shimonoseki. Several months prior to the Korean prince's departure for Japan, the Japanese crown prince (the future emperor Taishō) had visited Korea himself, and so Japanese newspaper readers had grown accustomed to following such tours. Unlike the Japanese prince's visit to Korea, however, neither the Korean prince nor his guardians wanted to go to Japan, a point most Japanese never knew.

In the case of Yi Yun, Japan's actions certainly could be described as a form of kidnapping. What is more interesting, though, is the extent to which the Japanese government did not hide its actions, but rather displayed its prize. By educating the boy in Japan in an "enlightened manner," the Meiji regime sought to generate domestic and international commentary on its relations with Korea. Two weeks after leaving Korea, the prince and his entourage arrived at Tokyo's Shimbashi Station to great fanfare.[66] With the Japanese crown prince at the head of the line, hundreds of well-wishers, including members of the Japanese imperial court's council, cabinet dignitaries, and school groups, as well as countless passersby, heralded the boy's arrival.

The significance of this event cannot be overstated. After centuries of Chinese dominance in East Asia—a region whose source of knowledge was located in the Chinese emperor's residence—for the first time Japan claimed the privilege of instructing a continental prince in an "enlightened manner." The era of colonizing politics did not inaugurate the practice of capturing foreign princes for political ends, but, in the discursive practices of enlightened exploitation, educating a foreigner of royal blood in the colonizer's capital city defined and sustained notions about higher levels of civilization vis-à-vis the visitor's homeland.[67]

At this point, the Japanese government seized its advantage. Japanese leaders from the imperial couple down through the ranks of local government employees manipulated the boy's seemingly innocent presence to anthropomorphize Japanese-Korean relations for the benefit of spectators and newspaper readers throughout Japan. What could have been better material to work with than a barely adolescent boy with regal manners who spoke only a few sentences of imperially inflected Japanese?

Following the formula concocted by Meiji statesmen in the 1870s to explain the then-new Japanese emperor's political existence to his unaware subjects, between 1908 and 1910 the Japanese government organized lavish tours throughout Japan for Yi Yun. Also following earlier practice, Japanese taxpayers footed the bill for the Korean prince's travels throughout Hokkaido, Aomori, Akita, Sendai, Morioka, Fukushima, Kansai, and the San-in Coast. Apparently Yi Yun and his guides enjoyed some places so much that his hosts took him two and even three times. Historian Takashi Fujitani has explained that the Meiji emperor's tours in the 1870s served to "bring the emperor down from a godly presence 'above the clouds' in Kyoto to become an active and visible agent in politics."[68] In 1908, the Japanese government did not need to bring the Korean prince down to earth, as it were, but it similarly needed to integrate him—on behalf of his country—into the realm of politics as usual for Japan, a politics that increasingly meant Korea as part of Japan. At each stop on Yi Yun's tours, local officials constructed elaborate welcome arches with Japanese and Korean flags and orchestrated their townspeople into cheers of "*banzai*," dances, and military drills in his honor. Although the process of introducing the prince followed the same methods as those used to introduce the young Japanese emperor in the 1870s, local dignitaries and newspaper reporters added an important new component to the mix. The Korean prince, they emphasized, had come to Japan to obtain an education similar to what all subjects of a rapidly "enlightening" Japan were by then privileged to receive.[69] Riding the still-surging patriotic waves that followed Japan's victory over Russia, the Meiji government proudly displayed its control of Korea.

The Japanese people who gathered at train stations from Nemuro to Matsue to Nagoya may have known little, if anything, of the Korean mission to The Hague, who Sunjong or Kojong was, or how this boy Yi Yun fit into the puzzle. Even if they did, they might not have cared. As the subjects of Japan welcomed the Korean prince into their neighborhoods, his presence defined and confirmed what local and national officials and journalists were publicizing: their country stood higher on the chain of enlightenment than the boy's native land. The Japanese government did not plot Yi Yun's tours as a covert means to justify the official colonization of Korea two years later. It did not have to. The descriptive reactions to the boy's well-publicized visits solidified into the fact of annexation when it finally took place. As Japanese leaders and newspaper reporters emphasized, Japan had come so far internationally that now foreign royalty came to Japan for enlightenment.

During the first few years of the twentieth century, in the self-legitimated taxonomy of the world's colonizing powers, Korea increasingly ranked as a dependent regime. In what we might productively reconsider as a colonial war, akin to numerous such wars around the world at the time, Japan defeated Russia and won Korea. In 1906, the United States recognized Japan's victory spoils by deleting "Korea" in the U.S. government's *Record of Foreign Relations* and placing it under the category of "Japan." The change inscribed a shift in political relations that neatly fit into national erasures occurring around the world at the time, such as those in Hawai'i, New Zealand, and Vietnam. In July 1907, frustrated by their nonreception at The Hague, the Korean envoys set sail for America, hoping to register a formal protest against Japan and plead their case in Washington, D.C.—a place many believed defined the meaning of independence at the time. When news of the Koreans' departure from London reached U.S. Secretary of State Elihu Root, he resolved that the men would not be received in any official capacity either in Washington, D.C., or in Oyster Bay, where President Roosevelt was spending his summer vacation. The United States, declared Root, "formally recognized the Japanese control of the foreign relations of Korea."[70]

Analyzing the colonial discourse surrounding Japan's annexation of Korea allows for a new approach to Japan's engagement in the politics of the Great Game. The following chapters give prominence to an intellectual history of international relations by examining how and when powerful terms of state interaction began to encircle the globe within a reflexive political discourse. To some, an exploration of such terms may seem excessively detailed, and to others it may seem coldly inconsiderate of human suffering, but this discussion is more than an academic exercise. Common understandings of this era in Japanese studies have long relied on theories of imperialism whose composition ignores the Japanese empire.[71] Many analyses, for example, trace a century of imperialist historiography by beginning with J. A. Hobson's famous 1902 treatise, *Imperialism*, never recognizing that the Japanese anarchist Kōtoku Shūsui predated Hobson by a year with his own scathing condemnation of colonizing politics, entitled *Imperialism: Monstrosity of the Twentieth Century*.[72] Comparativists and scholars of Japan alike tend to plug Japan into studies of Euro-American colonial projects, measuring Japan's performance against them in some way. Japan was "late." Japan was "similar" or "different." Language difficulties exist to be sure, but they exist for the Japanese scholar as well.

A far deeper problem persists. Historical theories of international relations sustain the Euro-American Powers and their former colonies as the standards by which historical pasts and presents are defined. By neglecting Japan in these formulations, the civilizational project endures. Only the nations first described as civilized manifest a *normal* history of imperialism.[73]

Another related problem arises in trying to fit Japan squarely into such existing imperialism studies. In the latter half of the nineteenth century, Japan did not come close to the national strength of the "Powers," according to what many historians since Marx—sympathetic and not—have valued as indicators necessary for imperial conquest.[74] Further complicating this problem, historians of Japan's imperialist development have divided themselves into fairly entrenched political camps according to whether they agree with or are critical of Lenin's understanding of imperialism. Because the numbers in Japan's case do not easily concur with Lenin's determination of imperialism as the highest stage of capitalism, scholars from one school of thought have tried to massage official economic statistics in order to amplify their critiques within a larger, Marxist frame of explanation.[75] Conversely, other historians who are dismissive of Marx—and also, vehemently, of Lenin—tend to revel in official statistics to discount these ideas as wrong-headed, proving that Japan's imperialist efforts were "political" and not "economic" in origin.[76] Now, at the beginning of a new century, the first group's line of reasoning feels hackneyed and defeated, while the latter group teeters close to apologism: Japan just did what everyone else was doing.

Japan's imperialist projects *were* political, but imperialist politics were not discrete from economic endeavors. Reasoning otherwise now works only to privilege twentieth-century Japan as a perennial victim of the times. To describe, for example, Minister of Finance Shibusawa Eiichi's Meiji industrialization plans as "economic" without connecting these plans to the Japanese empire's growth, or to remember Itō's restructuring of Japan into an internationally recognized sovereign state as "political" without acknowledging its economic dimensions, fails to acknowledge the interdependence of these actions. Moreover, separating this history as either economic or political—rather than insisting on both dimensions—encourages contemporary Japanese governments to continue to avoid responsibility for Japan's twentieth century. This history, of course, includes the forcible removal of millions from Korea, China, and elsewhere to work in factories and sex camps throughout Japan's empire. Yet the government of Japan can officially maintain that Japan's empire was politically necessary, and not based on economic considerations; therefore, it maintains that it owes no compensation to its victims.

Ironically, scholars overlooking the historical nature of international terms as useful tools for analyzing Japan's empire risk not only sustaining a sense of the transcendent value of the terms but also reiterate ideologies that once condoned Japan's expansionistic policies. For example, the legal expression "propinquity"—used by the United States government in the early twentieth century to sanction Japan's colonial involvement on the Asian continent—has been recycled into the enduring historiographic explanation of the difference between Japanese imperialism and other nations' imperialist pasts.[77] The "Japan-as-different-from-the-norm" approach argues that "as the only non-Western imperium of recent times, the Japanese colonial empire stands as an anomaly of modern history. . . . To maximize its strength, the effort to assert its presence in Asia—the creation of empire—would have to begin with the domination over neighboring areas close to home."[78] For many historians, this worldview—the "thinkable" story within the field—has defined modern history as Western history, and Japan's past is seen as an aberration within the expected flow of the linear chronology of modern history. In this book, I attempt to step around this line of reasoning by not presuming that Japan's colonizing past was a strange occurrence on a predetermined timeline. Japan's engagement in international terms demonstrates instead how the politics of enlightened exploitation germinated globally in capitalist modernity and how its forms endure.

Meiji political theorist Nakae Chōmin's famous treatise, *A Discourse on Government by Three Drunkards* (1887), provides a fitting segue into the chapters that follow.[79] The book's protagonist, Professor Nankai, holds great faith in the promise of Japan's new place in the international community. In his customary besotted state, he expounds on the possibilities of this world: "Despite the power of survival of the fittest . . . all more or less recognize international law. . . . Moreover, [the four Powers'] duty in maintaining the balance among nations and their agreement to uphold international law secretly binds their limbs."[80] Throughout the *Discourse,* Nankai describes a social Darwinist world of nations. Despite the intersection of this political theory with the workings of international law, Nankai (and arguably his creator) holds faith in the value of these terms to constrain such voracious appetites, concluding that international law would prevent "smaller nations from being annexed."[81] In practice, however, Japan's engagement with international law afforded the opposite result. As Japan engaged the terms of international law in describing its policies towards Korea, Meiji diplomats and legal theorists forged a legitimated path to the annexation of Korea in 1910.

# CHAPTER 2

# INTERNATIONAL TERMS OF ENGAGEMENT

*I*nternational terms won the twentieth century. Terms such as independence and sovereignty became the means of discursive exchange in markets and parliaments around the world, but their everyday usage has obscured the historical process that made them the vocabulary of modern international relations. Use of these terms has simply become common sense. The new, post–9/11 U.S. doctrine of "preemptive strike" introduces still-unmeasured dimensions to these terms; yet at the end of the twentieth century, the whole body of international terms was heralded as "the constitution of mankind," upheld by many as an ideal and untouchable form.[1] Disparate political interests, including the member states of the International Monetary Fund, North Korea's reclusive leader Kim Jong-il, and U.S. militia leaders (who incite fear of the United Nations), all speak in terms of the "sovereignty" of their own "independent" nations. Recent self-determination movements in East Timor and Kosovo defined their wars using these terms—which are the same terms their oppressor regimes used to constitute themselves—further attesting to the power of these expressions.

In the late nineteenth century, the young Meiji government engaged Japan in international terms, a decision that stands to this day as one of the most significant changes in Japanese modern history. In a short period of time, Japanese officials determined to establish their newly reorganized nation in the terms of international law, thus relocating Japan's place in the world and redefining power in Asia. These terms became Japan's new legal discourse of power. As aggrandizers of the Japanese empire described their policies in this

27

discourse, they legitimated their nation's imperialist expansion. As they did so, the vocabulary they used became the prevailing political terminology used throughout Asia.

It is important to bear in mind that the terms themselves did not make Japan imperialist. Rather, Japanese policymakers used the terms to describe their early-twentieth-century empire as legitimate. At the time, throughout the world, leaders of colonizing nations used international terms to describe their countries' imperialist expansions as legitimate, and the vocabulary they used became legal precedent. The terms of international law were, therefore, part and parcel of the terms of colonialism, and their global use at the beginning of the twentieth century embedded them as *the* dominant, discursive form in international relations at the time.

In the 1850s, American and European warships began to arrive off Japan's coastline. The Western method of opening Japan to commerce was to threaten war against the Tokugawa shogunate (1603–1868) should it refuse to sign trade treaties.[2] The documents that representatives of these nations brought with them were written in the vocabulary of international law, peppered with terms such as sovereignty and independence. A number of Tokugawa ministers, as well as their rivals, signed such papers without fully understanding the scope of their contents.

What was most remarkable about this episode—as will be detailed later in this chapter—was the ability of Japanese officials to negotiate with the so-called barbarians, in light of nearly 250 years of self-imposed isolation from foreigners that had existed under Tokugawa rule. The United States government had not prepared its demands in Japanese or even Chinese. Rather, these exchanges were made possible through the efforts of generations of Tokugawa-era scholars, who undertook linguistic studies based on their fascination with words. These scholars often worked in secret when the government deemed their scholarship heretical. The work of these wordsmiths enabled the initial negotiations with the barbarians, but more importantly it led to the transformative, Meiji-era outcome of making the new discourse of international relations meaningful in Japanese. Because these scholars' work made it possible to translate international terms into Japanese, Meiji leaders made informed decisions about engaging Japan in the "civilized arena" of the early twentieth century.

Writing international law into Japanese represents more than a reactionary response to prevent Japan itself from being colonized. The terms of international law embodied a pivotal element—a larger method of creating international order. Meiji political and legal theorists recognized in these terms a means by which Japan could engage in the power politics of the day.

By definition, international law is a performative discourse in which representatives, acting at the behest of sovereign states, negotiate with similarly entitled foreign envoys. In this relationship, the representatives mutually define one another in a politics of display. At the turn of the nineteenth century, international law classified the world in terms of "completely sovereign and independent" countries and places where sovereignty was "limited and qualified."[3] The "limited and qualified" regimes were, therefore, definitionally dependent in some way on alien regimes for their own identities. Responding to what the world's self-defined Powers proclaimed to be a universal means of exchange, Japanese state strategists resolved to use these forms. By the turn of the twentieth century, this decision created a perception among the "civilized" world that Japan was *the* modern, legal nation in Asia.

As the modern international system developed, international terms fed on and were fed by theories of the nation-state. Although international law presumed to transcend national distinctions with universalist claims, only governments that successfully subscribed to nation-state theories could participate. Carol Gluck's benchmark analysis of Meiji Japan richly demonstrates how Meiji officials reshaped the country in keeping with the substance and style of a modern nation.[4] As a matter of course, Meiji officials and their advisors refashioned Japan according to a broader discourse of power among nations. By examining how Japan engaged in these terms, we can deepen our understanding of the reflexivity of the modern form of nation building. Viewing the Meiji effort in an international context recalls various assumptions and limits of the nation writ large, as well as highlighting some present-day legacies.

Late-nineteenth-century theorists of the nation-state created what Prasenjit Duara calls "regime[s] of authenticity," which were fashioned by statebuilders who "invoked various representations of authoritative inviolability."[5] International terms afforded such immutable authority. Claims to national existence in one country mirrored similar claims in other countries; in conjunction they created an "authentic regime."[6] Only governments that described themselves in modernity's terms fit into the workings of international law, and Japan's decision to define itself within this discourse enabled the Meiji government to participate as a subject. In his 1875 *Outline of the Theory of Civilization,* for example, the famous Meiji-era enlightenment thinker, Fukuzawa Yukichi, repeatedly urged Japanese leaders to label the country "independent" in order to participate as a civilized state in the enlightened world.[7] At the same time, individual voices and groups that challenged the assumptions of such governments—like the Korean envoys to The Hague in 1907—found hope in international terms, but they were often rendered powerless from voicing what the "authentic regimes" judged as inauthentic claims. In other words, only the era's "thinkable" participants counted as "authentic" in international law.

So-called universalist ideas—including the concept of a sovereign state acting independently—were historically generated within the emerging dynamic of capitalist political economics. The vocabulary of international law could not be separated from the material conditions of industrializing capitalism. Nor, for that matter, were its terms meant to be distinct from such conditions. These terms, like others generated within this dynamic, rendered the conditions of the capitalist social order normative and legal, and Meiji internationalists made the terms commonplace in Japanese.

In any discussion of historical change from Tokugawa to Meiji Japan, it is critical to remember that Japan's Tokugawa economy prepared the way for Meiji entrepreneurs to capitalize quickly on the postrevolutionary era's newly available commodities of labor and materials.[8] At the same time, it is equally vital to grasp that the process of industrialization tore apart and refashioned all social relations (and still does) whenever and wherever it occurred.[9] The Meiji government's famous decision to erase prior social categories by outlawing distinctions between "high" and "low" generated the legal underpinnings for the creation of a new mass of Japanese subjects, who comprised, in Marx's phrasing, the "free, unprotected, and rightless" labor that would propel Japan into the twentieth century.[10] Marx's words are worth noting here. In *Capital*, written the same year that the Meiji government came to power (1868), Marx's critique of the social conditions surrounding him is replete with the terminology of "freedom" and "protection" that states increasingly relied on to describe the politics of imperialism as enlightened practice.

The 1868 Meiji *ishin* (variously understood in English as a "revolution" or "restoration") wove anew the terms of governance in Japan. The government's engagement in international terms has proved as important in the long run as its creation of a mass military and an industrial fiscal policy. Americans and Europeans arriving in Japan demanded that the Tokugawa government "open" Japan to the world. They also insisted that Japan agree to do so by signing the documents of "amity and commerce" brought ashore by the Americans and

Europeans. Students of European languages and technologies (known at the
time as "Western studies scholars," or *yōgakusha*) investigated the meaning of
the terms written in these texts and rendered Japanese expressions for words
such as "independent."

Although the leading antigovernment forces decried the Tokugawa government's diplomatic negotiations as treacherous—and despite their widespread
slogan to "expel the barbarians," at one of the first meetings of the antigovernment forces after the overthrow of the Tokugawa government—the new Meiji
government declared its intention to conduct itself with all nations "according to international law."[11] Soon after claiming control of the government,
the Meiji Council of State issued a series of instructions to the young emperor
concerning relations with foreign countries. Led by former "Revere the
Emperor–Expel the Barbarian" activist Sanjō Sanetomi, the council proclaimed its intent to "fix [its] eyes on the conditions of the times and avoid
corrupt customs of the past."[12] The following month, ministers gathered in
front of the emperor and swore to uphold five principles that the government's
financial planner, Yuri Kimimasa, and others drafted as the regime's famous
Charter Oath. Again, vowing to "break with the evil customs of the past, " the
officials proclaimed to accord their actions with the "just ways of the world"
*(tenchi no kōdō),* an expression that was just one of the phrases used to render
"law of nations," or "international law," into Japanese.[13]

The founding principles of the Meiji government, therefore, not only
negated the prior government's practices, but also indicated that Japan would
henceforth conduct foreign policy in terms that manifested the internal
reordering of the country. For the architects of Meiji Japan, building the new
nation-state necessarily meant creating one that would engage openly with the
world in international terms. The profound shift from distrusting all things
foreign to participating actively in the international system did not take place
easily or without confusion. The preponderance in the new government of
former retainers from Satsuma (a region in southern Japan) fostered an
approach to policy that reflected an awareness of foreigners beyond the Asian
world. In 1868, when the Satsuma men came to power, they knew firsthand
that during the previous several hundred years, when the Tokugawa government sealed off Japan from much of the world, the concept of "foreign" had
expanded well beyond a China-centered sphere to include in its practical
meaning Europeans and New Worlders . Because of this, these leaders were
disposed to build quickly on the efforts of generations of scholars from
throughout the country who had long studied the far-flung aliens, thus

enabling Japan to engage with the vocabulary of power dominant in a wider "foreign" arena of the time.

An even more direct way of understanding the Meiji leaders' conscious decision to engage Japan in international terms comes through knowing that the practical terms of this law were first introduced to the Chinese character world by China, but the Chinese chose *not* to reorder their policies by these terms.[14] In 1862, bureaucrats at the Zongli Yamen—the office established by the Qing court to cope with the dramatic influx of Europeans and Americans to China—began to read parts of the prevailing text of practical international relations of the day, Henry Wheaton's *Elements of International Law*. Wheaton, a scholar of government and law at Brown University, moved between academia and government service, working also as a young diplomat in Paris where he studied continental law firsthand. In 1863, the American minister to China, Anson Burlingame, decided to introduce a missionary friend of his, William Martin, to members of the Zongli Yamen because he knew that Martin had been working on a Chinese translation of Wheaton's text. Martin, a Presbyterian missionary from Indiana, later wrote of this moment: "The Chinese ministers expressed much pleasure when I laid on the table my unfinished version of Wheaton, though they knew little of its nature or contents."[15] Overall, there was slight interest in the book among the group of Qing officials who were on good terms with Americans and Europeans, but no one suggested using these different laws with their alien terms for relations with other Asian governments. As far as China was concerned, there was no need to redefine the terms of international relations within the region, because the long-standing formula sustained China at the apex.[16]

Rulers of countries of what is now East and Southeast Asia had long manipulated the influence of Chinese emperors. They either sent envoys to engage in subordinate exchanges with the Chinese leaders or, like the Tokugawa shogunate, actively degraded the emperors to elevate claims of their own rule. Early in the eighteenth century, the well-known example of shogunal advisor Arai Hakuseki's concern for naming the shogun, vis-à-vis the Korean king, revealed a desire to place Japan on a par with China by purposefully avoiding reference to China.[17] Nonetheless, whichever method of self-legitimation was performed, rulers in the region conducted written legal exchanges with other regimes through the common currency of mutually intelligible Chinese-character terms *(kanji)*. Diplomatic agreements, which defined centuries of protocol between Japan's Tokugawa-era and Korea's Chosŏn-era rulers, derived meaning from a shared diplomatic discourse, because the terms referenced a mutually comprehensible Chinese lexicon. Regardless of whether these contracts mentioned China, China's intellectual authority in the region was manifested through the continued use of its legal terms, derived from continental practice. Moreover, when there were disagreements, translators or negotiators themselves could write out disputed points to make them clear. This practice was known as "brush-talking," and the discourse of exchange relied on a shared comprehension and valuing of the continentally ordered terminology.[18] In short, the regimes in this region had long legitimated themselves and their policies in a common form that ultimately sustained the dominant position of Chinese knowledge, because they all relied on Chinese terms for exchange.[19]

In face of these traditional methods of exchange, the Meiji regime's conversion to international terms radically transformed the hierarchy of power within the region. Japanese officials wrested power away from the continent and became the definers of the new terms of exchange. This point may be illustrated by an example from a 1905 discussion of privileges that Japan wanted in Manchuria. Qing representatives, led by Yuan Shikai, expressed concern over the phrasing of a Japanese diplomatic note while meeting with Japanese envoys Komura Jutaro and Uchida Yasutoshi. According to the Japanese minutes of the conversation, Yuan asked for clarification of the term "protest" *(kōgi)*, a term that "was not usually used" in China.[20] His interpreter, Tang, asked Uchida, "What is the meaning of *kōgi?*" Uchida replied in English, "Protest." In English, Tang replied, "Have you this word?" "Yes," said Uchida. Tang inquired further, "Legally?" "Yes," said Uchida. "Legally and diplomatically." Tang responded, "We have not had it. This is a new word." Returning to interpreted Japanese, another Chinese minister mused, "The British Ambassador Mr. Satow like this term." Yuan Shikai added, "I learned this term from Mr. Satow." The Japanese minister Komura interjected, "It puzzles me to learn that you do not like this term." The minutes noted general laughter.[21] Despite the recorded levity of the moment, the men's conversation indicates a major historical shift. The Meiji emperor's representatives demonstrated that the government of Japan was officially conducting foreign relations in terms that were new to the *kanji* world and fluent with the terms the Powers used; thus, they were not deferring to China's long-held position in the region as definer of terms.

Ultimately, the Meiji decision to reorder Japan's foreign relations collapsed the distinction between contracting with *kanji*-educated and *kanji*-illiterate places. As early as 1798, Japanese political thinker and government advisor

Honda Toshiaki bemoaned the impenetrability of his native tongue. "The vast number and inconvenience of *kanji* render them unusable in exchange with foreign countries," he explained.[22] At the time, Honda already saw a double order of diplomacy, with the *kanji* world discrete from the "foreign" world. Within a mere century, however, Japanese legal and political scholars had translated the terms of international law into Japanese, either by redefining extant *kanji* terms (e.g., *hogo* [to protect] into *hogokoku* [protectorate]) or by creating new terms (e.g., *dokuritsu* [independent]). They created a vocabulary that made sense when it was translated back into the European languages that originated the terms, and also ensured that Japan could name itself in the *kanji* region as the definer of knowledgeable practice with the modern world. Although Japanese leaders ranged from hot to cold in sentiments and policies toward Asia during the final decades of the nineteenth century, the double-tiered terms of diplomatic interaction disappeared, and Japan legally contracted with all nations according to a shared lexicon.

Historians and literary scholars have long divided texts of Meiji international law texts into two categories: those that relied on the Chinese government's initial efforts and those that did not.[23] In the early 1930s in Japan, the desire to locate native origins in everything and anything encouraged literary critic Osatake Takeki to notice a particularly "Japanese theoretical stance" in one of the numerous books of international law consulted by the Meiji government.[24] Despite the fact that the Meiji government had adopted a text by the scholar of Chinese studies Shigeno Yatsusugu, Osatake found "truer" understanding of what was at stake in Japanese sources, including, for example, linguistic scholar Uryū Mitora's use of "*kōdō*" ("official way") over Shigeno's choice of "*kōhō*" ("international law"). These analyses highlight nuances among various schools of thought in the tempestuous atmosphere in which international terms became Japanese, as well as their historiographic legacy.[25]

Because the Meiji example of the interconnection of words and power is so tangible, my inquiry steps around a concern for origins and "true" meanings and focuses instead on how the terms were put into practice. Although the search for specific moments when thinkers finally translated certain words into Japanese may rectify the work of forgotten translators and scholars, approaching translation from such a perspective often leads to assertions of mistranslation. Furthermore, although analysis along such lines can yield compelling discussions of a particular language's past, it runs the risk of doing battle with a universal language—a pre-Babellian ur-lexicon.[26] The mistranslation approach assumes an eventual *correct* translation and can blot out the importance of the historical activity of preliminary attempts at new concepts. Therefore, I follow Pierre Bourdieu's observation of the futility of trying to understand "the power of linguistic manifestation linguistically," and instead I examine instead how international terms became what Bourdieu called "legitimate speech."[27]

There is an unfortunate and almost unyielding opinion that Japanese are simply copycats and have never invented anything of importance on their own. To imply even slightly, however, that those concerned with Meiji Japan's place in the world copied only silhouettes of alien knowledge would fail to understand how Japanese thinkers and diplomats engaged the discourse of international terms as a form of power. Moreover, the view that Japanese only imitate modern political forms—and, according to this logic, never really understand them—entrenches the idea that the Europeans and Americans who invented such forms created them in a pure vacuum or along the lines of some Platonic good.[28]

From its inception, the encoders of international law in Europe and the United States defined it as a domain exclusively practiced by nations that had achieved a certain level of civilization. In the late eighteenth century, political theorists began reworking an accepted notion of *jus gentium* (the law of nations) into a measurable discipline of positive law. In 1789, Jeremy Bentham coined the term "international" to redefine the ideas of law and ambassadorial protocol previously theorized by earlier thinkers such as Hugo Grotius, Samuel Puffendorf, and François de Callières: "The word *international,* it must be acknowledged, is a new one; though, it is hoped, sufficiently analogous and intelligible. It is calculated to express, in a more significant way, the branch of law which commonly goes under the name of the *law of nations.*"[29] Although many of its practitioners continued to use the expression "law of nations" along with "international law"—and many still do—Bentham designated a new phenomenon that was taking root at the time. He codified the intercourse among nations as a knowable and discrete science that could be studied, taught, and expanded on as a discipline, and he named international law as its attending terminology.[30]

Legal theorists conceived of the terms of international law in a discourse resonant with prevailing European and American theories of civilization, theories that named the independent nation-state as the perfect form of political achievement. In his 1836 tome—*Elements of International Law: With a Sketch of the History of the Science,* which ultimately formed the basis of international law in Asia—Wheaton asserted that "international law, as understood among civilized nations, may be defined as consisting of those rules of conduct which reason deduces, as consonant to justice, from the nature of the society existing among independent nations."[31]

Because Wheaton's text wound up in Japanese translation and was used as one of the sources in drafting the Meiji government's new foreign policy, it is worth noting how Wheaton himself described the importance of the law. Like most of his contemporaries, he did not presuppose a blank world, but rather emphasized how Christianity propelled the law and the civilization he espoused: "International law may therefore be considered a positive law. . . . The progress of civilization, founded on Christianity, has gradually conducted us to observe a law analogous to this in our intercourse with all nations of the globe, whatever may be their religious faith."[32] Such awareness directed the presumed "we" in Wheaton's thinking to write laws of international exchange that bespoke the inner meaning of "our" civilization's progress.[33]

Although Wheaton acknowledged that non-Christians had forms of exchange, he believed that such heathens would remain uncivilized until "we" brought them civilization and converted them to its more perfect methods: "It may be remarked, in confirmation of this view, that the more recent intercourse between the Christian nations in Europe and America and the Mohammedan and Pagan nations of Asia and Africa indicates a disposition, on the part of the latter, to renounce their particular international usages and adopt those of Christendom."[34]

Editors of subsequent versions of Wheaton's textbook never discussed whether the violence that European and American imperialists were unleashing upon non-Christians around the world might have propelled those people "to renounce their particular international usages." Rather, they affirmed that the science was spreading naturally as predicted.[35] In his 1866 edition of *Elements of International Law,* for example, Richard Dana wrote: "Already the most remarkable proof of the advance of Western civilization in the East, is the adoption of this work of Mr. Wheaton, by the Chinese government, as a textbook for its officials."[36]

Ascribing the terms of international law to the purview of civilized nations solidified the legality of practicing these terms. Expositors of civilizational theory maintained that civilization, like the terms that rode on its back, was a knowable thing. "I say *fact,* and I say it advisedly," declared the early-nineteenth-century French historian François Guizot. "Civilization is just as much a fact as any other—it is a fact which like any other may be studied, described, and have its history recounted."[37] Provided that an American or European permutation of civilization rested at the top, this "fact" underwrote the most fundamental assumption of international law: its terms were legal everywhere because the most civilized nations of Christendom had created them.

As mentioned earlier, the terms of international law scripted colonizing politics and inscribed them as the dominant form of international relations. It was in these terms that leaders of colonizing nations described their countries' takeovers and annexations of other countries as legal. Self-defined sovereign nations assumed legal control over nonsovereign entities, and this control over dependent countries defined the controlling regime as sovereign. These relationships—which defined their legitimacy as they were practiced—cemented the legitimacy of colonizing politics. When the Meiji government engaged Japan in this discursive order, colonizing politics traveled around the globe to what was considered the "far" end of civilization at the time.[38] Colonizing policies announced their legitimacy by announcing that they were legitimate. The circularity of the logic allowed the colonizer to explain his or her dominant position over the colonized by explaining the action of colonization according to an unseen, yet seemingly undeniable, higher authority such as "the natural order of things."[39] The terms of international law—the law of nations—afforded just such a transcendent authority to all its practitioners and enabled colonizers to make sense to each other. When Japan—the country on the world's "far" end, which built an empire to rival those built at the world's "center"—engaged with these terms, the discourse of enlightened exploitation became the internationally legal terminology of power.

For centuries, all knowledge in Japan—foreign and indigenous, ranging from botany to economics—was routinely rendered into some form of intelligible Japanese script (Chinese-style Japanese [*kanbun*] or Japanese) in order to be of use to the government or its critics. Moreover, and of most direct importance to the translation of international terms, Japan's history of Dutch and Western studies laid the practical foundations for translating these terms of power—terms that were arguably more alien than Chinese ones, but alien just the same.

The vast number of new terms floating through early Meiji Japan invigorated dictionary authors.[40] Debates spun around the viability of Japanese, and several authors reiterated Honda Toshiaki's earlier frustrations and suggested doing away with the language altogether. In 1872, educational reformer Mori Arinori pleaded with Yale University's William Whitney to help him create a new language for Japan because, as Mori saw it, Japanese was a "deranged Chinese" that was unusable in a modern nation.[41] Two years later, the inaugural journal of the Meiji Six Society, *(Meirokusha)* featured a lead article by the progressivist Nishi Amane in which he advocated writing Japanese in "Western letters" *(yōji)*.[42] Even nativist Kurokawa Mayori argued for a contemporary resurrection of *romaji*—the practice of writing Japanese in the Roman alphabet—from its sixteenth-century Jesuit missionary roots, so as to make Japanese more accessible to foreigners.[43] An environment in which opposing poles of the political spectrum challenged the future of the country's language for similar reasons—let alone its terms of governance—brings into relief the volatility of the moment.

In 1887, legal scholar Mitsukuri Rinshō spoke at the opening ceremony of the Meiji Law School in Tokyo. After thanking the school for inviting him, he introduced himself: "My grandfather was the Dutch studies scholar Mitsukuri Genpo, and ever since I was a little boy I also did Dutch studies. . . . Toward the end of the *bakufu* rule, however, when English studies came into fashion, I switched from Dutch to English. I worked diligently on my English, but because I didn't have [a textbook]—my school didn't have one either—I worked haphazardly. . . . I wanted to go to the West very much."[44]

Mitsukuri also recalled accompanying the shogun's brother, Tokugawa Akitake, at the Paris Universal Exposition in 1867: "I went to France. I became proficient at reading some French, and after a year I returned to Japan. The Meiji *ishin* occurred very shortly after that. I didn't have even a smattering of knowledge about the original texts, but in the second year of Meiji [1869], the government ordered me to translate the French criminal codes. . . . I didn't understand them. . . . There were no annotations, no glossaries, no instructors."[45] By invoking the legacy of his grandfather, Genpo, Mitsukuri pointed to the important intellectual lineage of Dutch and Western studies in Meiji Japan and drew attention to the basis for his government's ability to translate the prevailing, yet entirely confusing, terms of international politics.

Although the "closed" conditions of Tokugawa Japan fostered a firm, conservative official knowledge that sustained the Tokugawa order, the "opening" with Korean and Chinese envoys and with Dutch merchants at Nagasaki brought books that enabled scholars to examine their own system from within, even if such inquiry cost them their lives. Understanding Dutch studies from this perspective helps counter a tradition in the field that has viewed seventeenth- and eighteenth-century Dutch studies as merely an escape from the rigidity of Tokugawa's official Confucian thought. Scholars such as Tetsuo

Najita have criticized this opinion by stressing that the primary objects of Dutch studies were compatible with the Confucian ethic of "saving the people" *(saimin)*, asserting that any inquiry into language comprised a vital element of the teachings of Confucian studies.[46] In 1639, the Tokugawa regime banned travel abroad, as well as open contact with the Dutch merchants in Nagasaki. Soon afterward, several scholars and interpreters, intrigued by the Dutch, began compiling word lists derived from interactions with them. These forgotten scholars were described by Sugimoto Tsutomu as "soldiers of words."[47] In short, these "soldiers" constituted the intellectual frontline that paved the way for a body of knowledge to grow.

Over time, other scholars used these preliminary word lists to develop larger schools of thought concerning what the words described; these schools were first called Dutch and then Western studies. Historians in general agree on when these schools coalesced into recognizable forms. For example, in 1771, when Maeno Ryōtaku and Sugita Genpaku secretly dissected a corpse, they searched Dutch texts for information they found lacking in Chinese books in order to perform their experiment.[48] In contrast to the Tokugawa government's earlier policy of declaring such studies heretical and punishable by death, these men openly published their findings, the *New Text on Human Anatomy (Kaitai Shinsho)*, without penalty. This historical moment is widely considered the origin of Dutch studies.[49] In similar fashion, in 1855 the government officially renamed its Bureau for Translating Barbarian Documents *(Bansho Wagegoyō)* to the Bureau for Western Studies *(Yōgakushō)* to accommodate scholars busy with, among other things, the letters and treaties that Matthew Perry brought with him in 1853. Publications such as Hirose Takean's *General Description of America* (1854) and Masaki Toku's *General Description of England* (1854) further attest to the shogunate's open desire for texts about "the West" at the time, and mark this decade as the beginning of Western studies.[50] By the early Meiji period, the expressions "Dutch" and "Western" were indistinguishable in popular parlance, and decades later Japan's famous internationalist Nitobe Inazō reminisced that at the time "[the word] *Oranda* did not necessarily mean 'Dutch.' The term was comprehensive enough to include all of Europe and America. It was, therefore, a disappointing revelation to learn later on that Holland was not the entire Western world."[51]

Around 1800, the Tokugawa government began ordering new kinds of maps, which indicated an official desire to express their control of Japan in ways that made sense to foreigners who were not Korean or Chinese. Such demands, moreover, permitted new kinds of quests for knowledge outside the *kanji* world. Studies arising from matters that did not ostensibly threaten the Tokugawa way of governing—such as autopsies, astronomy, and plant and animal taxonomies—broadened into a riskier desire to know about and to engage the mechanisms of power that sustained alien regimes. Russia in particular had begun to challenge the Tokugawa claim that Ezo (present-day Hokkaido) was Japanese territory, and the Tokugawa government wanted to demonstrate its control.[52] A map of the world, dated 1792 and thought to have been made by either military theorist Hayashi Kōhei or painter Shiba Kokan, depicted Japan and Ezo as separate realms.[53] In the early 1800s, a Russian ship returned several Japanese castaways to Japan, along with a Russian world map in which Ezo was drawn as non-Japanese territory.

The terms of legal sovereignty did not yet concern the shogunate, but the process of delineating the official reach of Tokugawa lands caused great anxiety for the governing house. The shogunate wanted to make sure that Ezo was included in its lands. In addition, officials sensed the urgency of representing Great Japan's territory *(Dai Nippon)* on a detailed longitudinal and latitudinal map similar to the Russian one, so that the Russian "barbarians" would understand. In 1809, the government requisitioned a complete map of Japan from cartographer Inō Tadataka.[54] Until his death in 1818, Inō drafted numerous depictions of the territory of Japan that included Ezo and Kunashiri, the latter being a region that is in dispute to this day and continues to prevent the governments of Japan and Russia from signing a treaty to officially end World War II. Inō's maps depicted Japan so precisely and exquisitely that the German adventurer Philipp Franz von Siebold made free use of them to make his famous maps—maps that, according to most sources, reintroduced Japan to the world in the late 1820s, rendering it ripe for the external world's "opening."[55]

The shogunate wanted to make its territorial claims about the extent of the area of Japan understandable to all foreigners. This desire converged with the efforts of scholars who were just beginning to openly study alien forms of governance and military power. At the same time, it is critical to understand that, when the terms of international law arrived in Japan in the mid-nineteenth century, they did not suddenly reveal to Japanese officials that claiming land was the basis of ruling power. Maps from the seventh century C.E. (known as the "Gyogi maps," after the Korean monk who introduced them) reveal that this concept had been in place in Japan for more than a thousand years.[56] Despite long-standing Japanese knowledge of the territorial basis of power, the introduction of terms such as "sovereignty" fostered a new awareness that claiming land in international politics was a legally defined privilege. It was, furthermore, a privilege sanctioned as a form of "national" defense. The efforts of generations of scholars culminated in the Meiji declaration of national territorial sovereignty as one of its foundational terms of governance. Although the government strongly made this claim, Mitsukuri Rinshō alluded to the confusion of how this moment became possible during his 1887 speech at the Meiji Law School, when he recalled his frustrations at not having had a book for his English studies. A contemporary biography of Mitsukuri quoted one of his classmates to illustrate the mayhem involved in teaching and learning the languages and techniques of power prevalent in Europe at the time: "The students brought whatever books they had to school. One brought a book on physics, another brought an economics text. When one brought a geography book, someone else brought a book on law. Military texts, histories—the students brought their miscellaneous books [from home] and asked the teacher to instruct them."[57]

As Mitsukuri himself pointed out, many young Japanese who later became important Meiji diplomats and translators began their educations in this unsettled atmosphere. Whether the scholars and legal theorists who fashioned Japanese terms for the vocabulary of international law redefined existing *kanji* or coined new combinations, they clearly did not thwart their initial efforts by worrying whether the Japanese renderings fully captured the original French, English, or German.

The texts of international law available in Japan by the early Meiji era— along with the jumble of scripts in diplomatic notes—reveal the creative volatility that existed regarding the shaping of new terms in something as apparently normative as the legal vocabulary among nations. At the time, for example, there was not even a standard term for "international" (most often *bankoku* was used, but increasingly today's term, *kokusai*, appeared). The first books in Japan concerning the practice of international law—what literature scholar Sawa Ōmi has described as "the epitome of *bakamatsu*-era Western political thought"—appeared at this time of makeshift language studies.[58]

In 1862, the Tokugawa government sent Nishi Amane and Tsuda Mamichi to Leiden University, in the hope that what they learned there would yield the knowledge to help resurrect the disintegrating regime. When Nishi returned to Japan in 1866, he turned his notes from Simon Vissering's tutorials on international law into the basis for his compilation *Bankoku Kōhō Yakugi*. The Tokugawa government's now twice-renamed Bureau of Translation and For-

eign Affairs (the *Kaiseijo*) published the text in *kanbun* in 1868.[59] The same
year that Nishi published his book, Tsutsumi Kokushishi wrote a synopsis of
William Martin's Chinese rendition of Henry Wheaton's *Elements of International
Law (Bankoku Kōhō Yakugi)*, offering the first description of the terms
of the science fully rendered in the Japanese language.[60]

Nishi and Tsutsumi's efforts to translate into Japanese the terms that dominated international and diplomatic discourse indicate how both men understood the power inherent in these terms. For his part, in the opening statements of his book *Bankoku Kōhō Yakugi*, Tsutsumi proposed that "a translator
earnestly searches for the spirit" of the text.[61] Nishi, on the other hand, had
worked as the shogunate's interpreter during the treaty talks with American
consul Townsend Harris, negotiating in Dutch with Harris's interpreter.[62]
Nishi and Tsutsumi wrote descriptions of international law, not practical
manuals for how to use the terms. Their work was, therefore, akin to the early
Nagasaki translators—the "soldiers of words"—who enabled later schools of
thought to flourish.

To compound the confusion, in an effort to make international legal terms
meaningful in actual use, an anti-Tokugawa regional daimyo—the Satsuma
ruler Shimazu Hisamitsu—commissioned the first text of international law
in Japan that attempted to render the terms practical in Japanese. By the mid-
1860s, the Tokugawa shogunate's hold on government had almost collapsed,
and envoys from several of the "first-rank" nations tried to align themselves
with various regional daimyo—in particular those critical of the shogunate.
These local rulers, in turn, wanted to understand the international terms used
by the foreign envoys. Especially after British ships firebombed Kagoshima in
1863, to avenge the murder of merchant Charles Richardson, the powerful
Satsuma daimyo ordered Shigeno Yatsusugu, a teacher in the realm's Confucian academy at the time, to negotiate with British representatives. When the
talks ended, Shimazu (an outspoken advocate of "expelling the barbarian")
then ordered Shigeno to translate into Japanese a complete version of Martin's
Chinese rendering of Wheaton's *International Law*.[63] Shigeno was a scholar of
Chinese studies by training, and, in response to Shimazu's request, in 1869 he
produced a facing-page rendering of the text, which juxtaposed his own Japanese translation of Martin's Chinese version with Martin's original translation of Henry Wheaton's book. Unlike Nishi and Tsutsumi, Shigeno did not
attempt to describe or generalize broad features of international law or its
historical place in European thought. Rather, he offered working definitions
in Japanese of the fundamental terms of international law. Shigeno's book

explained international terms through the medium of what had been the legal-reference language in the region until that time: Chinese. Shigeno made the terms workable in Japanese by providing ready, comparative explanations that were comprehensible to most educated members of his domain at the time.

Less than a generation later, Mitsukuri Rinsho played historian and even made light of the random atmosphere in which such international vocabulary became Japanese:

> There were, in fact, many parts that I didn't understand. And even when I did understand, I was at a loss because there were no words to translate the terms. Today young men use terms such as right and obligation with ease. But when I was young, I used these terms with great difficulty in translation. I didn't claim to have invented anything, however, so I wasn't able to get a patent. (Laughter. Applause.) The words *raito* [right] and *oburigeshyon* [obligation] were translated as *kenri gimu* in the Chinese version of *International Law*, and I took them, but I wasn't stealing.[64]

Mitsukuri's academic career as one of the foremost scholars of French law in Japan in the 1870s and 1880s stemmed in part from his language studies and his timely "command" of French.[65] During these decades, the Meiji government reworked Napoleonic criminal codes into Japanese, and legal thinkers debated whether the regime should adopt German or French civil codes. Mitsukuri actively participated in these projects. Granting him the privilege of hyperbole in memory, as a writer of the terms around which this activity revolved, he was very much a part of the process of making these legal terms Japanese. Mitsukuri described how recently radical concepts such as "right" and "obligation" had fallen asleep in the language, as it were—how they had become normative terms.[66] In using the terms of international law for Japan, legal theorists, policy writers, interpreters, diplomats, journalists, and others rendered terms such as "sovereignty" and "independence" commonplace. Mitsukuri's admonition to the young students who "use[d] these words with ease" brings into relief a landscape in which terms that totally transformed political interaction in Japan had become customary within twenty years.

Before moving on to the next chapter to consider how Meiji diplomats transformed international terms into Japanese practice, by way of closure here it is instructive to think about the government's official measure of itself vis-à-vis such terms at the outset of the twentieth century. Beginning in 1874, the

Japanese Foreign Ministry began publishing an English-language compilation of its activities—treaties, agreements, protocols—that it conducted with the Powers. By all measures, the book was a dry, chronological compendium that made a convenient reference book for foreign legations or students interested in developments in the "far" end of the world. By 1899, the preface to the fourth edition recounted the text's history, as well as self-consciously indicating how far the Japanese government believed it had come: "In order to afford an easy opportunity to consult the Conventional Agreements regulating foreign intercourse of this Empire, a volume containing the Treaties and Conventions concluded between Japan and *other* Powers was first published by this Department in 1874; a revised edition was issued in 1884 . . . and the latter publication was followed by a supplementary volume in 1899."[67] The promoters of Japan's newly expanding place in the world clearly defined Japan among the Powers by referring to them as the "other" ones. Meiji leaders had made international terms Japanese in practical application and law; such terms enabled Japan to conclude new trade treaties with England and Germany, for example, and they confidently displayed the transformation abroad.

CHAPTER 3

# THE VOCABULARY OF POWER

For centuries, a shared knowledge and practice of *kanji* had facilitated official relations in what is now called the East Asian world. When the Meiji government chose to engage Japan in international terms, however, it ruptured this order. Politicians and diplomats went beyond scholars' word lists and dictionaries and entrenched the terms in practice. They made these international terms legal precedent.

During the final years of the Tokugawa regime, the United States and the European nations bound Japan with the so-called unequal treaties. As historians have long explained, these treaties mirrored similar arrangements elsewhere and granted extraterritorial privileges for foreigners in Japan. Some Meiji statesmen accepted these arrangements as a temporary condition, but others decried them as an affront to national dignity. Most political biographies and general histories of this period make it clear that debates over treaty revision preoccupied the generation running the country.[1] From the perspective of international terms, because the Powers imposed conditions that restricted Japanese sovereignty through these treaties, Japan was not a full subject in international law. All of the Japanese texts on international law at the time quoted Henry Wheaton's basic explanation: "states which are thus dependent on other States, in respect to the perfect external sovereignty, have been termed semi-sovereign States."[2] Evocative of the privileges that still benefit members of the U.S. military in many places around the world, for example, extraterritorial privileges at the time meant that certain foreigners in Japan (Americans, French, English, Germans, Dutch, and Russians, for example) were not subject to Japanese law. According to the logic of the day, this provision strongly indicated that members of the international arena did not consider Japan civilized enough to fully belong in their sphere.

Examining pressing debates in Japan at the time from the vantage point of international terms reveals a significant yet underappreciated historical transformation. The ability of Meiji state aggrandizers to engage Japan wholly as a fully sovereign state in the international community depended heavily on its newly chosen discourse of power. From 1868 onward, policymakers used these terms successfully vis-à-vis the Powers, eradicating the remaining tendrils of extraterritoriality by 1911. Not coincidentally, during the same forty-year period—Japanese leaders also relied on international terms to rewrite policy within Asia. In particular, Meiji rulers used these terms to forge the path to Japan's annexation of Korea in 1910.

The intellectually volatile atmosphere of the early Meiji period prevailed when Japan embarked on its mission to redescribe the country's place in the world. Scholars did not yet agree on translations for even the most fundamental terms, and the statesmen required tutors at almost every step of policymaking. An example from a preliminary stage in Japan's new relations with Korea brings this condition into relief. The 1876 Treaty of Kanghwa established Japanese settlement areas in Korea. Needless to say, Koreans did not calmly accept these unprecedented incursions. In 1882, in an incident known in Korean as the *Imo Gullan,* several hundred unpaid and unfed Korean troops protested the Japanese presence in Seoul, as well as the Korean court's failure to pay its soldiers, killing some twenty Japanese soldiers and setting fire to the Japanese legation building.

Meiji Council of State members Itō Hirobumi and Inoue Kaoru consulted the government's French legal scholar, Gustave Boissonade, on how best to respond according to international law.[3] Several years earlier, the Japanese ambassador to France met Boissonade and invited him to Tokyo to advise scholars and policymakers in drafting new legal codes.[4] Soon after his arrival, Boissonade's role broadened, and politicians and law students alike came to rely on him as an encyclopedia of civilized and modern European legal practice. In 1882, Boissonade answered Itō and Inoue's questions in a series of memoranda that explained the nature of relations between what he termed "unequal states."

Ukawa Morisaburō, a student of French language and French law, translated Boissonade's notes for Itō and Inoue. Ukawa's efforts reveal the wordy sediments that often collected in official documents, as scholars and diplomats wrote new terms within the same legal and diplomatic procedures that explained their meanings. For example, Boissonade's "Opinion Concerning the Korean Incident" defined the rules for contracting with "semi-tributary states" *(han zokku)*. In his translation, Ukawa juxtaposed the spelling of a *katakana* word, *shusurenti* (transliterating the French *suzerainté* from Boissonade's original), next to the *kanji* compound, *kankatsuken*. In another essay, however, *suzerainté* was written into *katakana* as *shūzurenute*, and *kankatsuken* had become *jōkuni no kankei* (relations with a higher/superior country).[5] French words such as *violation, réparation,* and *annexation* were transliterated into *katakana* and either printed next to *kanji* or left as is. In most cases, the names of the translators remain unknown, but their creations reveal the practical possibilities of one of the era's most challenging intellectual fields.

In stark contrast to the confusion of the early 1880s, little more than thirty years later, in 1905, Itō—now special ambassador to Korea—recounted in international terms his version of Japan's recent history in Asia.[6] On the eve of establishing Japan's protectorate relations with Korea in November 1905, Itō summoned Korean cabinet ministers to his hotel room in Seoul and, according to the Japanese Foreign Ministry's record of the moment, gave the following lecture:

> Diplomatic relations between East and West have developed remarkably, especially in this region, and diplomatic techniques [*gaikōjutsu*] have also made great progress. The days of indulging in dreams of closed ports are over. Those dreams inevitably invited a country's ruin. As you are all aware, Korea is no longer a Chinese tributary state. . . . In the eighteenth year of Meiji [1885], I went to Tianjin entrusted with [Japan's] mission and succeeded in establishing Korea's [new] status. Although [China] formally altered [the status of] its notorious Korean dependency system, it continued to harbor intentions of restoring Korea as its tributary state in name and in reality. . . . At the time, I explained that should China act according to those wishes and return Korea to dependency status, it ought not to have voiced fears that other countries would annex Korea. I firmly advocated your country's independence, and in the end I attained it and dashed China's ambitions.

Fully aware that the international arena sanctioned Japan's increasing rule of Korea, Itō did not miss this chance to slight what he knew the Powers perceived of as the Koreans' inability to govern themselves. He drew attention to Korea's domestic turmoil of the 1890s and described how Japan had then acted as what the international community might call a "friend" of Korea:

In the twenty-seventh year of Meiji (1894), the Tonghak disturbance occurred in your country, and China could not pass up this opportunity. In the name of suppressing this disturbance, China attempted to fulfill long-cherished desires [of conquest] by dispatching large numbers of troops to your country. The result of which was the origin of the dispute between Japan and China. China's defeat in war brought about the Bakan [Shimonoseki] Peace Treaty in which we established Korea's status as independent.

Having redefined the Sino-Japanese War as the Korean War of Independence, Itō explained that Japan was dragged into its recently victorious war with Russia for similarly humanitarian principles:

> Russia grew more aggressive ... and made a grab for Korea besieging by land and sea. Watching Russia try to annex the peninsula, who became alarmed for the sake of your country? For the fate of the Orient [*tōyō*]? It was Japan. Japan took up arms and sacrificed life and property.

Deftly precluding the issue of whether the Koreans had any say in what was happening, Itō concluded that the current events were *faits accomplis*, a style endemic to the discourse of enlightened exploitation. Japan was on the verge of robbing Korea of its international existence, and Itō explained this process as not just inevitable but as already having taken place. Again in the circular logic of this discourse, Japan's establishment of Korea as its protectorate was made legitimate before it happened: "So now, the preservation of your country's territory—a result of our victory in that war—manifests the state of things as well as the opinion of the world. As the territory of Korea is now wholly preserved, and the peace of the Orient restored, we will encourage the progress of peace into perpetuity. We accept the mandate from your country [to take over Korea's] foreign affairs because there will be increasing interruptions in the future of the Orient."

As narrated by Japan's greatest statesman of the day, the country's recent and future international history was that of a nation with an intimate near-past with Korea, both as its victorious liberator and benevolent protector. Before turning to Itō's encounter with Korean officials at the time, I will examine how he and other Meiji politicians and scholars practiced their new "diplomatic techniques" *(gaikōjutsu)* during the late nineteenth century to enable Japan to arrive with such confidence at this moment. Meiji state aggrandizers negated the old regional order during this period, and they did so in the fully legal terms of enlightened exploitation.

Although the unequal-treaty debates ostensibly revolved around Japan's stature vis-à-vis the Western world, by engaging in international terms, Meiji state-theorists demonstrated their determination to rewrite Japanese policy in a way that did not distinguish between the Western world and Asia. As a result, other important debates taking place at the time naturally became entangled with Meiji politicians' overarching obsession with treaty revision. In particular, what came to be known as the Conquer Korea debates of the early 1870s rivaled the passions over the unequal treaties. Examining the outcome of these debates through the lens of international terms makes it possible to see how Meiji leaders measured the world around them.[7] These politicians' new policies toward Korea reveal how international terms formed the basis of Meiji Japan's worldview, an important point to remember when considering that Japan ultimately colonized Korea in the open and with the approval of the global community.

Not unusually, domestic problems fanned the fires of many foreign policy debates in Meiji Japan. In the early 1870s, resentment by some participants in the overthrow of the Tokugawa, who had failed to gain powerful positions in the new government, compounded with other dissatisfactions and climaxed over the Meiji decision to strip former samurai of their right to bear arms. In the Conquer Korea debates, some of these disgruntled participants took advantage of a diplomatic dispute—in fact, a terminological dispute—to advocate for war against Korea.

The dispute arose when the Korean king refused to acknowledge the new Meiji regime and its emperor because, in the region's traditional relations, Korea recognized only China's emperor as the "son of heaven." (The Tokugawa shogunate had avoided this problem because its "shogun" contracted with Korea's "king," ranks the Chosŏn court viewed as compatible and beneath China's emperor.) The famous revolutionary Saigō Takamori declared Korea's rebuff a greater affront than the unequal treaties with the West, and he urged war with Korea—a war that would enable him in midlife to again wield arms.

In his late forties, Iwakura Tomomi was also arguably an elder, serving in a government comprised of mostly very young men. He opposed Saigō and rushed home from his renowned world tour to prevent Saigō from acting. Iwakura's opposition to his fellow revolutionary firebrand was *not* because he agreed with Korea's refusal to recognize the legitimacy of the Meiji ruler. Rather, to stop Japan from going to war, Iwakura and his fellow travelers— Ōkubo Toshimichi, Kido Takayoshi, Ōkuma Shigenobu, and Itō Hirobumi— cut short their famous world odyssey, known as "the Iwakura Mission" (1871– 1873), because in Europe they had learned firsthand the material conditions substantiating the furious rhetoric of the Great Game.[8] They visited Western parliaments and congresses wherever they traveled and also inspected the militaries and industries interwoven with the Great Game debate, confirming what they had imagined before their tour and learning much more. They returned to prevent Japan from starting a war abroad with Korea because they knew that such action might invite military intervention by colony-hungry Europe, an intervention their young government's disorganized infrastructure could not match.

The participants of the Iwakura Mission learned without a doubt that Japan needed a mass military to maintain its claim to sovereignty, but they also redoubled their sense of the importance of describing Japan as a sovereign power in international terms. As part of his contribution to the debate over treaty revision with the West, even before he left for Europe, Iwakura prepared a document, entitled "Opinion Paper on Diplomatic Relations," in which he decried the inequity of the treaties that "disgraced the Japanese Empire."[9] He asserted, "We should not endure the affront. We must expand our sovereignty [*kokken*]."[10] The world tour of imperialist debate that Iwakura and his comrades experienced only intensified Iwakura's convictions. Obsession with treaty revision did not, however, efface the nearer "Korea problem," as it was often called. Because the problem arose during discussions of how to create a wholly new international policy for Japan, the drafters of Japan's Korea policy made these policies compatible with those that Japan would maintain with the rest of the world. At a practical level, Meiji's foreign policy authors articulated policies toward Korea that were fluent with general policies they wrote with the international arena.

In February 1874, discussing the humiliation that the Meiji government continued to endure as the Korean court still refused to recognize it, statesmen and recent world travelers Ōkubo Toshimichi and Ōkuma Shigenobu issued the joint "Protocol Concerning the Sending of Emissaries to Korea."[11] The authors detailed several new diplomatic policies. They drew specific attention to the *Sōryōkan,* the trade office in Pusan, which had been known throughout the Tokugawa period as "Japan House" *(Wakan/Waegwan)* and, as far as Japanese records were concerned, had been under the Tsushima daimyo's control.[12] Two years before they wrote their report, the Meiji government renamed and assumed control of this building and its functions. As Ōkubo and Ōkuma explained, the *Sōryōkan* should be viewed as "an extension of our country's sovereignty [*kokken*]. It occupies the land for one office, it protects [*hogo*] the officials and secures trade routes."[13] The trading center had existed for centuries, but the new government emphasized how they now controlled it, and they redefined it in new terms to manifest Japan's national, sovereign rights.

At the same time, however, Meiji leaders became increasingly impatient with conducting negotiations from this office in Pusan and finally determined to establish a base in or near Seoul. In September 1875, in a maneuver reminiscent of Saigō Takamori's offer early in the Korea debates—to get himself killed at the Korean court in order to provoke war—the Japanese warship *Un'yo* sailed uninvited into the waters around Kanghwa island, off the western coast near Seoul. The *Un'yo* sailed close enough to sustain the shelling that legitimated under international law Japan's subsequent invasion of Kanghwa, slaughter of Korean soldiers, and decimation of the buildings there. Japan's official *History of National Defense (Kokubōshi)* records the incident as the Imperial Navy's first engagement in foreign waters.[14]

Arguably, therefore, gunboats opened modern diplomatic relations in Korea just as they had in Japan.[15] In the wake of the *Un'yo* adventure, Itō, Inoue Kaoru, and others consulted Gustave Boissonade—several years prior to the incident described at the outset of this chapter—before orchestrating the diplomatic talks that followed the warship's maneuver. Having only just arrived in Japan, the French scholar laid out a comprehensive Korea policy for Japan. Boissonade suggested three primary objectives the Meiji government should secure in its upcoming negotiations: (1) establishment of a trading port outside of Pusan, at Kanghwa; (2) unimpeded travel of Japanese ships in Korea's waters; (3) apology for the Kanghwa incident.[16]

In a separate memorandum, Boissonade listed eight more points the Japanese government should consider concerning the establishment of "the independent status of the Korean king" in order to declare his and Korea's "sovereignty" (*kunshuken* and *kunshukuni*).[17] The French advisor focused on the problem of international "diplomatic custom" (rendered as both *kōsaijō* and, more phonetically, *jzipuromachikku no shudan*), in which only sovereign states could contract with one another. According to Boissonade, Japanese policymakers faced particular difficulty in this matter because, "in relation to China, Korea is neither completely a vassal state [*shinzoku no kuni*], nor is it completely independent [*dokuritsu no kuni*]—it holds a position in the middle."[18]

He further stressed that the delegation to Seoul should make clear that the powers of the Tsushima daimyo—the Sō family—no longer existed. "As far as the government of Korea was concerned, His Imperial Majesty's government will succeed the Sō's rights and trading privileges."[19] To align their new Korean policy with the standard of international law, Meiji policywriters had to contract with the Chosŏn court as a "sovereign," "independent" entity. They also had to impress upon the Koreans that, beginning with the *Sōryōkan* in Pusan, the new Japanese government-controlled areas of trade and intercourse in Korea were the spaces of legal contact with Japan. Boissonade's explanations were crucial. He instructed Meiji Japan's new inscribers of international law in its rules as they implemented its terms, helping them to naturalize the terms in practice as Japan's discourse of power.

The military threat issued by the United States to Japan in the 1850s, and in turn mirrored by Japan to Korea twenty years later, sped up and determined the shape of the countries' respective trade negotiations. The terms of the treaties themselves, however, bound Japan to the United States and Korea to Japan in ways more enduring than the threat of imminent military attack. In 1876, Kuroda Kiyotaka commanded three warships and three transport ships with more than 800 men into the same waters that the *Un'yo* had entered, demanding that Korea begin new diplomatic relations with Japan.[20] Photographs of the *Takao, Nisshin,* and *Mōshun* anchored in the waters off Kanghwa Island are jarringly similar to the sketches published in 1854 of the *Susquehanna, Mississippi, Saratoga,* and *Macedonia* under Matthew Perry's command.[21] Echoing the terms that the United States and other Powers imposed on Japan two decades earlier, Japan legitimated its subsequent course of action in Korea according to the standards followed by the colonizing nations of the world.

The purpose of Kuroda's 1876 mission to Korea, as Perry's had been in Japan, was not to wage war but to establish trade relations. Numerous members of varying rank from Japan's Ministry of Foreign Affairs and Colonial Ministry accompanied the soldiers and sailors.[22] As Kuroda and his entourage waited to learn whether the Chosŏn court would receive them in Seoul, some of Japan's lesser emissaries had occasion to discuss the proposed treaty with their Korean counterparts. On 2 February 1876, Moriyama Shigeru, a secretary from the Foreign Ministry, recorded the minutes of a conversation he had earlier that afternoon in Incheon with Yun Chasŭng, aide to the Chosŏn government representative Sin Hon.[23] He noted that Urase Hiroshi was present as interpreter.[24] Like Perry to the shogunal officials in Shimoda, Moriyama emphasized to Yun that Korea would surely incur the enmity of the "nations" *(bankoku)* should its government refuse to trade; he also threatened Yun with the wrath of Russia, America, and France.[25]

Moriyama explained that only by concluding this treaty with Japan as an "independent" and "sovereign" country could Korea survive.[26] The surety with which Moriyama recalled his words suggests the confidence with which he might have uttered these new expressions during his actual meeting. In response to a question about the meaning of "sovereign," he remembered saying that, "More than the fixed expression 'emperor' [*kō*] or 'king' [*ō*], the ruler is the sovereign [*kunshu*] of a country. The sovereign of a country namely makes it an independent [country]. And when you call [the country] independent, both emperor and king have comparably equal rights [*dōtōhiken*]."[27] Moriyama wrote that Yun then asked how this concept would be written into formal state correspondence and that he (Moriyama) obliged by writing out the following equation for him:

DaiNipponKokuKōteiChishō      ChōsenKokuōKeifuku

ChōsenKokuōDenka              DaiNipponKokuKōteiHeika

At face value, the moment between Moriyama and Yun reveals an informal way that diplomats wrote new international terms into practice. The moment also indicates, however, the Meiji government's deeper objective of extracting Korea from the long-standing *sadae* (lit., "serving the greater") relations with China, which prevented Korea from being the fully independent nation needed by Japan for making treaties. According to the legal theory that Japan wanted to practice in the region, only such independent states could freely conduct relations with each other; or, as many scholars understood and translated Henry Wheaton's terms into Japanese, only such independent nations could that "govern [themselves] independently of foreign powers."[28]

During the official negotiations several days after the conversation between Moriyama and Yun, Japanese diplomats wrote their new terms into practice and precedent for relations with Korea. Japan's envoy Inoue explained to Sin and Yun that the proposed treaty meshed with a larger international order, and that although the terms might be new to them, the treaty derived its legitimacy from this greater mean. According to the minutes, when Yun asked to see the treaty, Inoue responded that he had written the treaty in Japanese *(kokubun)* but that he would request a translation from the Office of Translation.[29] Inoue assured Yun that "this treaty makes your country independent [*jishu*] as well. It relies on the precedent of customary exchange among nations and is based on the just ways of the world [*tenchi no kōdō*]." Next, the transcript credits the translator Urase Hiroshi with explaining the treaty "point by point," where-upon Sin requested a Chinese text of the treaty.[30] Quibbling began about whether it sufficed merely to attach a translation of the treaty to the final ver-sion, until Kuroda interrupted and reiterated Inoue's claim of the "precedent" of international law and "the just way of the world."[31] Both Inoue's and Kuro-da's remarks may seem mechanistic, but their statements point to the new way in which the Meiji government ordered its world, a way that allowed its rep-resentatives to define Japan's policies as both a departure from past practices and rooted in international precedent.

The Meiji delegates explained the treaty's terms to the Korean representa-tives before and during the sealing of the treaty, but as far as Korea's traditional relations with China were concerned, Japan's attempt to designate Korea inde-pendent at this time was not particularly successful. Sin responded by saying, "Until now, our country has conducted exchange only with your country. We had no trade with foreign countries, and for this reason we are unfamiliar with the laws of exchange among nations [*bankoku kōsai no hō*]."[32]

Despite whatever remained "unfamiliar" to the Korean men, two weeks later, on 26 February 1876, Kuroda and Inoue sealed the Treaty of Peace and Friendship with Sin and Yun.[33] Only independent governments could initiate and conclude treaties with each other according to international law, and the treaty's first clause announced that "Chosen being an independent state enjoys the same sovereign rights as Japan" *(Chōsenkoku wa jishu no ho ni shite Nihon-koku to byōdō no ken wo hoyū seri).* (In the official translation, quoted here, the Japanese expressions *jishu* and *ken wo hoyū* were used to embody the con-cepts of "independence" and "sovereignty.")[34] The terms with which the Japanese government declared Korea independent, however, reveal various tensions pulling at Japan's desire for power. They also show some of the prob-lems that could arise from relying on older *kanji* to express new concepts. The literal translation for Japan's choice for independence in this document—*jishu* (自主)—expresses the idea of "self-rule." The term did not, therefore, threaten the existing practice of Korea's homage to the Chinese court, a rela-tionship that permitted Korea the privilege of administering itself.[35] As sub-sequent efforts by Japanese negotiators and politicians reveal, however, the

Japanese did ultimately locate a term for independence that dislodged Korea from tributary status as well as leaving the country susceptible to new forms of domination.[36] Nevertheless, Japan declared Korea an "independent nation" in the Treaty of Kanghwa, displaying that the Meiji regime had begun to conduct even its regional relations according to international law.[37]

Of equal significance, and in the fashion of emergent colonizers around the world, the Japanese government simultaneously impinged on the independence that it declared for Korea. Defined by Japan, Korea's new independence allowed Japan to establish a colonial outpost in Korea, a privilege independent Japan could contract only with independent Korea. Article 5 of the treaty designated two "treaty ports" at Incheon and Mokpo, in addition to the area around the *Sōryōkan,* in Pusan, where Japanese laws would prevail. Article 10 introduced the term "extraterritoriality" *(jigaihō)* to the Korean peninsula, ensuring that Japanese soldiers and businessmen would not be subject to Korean laws. Despite Japan's assertions of power, however, the treaty agreed to the condition that "official correspondence" from Japan to Korea would continue to arrive with Chinese translations attached, and also that Korea's communications to Japan would continue to be written in Chinese. Although pleased with the success of the treaty, Meiji state aggrandizers knew their discourse would not be a powerful currency in the region until China acknowledged Japan's newly chosen terms as meaningful.

## DIPLOMATIC TECHNIQUE

In 1885, during diplomatic negotiations with China in the port city of Tianjin, Meiji envoys resolved a stronger means to dislodge the old order—a contrast to Japan's 1876 accession, which permitted Korea to rely on Chinese translations in order to make its interactions comprehensible in the Asian region. In a remarkable example of what he would later call "diplomatic technique," Itō Hirobumi negotiated the Tianjin Convention in 1885 in English. Itō spoke in a radically different language from anything that had ever been used before in diplomacy between Japan and China. English was the language of countries with which both Japan and China had difficulties at the time (England and the United States). In short, English was not a comfortable choice for anyone at the talks, but it was the European language Itō knew best. By speaking English, Itō confirmed Japan's desire to change forever the order of the regional discourse of power. Had Itō spoken in Japanese and attempted to use Japan's new Chinese character terms for "independence" or "sovereignty," for example, Chinese negotiators could have dismissed Japan's use of the *kanji* as meaningless misinterpretations of the characters' true meanings—as defined by them. Brush-talking was useful, but the Chinese were its champions. Articulating the same concepts in a wholly alien language allowed international terms to retain their distant authority. Thus, English made the terms nonnegotiable. Itō demonstrated that the national language in which the new concepts were uttered—he used English in this instance, and in the future others would use Japanese—did not matter as much as the relations that sustained their meaning. In so doing, Itō trumped the Chinese at their own long-held game.

The need for the high-level meetings in Tianjin in 1885 arose from an impasse over how to resolve what Japanese and Chinese representatives euphemized as "the latest disturbance in Korea." On the evening of 4 December 1884, Kim Okkyun, Pak Yŏnghyo, and Hong Yŏngsik led members of their "progressive faction" (the *Kaehwa'pa*, also sometimes referred to as the "pro-Japan faction") in a coup attempt against the Min faction at the court in Seoul. Takezoe Shinichirō, the Japanese representative in Seoul, promised Kim that should his men go forward with their attempt to rout the pro-China Min group, 200 Japanese troops would back him up. After the coup began, however, Takezoe quickly forgot his promise, and the coup failed horribly. During the ensuing mayhem, Takezoe not only fled for Japan with some of the progressives but also set fire to the Japanese legations in Seoul to cover his tracks. Chinese, Korean, and Japanese soldiers shot in all directions, inflicting casualties on all fronts. The Yi court (with China's backing) denounced Takezoe and accused Japan of trying to overthrow the legitimate Korean government. Foreign Minister Inoue failed to reach an agreement with Korea in Seoul, so the Meiji government decided to send a delegation to the Chinese court. In late February 1885, as Ambassador Extraordinary, Itō embarked on negotiation of what was arguably modern Japan's first disarmament treaty.[38]

The negotiations in Tianjin resulted in a rare text prepared for the Meiji emperor, unusual not because it was bilingual (Japanese-English) but because it was largely the Japanese half that was translated.[39] The author of the *Report* (most likely Itō Hirobumi's aide, Itō Myoji) created a playbook-like volume, transcribing the minutes of Itō Hirobumi's meetings as perfect dialogue and noting the closure of each day almost with a curtain cue. Descriptions abound, for example, of the men adjourning to dinner parties or to their quarters. Itō and Li Hongzhang held six meetings throughout April 1885, but the *Report* noted Itō's daring diplomatic technique of speaking English only once at the beginning of the first day: "The Minutes of the Conversation that follows, as well as those of subsequent ones, were taken down in English and afterwards translated into Japanese by Mr. Ito Miyoji."[40]

The men's conversation ensued, with Itō Hirobumi playing "The Ambassador" and Li Hongzhang as "The Vice-Roy":

> *The Ambassador:* (He spoke in English).
> *The Vice-Roy* [sic]: (He spoke in Chinese and his remarks were interpreted by Mr. Rahoroku in English.)[41]

Also only once on that day (and the only time in the proceedings) was there any indication that the Chinese representatives even acknowledged the unusual skill of Itō's maneuver:

> *The Vice-Roy:* I must ask Your Excellency to be patient and conciliatory, and not cast upon me too much difficulty (smiling).
> *The Ambassador* (to Rahoroku, the interpreter): I will proceed to make a general statement of the points of my negotiation, through my Chinese interpreter and so I will not trouble you for the moment.[42]

In fact, Itō's action did not completely take the Chinese negotiators by surprise. They had been notified ahead of time and brought along their own English-language interpreter. Before these negotiations, however, Chinese diplomats had never brought English interpreters to meetings with the Japanese. They brought Japanese interpreters or no interpreter at all. The ingenuity of Itō's technique was made even greater by his not dwelling on what he was doing, that is, by simply performing the negotiations in English and writing his actions into practice.[43]

More than anything, Itō wanted to conclude a treaty with China in international terms, but he continued to acknowledge China's position of power in the region. Following a month of talks, Itō and Li wrangled over how to prepare the final form of their agreement:

> *The Vice-Roy:* All other modifications in your draft are very insignificant. Now I can agree to this draft.
> *The Ambassador:* Very well. I have no objection to any of them, they are nothing but modifications of composition that do not affect the meaning at all. So, we mutually agree to the draft.
> *The Vice-Roy:* Now I have to consult with Your Excellency about the details of this Convention. When we enter into a treaty or convention

> with a foreign Power, it is customary with my Government that the Chinese text is prepared by our hands, leaving the preparation of the other text to the Plenipotentiary of the foreign Powers, with whom we are treating. So, in this case you have to prepare the Japanese text.

When Li asked about the meaning of the second article in a draft of the treaty, Itō responded:

> It simply means the right of war that every independent nation enjoys. . . . Thus, the present arrangement cannot effect in any way our right of waging war according to the Law of Nations. That clause may be modified thus: "It is understood that the right of warfare according to the Law of Nations, shall not be affected."[44]

Unlike the Korean representatives at the Kanghwa negotiations, the Chinese negotiators could not and did not plead ignorance of these rules. After all, two decades earlier Shigeno Yatsusugu had translated his text of international law from the Chinese government's version. Throughout the negotiations in Tianjin, however, Chinese diplomats insisted Japan must continue to recognize China's long-standing relations with Korea:

> There is a striking difference between the position of Japan and that of China towards Corea. To China, Corea is a tributary state and has the obligation to report to her every matter that takes place in her country. But Corea has nothing more than a treaty obligation towards Japan.[45]

At Kanghwa, Japanese delegates named Korea independent. Ten years later, the Japanese envoys in Tianjin had no gunboats with which to reinforce their demands. The new terms that Itō wanted to write into practice, to equate Japan and China in independent state relations with Korea, had to be ignored or designated differently.

One of the very few discrepancies between the English and the Japanese in the *Report* is useful to mention here, in light of Itō's dilemma about describing China vis-à-vis Korea. In the midst of the conversation over the final version of the treaty, the author included the following parenthetical note in the Japanese section:

> The modifications in wording [included] changing *Dai Shin Koku* [the Great Qing Realm] to *Chūgoku* [the Middle Kingdom, China] and deleting the *Dai* [Great] from *Dai Nippon Koku* [the Great Japanese Realm] in the first clause. . . . As there was no difference in meaning, this does not appear in the English written text.[46]

The author was not devious. There is no substantial difference in the English meaning. Throughout the English version of the *Report,* the names China and Japan are used. In Japanese, however—consonant with Chinese—*Chūgoku* is a different name for China from *Dai Shin Koku,* one that transcends dynastic labels without getting entangled in the name of a particular ruling family. Importantly, though, *Chūgoku* posits the centrality of China vis-à-vis the realms surrounding it according to its worldview, countries including Japan, Korea, and Vietnam. The term the Japanese wanted to use—*Dai Shin Koku*—would have made the name for the country read more like the one they wanted to use for Japan—*Dai Nippon Koku.* The Japanese lost their gambit in this instance to de-center China in Chinese characters, but, as the author of the *Report* noted, it did not matter internationally for those who would read this text in English, "as there was no difference in meaning."

Throughout the twentieth century, English operated as the higher authority in numerous state-level diplomatic treaties in Asia.[47] Although the Meiji government's decision to introduce English into its diplomatic arsenal sheds light on the subtle connection between words and power, it is a connection that has remained surprisingly undervalued. From a balance-of-power perspective, the treaty negotiations in Tianjin were not about words but about the net reduction of troops in Seoul. And yet, China's position in the region to define law held only tenuously, because the Japanese cemented their new terms to effect even without soldiers present.

A decade later, in 1895, meetings held in Shimonoseki to sign a peace treaty concluding the Sino-Japanese War (1894–1895) confirmed that Itō's diplomatic technique at Tianjin had transformed international relations within the *kanji* world for good. The fact that, at the end of the nineteenth century, China concluded treaties in English with delegates from London or Washington (or any European capital for that matter) could be argued (although somewhat paranoiacally) to be a means of protecting the regime's interests from the "cheating barbarians" and their foreign words. Even if accurate, such an understanding would not explain how this practice came to order relations among places that shared a mutually communicable past. On 17 April 1895, Itō Hirobumi and Mutsu Munemitsu sat on Japan's side of the table, and Li Hongzhang and Li Qingfang sat on China's, to sign the peace treaty of Japan's first modern war. The treaty stipulated that an English translation be attached to the Japanese and Chinese texts, and article two of a protocol note further announced, "Should any differences in interpretation arise between the Japanese and Chinese texts, we agree to sanction the aforementioned English version."[48]

The influential historian of Japanese imperialism W. G. Beasley mentioned in passing that an English text was agreed to at Shimonoseki, but he explained that "as a matter of national dignity it was the Chinese and Japanese texts that were signed."[49] By downplaying the importance of the linguistic maneuver, Beasley appears to consider the Japanese action inevitable or insignificant. In doing so, however, Beasley unwittingly naturalizes the use of English onto the larger plane of international relations where it is now, of course, wholly unremarkable to know and conduct relations in English.

In addition, Akira Iriye, the well-known historian of U.S.–Japan relations, has also belittled the significance of Japan's strategy. Instead, Iriye focuses on the fact that because Japan's delegate Mutsu Munemitsu could "read and comprehend what the Chinese delegate Li Hung-chang wrote in Chinese . . . the episode revealed not so much a cultural sharing as a cultural dependence on China even while its military might was proving superior. Mutsu's example, which can be multiplied, suggests that no matter how much one was influenced by Western civilization, Chinese learning was still considered the prerequisite for Japanese leaders."[50] Of course, Chinese learning was essential for educated Japanese—it remains impossible today to work effectively in government in Japan without knowing thousands of Chinese characters—but Itō's insistence on using international terms underscores Japan's shift to a *non-*Chinese referent of order. The discursive technique performed at Shimonoseki yielded a prize less concrete than the 200 million taels China paid Japan in indemnity for the war, but the prize set the terms of international relations within the *kanji* world for the twentieth century.

## KOREA IN LEGAL TERMS

Between February 1904 and August 1910, the Japanese government wrote a variety of diplomatic agreements and policies with Korea that gradually erased the existence of the country. In November 1905, the Meiji emperor's envoys in Seoul usurped the Korean government's ability to conduct diplomacy. In the summer of 1907, Itō overthrew Emperor Kojong and paraded his son, Sunjong, as Korea's new emperor. In short, Japan wholly gutted Korea's sovereignty by the time it announced the formal annexation in 1910. And, most importantly, it had done so in legal terms.

In 1895, the Treaty of Shimonoseki redeclared Korea's independence when Japan and China agreed to recognize an "independent Korea."[51] By this time, the *kanji* for the recently alien term, *dokuritsu*, had gained currency in Japanese, Chinese, and Korean. Moreover, two years later, on 12 October 1897, the king of Korea renamed his country Great Korea *(TaeHan)* and himself its emperor *(hwang'che)*. In doing so, the new emperor Kojong made official what members of various progressive groups had been working toward for more than a decade. He made the concept native practice in Korea when he announced, "The foundation of independence has been created and the right of sovereignty exercised." Historian Andre Schmid argues that with Kojong's proclamation, "The source of sovereignty rested unambiguously within the peninsula. In his first edict as emperor, Kojong reversed a five-century-long tradition" of tributary relations with China.[52] The declaration emanated from within Korea and equated Korea with China and Japan in the terms of international law. On 22 August 1910, however, the Japanese government used terms of the same discourse to execute a reverse technique that assumed Japan's complete and internationally legitimated sovereignty over Korea.

On 16 November 1905, the day before the Japanese seized control of Korea's foreign relations, Itō called Korean cabinet members together in his hotel room in Seoul. "I advocated your country's independence," he lectured, and "in the end, I attained it. . . . [But] we accept the mandate from your country [to take over Korea's] foreign affairs because there will be increasing interruptions in the future of the Orient."[53] Korean Prime Minister Han Kyusǔl objected. "Korea's independence," Han said, "should be based on the country's own strength, yet we could count on Japan's aid and protection [*fuchihogo*]." Education Minister Yi Wanyong quieted Han and said what Itō wanted to hear. "Japan," Yi countered, "has fought two wars over the Korea problem. . . . [By] crushing Russia . . . the time has come for us to choose [Japan]."[54] Agricultural Minister Kwǒn Chǒnghyun speculated that, if Korea were to lose its "independence in both name and reality," such a condition would be "worse [for Korea] than when Korea was a Chinese tributary state." Itō replied, "Your country does not have the necessary ability for its own independence. You haven't surpassed a false [state of] independence."[55] Itō's remark pointed to the prevailing and legally encoded view of the day, which historian Prasenjit Duara has explained as follows: "The right to maintain empire [as a] nation was centrally dependent on the ability to demonstrate that the colonies continued to remain non-nations."[56] As Japan redefined Korea as quasi-"independent," Korea became again such a "non-nation," and Japan inscribed its right to empire.

Unlike the Yi representatives in 1876 at Kanghwa, who pleaded that Korea was "unfamiliar with the laws of exchange among nations," the conversation recorded thirty years later between Itō and the Korean ministers displays how commonplace working notions of international law had become in Korea as well. When Itō declared, "With the establishment of the second Japan-Britain Alliance [1905] and the Japan-Russia Peace Treaty, this [agreement] is the next step in recognizing Japan's position towards Korea. The world powers will not consider such a proposal from Japan at all irregular," Han Kyusŭl again took exception: "Korea is on the verge of death, gasping for breath. The one thread of our remaining days exists in conducting foreign relations for ourselves. When you mandate our diplomacy to your country, we will submerge in despair as you sever our lifeline [to the outside]."[57]

Han, however, spoke into the wind in facing Japan's declaration to protect Korea. Although Japan positioned itself as the definer of international relations in Asia when it defeated China in 1895, the Powers paid much more approving attention when it beat Russia in 1905; and when it came to Korea, they pretty much gave the Japanese free reign with regards to international terms.[58]

Japan achieved victory against Russia by early spring 1905, and the now well-known "secret agreement" made shortly thereafter, between U.S. Secretary of War William Howard Taft and Prime Minister Katsura Tarō, displays a mutual ease with discussing Japan's policies in the region through the discourse of enlightened exploitation. A secretary at the Foreign Ministry cabled an English text describing the 27 July 1905 meeting to Komura Jūtarō, Japan's head delegate to the upcoming talks in Portsmouth, New Hampshire:

> Secretary Taft observed that Japan's only interest in the Philippines would be, in his opinion, to have these islands governed by a strong and friendly nation like the United States. . . . Count Katsura confirmed in the strongest terms the correctness of his views. . . . In regard to the Korean question Count Katsura observed that Korea being the direct cause of our war with Russia, it is a matter of absolute importance to Japan that a complete solution of the peninsula question should be made as a logical consequence of the war. . . . Secretary Taft fully admitted the justness of the Count's observations and remarked to the effect that, in his personal opinion, the establishment by Japanese troops of a suzerainty over Korea to the extent of requiring that Korea enter into no foreign treaties without the consent of Japan was the logical result of the present war and would directly contribute to the permanent peace of the East.[59]

Katsura's agreement with Taft was concluded in an amorphous space, similar to the hotel room where Itō described Japan's plans to Korean ministers the following November. The agreement revealed that Japan's ultimate usurpation of Korea would read legitimately in the terms of international law. In other "secret" talks the following week, Japan updated its 1902 friendship agreement with Great Britain and traded India for Korea in the process.[60]

Japan's determination to make Korea a protectorate before annexing it outright was not an unusual practice in imperialist politics. In light of the fact, however, that all the world (except Russia) was applauding Japan's actions in Korea, it is noteworthy that Japan even bothered to follow this cautious path instead of simply annexing the country right away, as it had Taiwan in 1895 after defeating China. Japan's decision to establish the protectorate arrangement underscores the Meiji leaders' determination to describe its Korea policy in internationally recognizable terms. At the same time, I believe it indicates apprehension about exceeding potential limits the Powers might have set for Japan's privileges there.

In 1895, Japan did not hesitate to annex Taiwan, but it failed to secure what was arguably the bigger prize—the Liaotung peninsula on mainland China—when Russia, Germany, and France demanded Japan's return of territory to Chinese control, in what is known as the "Triple Intervention." Japan's defeat of Russia in 1905 drew much greater international attention than Japan's victory over China in 1895, because at the height of the politics of the "white man's burden," a "nonwhite" nation defeated a "white" one—a victory John Dower has described as "stunning" to the Powers.[61] With intense focus from an international audience, therefore, Japan's domestic turmoil directly resulting from the war with Russia presented a delicate political situation in Tokyo. The Hibiya Riots manifested the collective indignity stemming from Russia's refusal to pay Japan the customary indemnity due to the victor under international law. These riots were directed generally at the huge price Japan had paid for its victory: hundreds of thousands of dead Japanese soldiers, military arsenals voided, and almost the entire budget of the country wasted, bringing about conditions of hyperinflation in rice prices, Japan's staple food. And more, Japan failed to gain the full international stature many thought Japan deserved. It is likely that the Meiji government's hesitation to annex Korea outright stemmed from fear that should the international arena reject such a move—as it had the 1895 attempt to take part of mainland China—Tokyo's leadership would fail to withstand the domestic turmoil that might follow.

Japan's discursive steps to describe its Korea policy in the international arena, therefore, deserve more consideration than they have been given in the past. Moreover, examination of these actions may usefully redirect entrenched positions concerning Korean colonization. Several historians have noticed Japan's anxiety over terminology when the country ultimately annexed Korea in 1910, but they have done so at the expense of examining a similar preoccupation over declaring the protectorate in 1905. In the field of Japanese imperialism studies, these historians have generated a prevailing view that Japan did something unusual or even sneaky in 1910 when it used an oblique *kanji* expression *(heigō)* to define the annexation of Korea. This scholarly suspicion has occasional contemporary political ramifications—for example, when South Korean opinion makers denounce Japan's colonial period as "illegal," asserting that Japan hid its policies by using a term unknown at the time in the *kanji* world. The scholarly and politicized lines of reasoning collapse, however, in considering the terms of 1905 and 1910 together, revealing that Japan did not act treacherously, but rather that it acted imperialistically and with the approval of the international arena.

Hilary Conroy was one of the first historians to examine the importance Japanese state aggrandizers gave to naming the colonization of Korea. He assessed Japan's choice of terms for the annexation *(heigō)* in light of Pan-Asian thinkers and their involvement with the takeover.[62] In his elaboration, Conroy relied on a pamphlet written in 1939 by a former secretary at the Foreign Ministry, Kurachi Tetsukichi, who claimed to have coined the term specifically for the Korean annexation: "Having newly invented the word *heigō*, I did not stress it too much, knowing there would be argument about it."[63]

Conroy credited Kurachi as having "undoubtedly had the inside story on *heigō*, since he composed it himself."[64] This explanation does not hold, but I want to be clear that I am not seeking to debunk Conroy's source for its own sake. In his analysis, Conroy himself mentioned four terms Japan could have used to designate the takeover of Korea: *gappō, gappei, heidon,* and *heigō*. The term *gappō*, however, did not surface in Kurachi's recollection of the terms: "Korea was to come completely to Japan and there would be no treaties between Korea and other countries. [However,] the word *heidon* (annex, devour, swallow up) was too aggressive for use, so after various considerations I thought out a new wording, *heigō*, which until that time had not been used. This was stronger than *gappei*, meaning that the other's territory should become part of Japan's."[65]

Conroy believed that the Japanese should have chosen the term *gappō* (merger, amalgamation), because it embodied to him the "ideological basis of the partnership between Japanese reactionaries and their friends." In Conroy's view, the Foreign Ministry's term *heigō* circumvented what he saw as the real nature of the relationship between Japan and Korea.[66] In 1939, Kurachi probably had a spotty memory of the history of Japan's takeover of Korea. The 1905 protectorate agreement—not the 1910 treaty—ended the Korean government's ability to make treaties between Korea and other countries. Kura-chi's failure to consider the term *gappō*, however, led Conroy to conjecture that Kurachi was "perhaps too well educated to appreciate the meaning of *gappō*, at least the way the reactionaries used it."[67] Despite his well-documented importance of Asianist thinkers to the colonization of Korea, Conroy con-ceded that because his then-contemporary English-Japanese *Kenkyūsha* dic-tionary (the *Webster's* of Japanese) did not list *gappō* for "annexation," the official elision suggested that the government—its well-educated members— "ran the annexation show."[68]

I agree with Conroy that the Foreign Ministry designated the particular term it wanted to use, but I am not convinced that the government used the term *heigō* because its functionaries were well bred. In 1906, Ariga Nagao, the most famous scholar of international law in Japan at the time, published a book entitled *A Treatise on Protectorate Countries (Hogokokuron)* immediately following Japan's designation of Korea as its protectorate.[69] In this mammoth work, Ariga discusses a wide range of colonial forms and uses the term *heigō* to describe the annexations of South Africa and Monaco.[70] Ariga also quotes Jules Ferry's speech concerning future French policy in northern Africa, again using the term *heigō* to explain the debate over whether France should annex Tunisia.[71] It is entirely possibly that Ariga himself did not coin the term *heigō* in 1906, but the expression he used to translate the policies of other imperial-ist countries surfaced in Japan four years prior to his country's annexation of Korea. Rather than believing that the Foreign Ministry's secretary, Kurachi, coined a new term for the takeover of Korea that was purposefully vague, I believe it much more likely that the Foreign Ministry chose this term in 1910 because they knew it already resonated in international meaning.

In his recent discussion of Japan's "penetration" of Korea, Peter Duus rewords Conroy's conclusions and focuses on the importance of understand-ing the "annexation" as "amalgamation." Duus's emphasis moves away from Japanese creativity, however, and toward a loosely worded suspicion that the Japanese government knew it was concealing its intentions: "Indeed the term *heigō* is probably not best translated as 'annexation,' which implies adding one thing to another; it *really* means 'amalgamation,' a process of merger rather than accretion. The colonial takeover, legitimized as an act of reunion, was thus hidden behind a façade of putative commonality between the domina-tor and the dominated [emphasis mine]."[72]

I have emphasized the word "really" in Duus's quotation to underscore how he posits the idea of mistranslation as more significant than what the Japa-nese bureaucrats actually produced at the time. Despite a repertoire of colonial "annexation" treaties in English, French, and German, and despite the Meiji government's official English publication of the Annexation Treaty in 1910, Duus contends that the Japanese version "hid" the term's intended meaning. Pushed further, such reasoning necessitates seeing Japanese imperialist effort as intrinsically different from American and European standards. For Duus, the Japanese term for annexation really meant something else: amalgamation. From an alternative standpoint, however, the particular term actually used might reveal that the Meiji regime defined Japan's actions to the world in a way that intersected with terms used by other nations. Both Conroy and Duus (though Duus more explicitly so) have argued that the Japanese government's designation of the Korean annexation as *heigō* was strange, and that the term shielded a deeper meaning. But how is it that only European and American colonial "annexations" were normally defined, whereas the Japanese effort was a façade?

The international terms of enlightened exploitation blurred the rationale of colonial domination with numbing consonance around the world, demonstrated by Ariga's publication on protectorates the year after Japan's open theft of Korea's foreign affairs. Begun as an arcane academic inquiry, the discussion of the terms of imperialist politics developed into a full-blown scholarly debate in the wake of Japan's new powers in Korea. Moreover, such discussion suggests that because Japan did not shield its intentions in Korea in 1905, it was unlikely to hide them all of a sudden in 1910, when there was more international approval for Japan's policies. The term *hogo/poho* (保護 "protect") appears in both Japanese and Korean versions of the 1905 agreement, which is now known commonly in Japanese as the "protectorate agreement," and in Korean by the corresponding calendrical year name, *Ulsa*.[73] The term itself had a long history within the *kanji* world, denoting military or police control of a particular place or group. In the 1876 Kanghwa Treaty, Japan used the term to refer to the protection of its new legation and troops in extraterritorial settlements in Korea. In 1905, however, policymakers gave the term new meaning by translating a recognized element of enlightened exploitation—the "protectorate"—into Japanese practice. In addition to redefining *hogo* in this diplomatic agreement, the Japanese Foreign Ministry invented a wholly new term—*tōkanfu*—to explain the form of colonial rule it would pursue in Korea. The Japanese version of the agreement transliterated the term in *katakana*— although it did not explain it in the Korean version—as *Rejidento Generaru* (Resident General, as in the French regime in Morocco) to designate its new branch of government in Seoul.

Itō Hirobumi assumed the post of Japan's first Resident General in Korea, and many scholars who have maintained a rosy glow for Itō argue that he never intended to "annex" Korea. Such logic blends into a larger line of argument that places blame for the annexation squarely onto Japan's notorious Pan-Asianists and their amalgamation plans.[74] According to this reasoning, Itō was content with the protectorate agreement. Whether Itō would ever declare Japan's rule of Korea an "annexation" can never be known, because Korean patriot An Chŭnggun assassinated him in 1909, a year before annexation took place. Personally, I believe that Itō wanted to rule Korea under any name; but regardless of the timing of his death, what can be known is that Itō presided over the total erasure of Korea's sovereignty during his rule there (1905–1909). In early 1906, he formally ascended to the position of Resident General, a new rank that Itō himself defined as answerable only to the Meiji emperor, thus legally marking the start of the Japanese colonial rule of Korea.

Like the early Meiji theorists and translators who tutored politicians step by step in foreign policymaking, scholars at the beginning of the twentieth century introduced the concept of the protectorate into Japanese practical usage, bringing into relief the conjunction of academic inquiry and policymaking. The broad readership these late Meiji scholars enjoyed, however, shows the exponential growth of their studies into a disciplined field in a half-century's time. Theorists of Japan's new place in the world worked as their predecessors had—as advisors to particular politicians—but they also published best-selling books, which well-informed Japanese subjects rushed to purchase.

Moreover, these efforts of scholars in the late Meiji era underscore the importance of the laws of war in international terms of engagement at the time, and also how such words interrelated with power at the outset of the twentieth century. Considering these scholars' work in international and domestic contexts further demonstrates the new naturalized order of nations in Asia at the time Japan annexed Korea in 1910. Ariga Nagao's fellow legal scholar, Takahashi Sakue, wrote a best-selling book the year before the Russo-Japanese War, entitled *A Treatise on International Law during Peacetime (Heiji Kokusaihōron)* (1903), in which he elaborated upon protectorate arrangements.[75] The book became such a standard that it was reprinted at least ten times. Throughout the text's thousand pages, Takahashi quoted from English, French, German, and Chinese sources and referred to numerous British, continental European, and American authors and historical examples. In straightforward (albeit bone-dry) prose, Takahashi explained aspects of the "protected state/the protectorate" *(hihogokoku)* in sections entitled "Partially Sovereign States" and "Rights of Occupying Territory."[76] Although such a publication might seem wholly unremarkable now, it is important to remember that only half-a-century earlier, the Japanese revolted against the Tokugawa regime for negotiating in the barbarians' terms, and the government often had difficulty finding anyone to explain them.

As Ariga made even clearer in his text on protectorates, these scholars' personal encounters with the Powers' use of such terms gave unequivocal authority to their research. Similar to the members of the Iwakura mission who traveled to Europe in the early 1870s and found European parliaments embroiled in the Great Game, when Ariga visited Paris in the late 1890s his trip coincided with what he described as a "clamorous debate about protectorate countries."[77] As a result, he wrote that he was able to purchase "a mountain of pamphlets, books, and treatises" concerning France's forays into Madagascar to use for a book of his own on the legal principles of protectorate arrangements that would include Japan.[78] Furthermore, he noted that he collected materials on European policies towards Bosnia-Herzegovina and Cypress for a future study of "mandate territories" *(inin tōchi),* not coincidentally the term that would soon define Japan's interests in Manchuria.

During the 1890s, Ariga and Takahashi gained not only domestic authority but also substantial international reputations. A brief examination into how they became Japan's articulators of international terms to such widespread audiences reveals the intrinsic relationship between such terms and how power was measured. Historians of modern Japan have long held that the country's victories against China and Russia at the turn of the century were the touchstones for proving Japan's power to the world, and it is also useful to consider how Meiji leaders described these wars.[79] Japan's engagement in the laws of war was an equally vital component to securing the country's foothold among the colonial powers: in short, international terms defined Japan's victories as legal. In 1894, when Japan declared war against China, then–Prime Minister Itō summoned Ariga to advise him. Ariga had studied law in Germany and at the time was a professor of international law at the Army War College in Tokyo, Japan's West Point.[80] Because he was widely considered to be the country's most respected scholar of international law, Itō questioned him about the legality of Japan's declaration of war.[81] Defining Japan's first modern war according to the just-war principle required technique from a thinker most familiar with its terms, and Itō knew to seek out Ariga because he was teaching a course on the laws of war to young officers headed to battle. Ariga's explanation so impressed the prime minister that Itō dispatched him to the battlefield on 16 October 1894, to act as ongoing advisor to the commander of the Second Army, Minister of War Ōyama Iwao.[82] Throughout the winter, Ariga elucidated Ōyama and his staff on questions of the legality of Japan's battles in Xinjin, Lushun (Port Arthur), and Weihai.

Immediately following the war, Ariga described his experiences in a surprisingly popular book.[83] What was even more surprising, however, was that Ariga's book—like Itō's text for the Meiji emperor on the Tianjin talks, which was first written in English—was written and published in French in the first version of the text, with the Japanese text for domestic consumption appearing several months later.[84] Creating the perception that Japan fought a just war with China required displaying the war in terms that made sense to Great Power consumers, but Ariga made sure that the Japanese text mirrored the French. From the opening line of both versions of his book, Ariga made it clear to readers that understanding the war in terms of law was simple: "The important point in the conflict between Japan and China . . . lies with the nations themselves, one did not observe the laws and customs of war, whereas, the other, on the contrary, enforced their respect as strictly as possible."[85] Moreover, he assured his readers that the "ignorant Chinese" failed entirely to understand international law. Although some Japanese soldiers were unschooled in the finer points of international law, the commanders of Japan's military knew "to practice benevolent and humanitarian policies unparalleled even in the wars of Western states."[86] Ariga served both as advisor to military commanders, explaining when it was legal to fire, and as propaganda scribe, detailing the army's actions as legitimate in international terms, which was a critical dimension in measuring the connection between words and power.

Ariga's books were not official government records, but his terms helped engender the perception of Japan as the legal nation in Asia, especially because he explained the war to a European audience. Significantly, during one of the first battles of this war—Japan's first modern war abroad—Japanese soldiers butchered people on the streets and in their homes in Lushun (Port Arthur). The army massacred Chinese civilians to such a degree that historian Inoue Haruki has recently suggested this moment eerily foreshadowed the horrors later and more famously remembered from Shanghai and Nanjing in the 1930s.[87] The chaos in Lushun in 1894 caused a small stir in British and American newspapers at the time, but the prevailing, so-called informed opinion quieted criticism, assessing that Japan acted according to the laws of war and defining China negatively in the same terms. Ariga's colleague, Takahashi, wrote his own description of Japan's legal engagement in this war—in English —in which he used his experience as advisor to Japan's navy to explain the war record according to prevailing international standards. Moreover, and ultimately perhaps to more effect than Ariga's work, Takahashi secured renowned Oxford legal scholar John Westlake to write an introduction to his text. Despite the known horrors in Lushun, Westlake had only praise for Japan's conduct: "In her recent war with China, [Japan] displayed both the disposition and the main ability to observe western rules concerning war. . . . Japan [thus] present[ed] a rare and interesting example of the passage of a state from the oriental to the European class."[88]

Like many of his fellow Japan-boosters in England, Westlake drew his conclusions without firsthand observation or, in fact, without any knowledge of what was occurring other than what the newspapers reported or what acquaintances—Japanese and not—told him. Not unusually, he learned of Japan through its national promoters such as Takahashi, people who could explain Japan's new international actions in terms that already made sense, and so he praised Japan's actions as a result. And, with far-reaching ramifications, the late-nineteenth-century idea of describing wars as legal according to an international standard spread around the world along with imperialism, defining through its terms the countries and peoples at war as legitimate or not.[89]

Westlake's conflation of evolutionary success with the ability to perform international law—Japan's "passage" to the "European class"—demonstrates how the notion of a legal nation took form and shaped itself into a preceding-setting worldview. Moreover, the image of Japan-as-specimen reveals the upward route amidst the hierarchy of the world's people as presumed in international law. A decade later, Japan's victory against Russia rapidly propelled the country up the great chain of being, and an illustration from *Tokyo Puck* printed during the final weeks of that war suggests the extent to which such reasoning was ingrained in Japanese audiences.[90]

In Figure 2, five men crowd around a table scattered with laboratory equipment, and one of the men (perhaps Russian) intently holds a pipette filled with liquid poured from a nearby bottle. The Imperial Navy's flag and the characters for *Dai Nippon* (Great Japan—like Great Britain) appear on the bottle label. While the men scrutinize the vial, John Bull and Uncle Sam approvingly look on with a gaze, which I think resonates with Euro-American treatment of Japan much later in the century as "miraculous" and "enigmatic."[91]

Despite Ariga's international reputation and predilection, he made it clear that he placed ultimate value on making the discourse of international terms in Japan normative in Japanese. In the preface to his book on protectorates, he stressed that, "although [he] culled facts from foreign countries to write [his book,]" he used "comparative examples from Japan to make the points readily understood."[92] He placed Japan's endeavors on equal footing with other imperialist powers and challenged his readers in the book's opening line, "Should Korea be declared Japan's protectorate?"[93] Ariga did not let them think too long and answered right away: "My purpose for readers has been to develop a fair and uniform consideration of the question, 'What is a protectorate?' and also to create a solid foundation for future Korea policy. In the coming years, I hope to make 'protectorate' a common expression."[94]

In the orderly fashion of a good social scientist, Ariga delineated four classifications of protectorates (with examples for each) and detailed the legal principles and respective positions of each classification according to international law. He determined that the agreement made between Japan and Korea on 17 November 1905, was a "protectorate treaty, validly [yūkō] concluded as expected," and he defined Korea in his second class of protectorates.[95] This type, Ariga explained, "does not fully manage its sovereignty by itself. Instead,

**FIGURE 2.** "Japan's Enigmatic Passage to the European Class," an illustration from *Tokyo Puck*

in place of the protected state, the protector state manages diplomatic and military rights."[96] In a section entitled, "Korea's Rights of Dignity," however, Ariga seemed to want to mollify the effects of the protectorate by writing, "Korea essentially possesses its sovereignty . . . mandating only a little portion to Japan."[97] Although ambiguous at times, Ariga offered lengthy legal explanations of Japan's policy, broadly situating Japan's control of international terms—in addition to its control of Korea—as a form of knowledge.

Indicative of the growth of the academic field of international law, Ariga's hypotheses and, in particular, his placement of Korea in that scheme did not go unchallenged. Tachi Sakutarō reviewed Ariga's book in the October 1906 issue of *Diplomatic Review (Gaikō Jihō),* the international affairs journal that Ariga had started in 1898.[98] Unlike Ariga, who learned international law amid everything else new to early Meiji Japan, Tachi could specialize in international law as a student at Tokyo Imperial University because this discipline had come into existence by his time.[99] Tachi reviewed his mentor's work by first assessing the basic aims of Ariga's book and noting in praiseworthy terms that "Professor Ariga's love of learning cannot be separated from his considerations of matters of state."[100] Tachi grew critical, however, as he questioned Ariga's classification of protectorates into four groups. He wondered whether, for example, "The native people of India, the third kind [of protectorate], or those in Africa, the fourth kind . . . should not be counted among the first kind of protectorate country?" He also challenged Ariga's unsophisticated grasp of lofty theoretical issues.[101] Finally, Tachi zeroed in on Ariga's vague use of the terms "sovereignty" and "independence" and criticized him for "having lapped up the dregs of European and American scholars."[102] Ariga did not ignore Tachi's review, and a pointed debate between the two continued for the next several months in the pages of *Diplomatic Review,* the *Journal of International Law (Kokusaihō Zasshi),* and the *Journal of the Association of Political and Social Sciences (Kokka Gakkai Zasshi).* Neither scholar altered his position much (Ariga maintained, for example, that "while Korea is independent in name . . . it is not an ordinary independent country"), but ironically their squabble only served to strengthen Ariga's initial purpose: to make the term "protectorate" become a common expression.[103] As the two argued about Korea's legal status, their debate confirmed the understanding that Japan's foreign policy read fluently in terms of a larger, global praxis.

Although none of the Powers officially challenged Japan's declaration of the Korean protectorate agreement, in 1906 Parisian legal scholar Francis Rey wrote an article for the *Révue Générale de Droit Internationale Public* condemning Japan's deplorable behavior in forcing the Korean government to sign the protectorate agreement.[104] Rey declared that, because the Japanese diplomats had physically and mentally harassed the Korean emperor and had failed to obtain his signature to the agreement, they had violated the internationally sanctioned method of concluding treaties. "Because of the particular circumstances in which it was signed," he wrote, "we do not hesitate to affirm that the treaty of 1905 is null."[105] Rey also expressed disappointment in Europe's far-off protégé. "It must be regretted," he wrote, "that Japan's protectorate over Korea, organized according to the rules admitted in the practice of civilized States, has in its origin a violation of rights. . . . This act constitutes the primary defect in policy on the part of Japan."[106]

As described above, Tachi Sakutarō questioned Ariga Nagao's methodology and sloppy diction, *not* the legality of the protectorate system. Similarly, Rey declared Japan's agreement "null" because of aggressive behavior, *not* due to the illegality of colonization. The debate over Japan's actions in Korea revealed the success of the Meiji policymakers' larger project of placing Japan legally among "the civilized States."

A 1908 American assessment of Japan's relations with Korea voiced what I believe was the prevailing international opinion at the time and commented on the protectorate arrangement in the wake of the incident at The Hague in 1907, when Koreans had tried to disobey the conditions of this arrangement. Yale professor George Trumbull Ladd wrote what can really only be described as a paean to Itō Hirobumi—*In Korea with Marquis Ito*—in which he made the following judgment of 1905: "If all treaties made under such conditions may be repudiated . . . the peace of the world cannot be secured or even promoted by any number of treaties."[107]

The text of Japanese-Korean relations between 1904 and 1910 became legal precedent through the terms "admitted in the practice of civilized States," a practice which did not necessitate that Japan act in a morally justifiable manner or in any way different from the actions of other, so-called civilized states. That the imperialist nations justified their actions as legitimate in these terms is precisely what calls the terms themselves into question, along with the legacies of their practice in the postcolonial world of the present. The following chapter examines this problem further and considers how Meiji officials restricted various individuals who tried more directly and more daringly than Rey to call into question Japan's use of international terms.

# CHAPTER 4

# VOICES OF DISSENT

𝐼nternational terms empower the strong. At the same time, the potential represented by these terms inspires those who resist domination. For the architects of the Japanese empire, any debate over the relationship between power and words would have seemed nonsensical. The terminology of statecraft, through which modern Japan made sense internationally, defined power itself. Controlling Japanese sovereignty meant controlling the legal terms of governance wherever Japan ruled. This included obvious censorship such as banning books, but on a deeper level it meant negating definitions that challenged Japan's sovereignty, both within Japan and abroad. International terms could only reflect those meanings that inhered to the government's range.

Most translators, politicians, professors, and others who engaged with the terms of international law used a vocabulary that provided the legal structure used by Japan, at home and abroad. The terms of foreign relations used by Japanese officials made sense with a coterminous reformulation of domestic political vocabularies. Diplomats and international legal scholars understood "equality" among nations, for example, in ways that aligned with how parliamentary politicians settled the meaning of the terms within Japan. In discussing what he calls "the metaphor of censorship," Pierre Bourdieu argues that "censorship is never quite as perfect or invisible as when each agent has nothing to say apart from what he is objectively authorized to say."[1] The permitted discourse of legal Japan circumscribed expression throughout the geographical realm to which the new regime aspired. Therefore, the few people who challenged the discursive range determined by the state contested what most of society presumed to be a normatively defined, legal terminology.[2]

A variety of dissenting voices tried to subvert how international terms were understood and used with regard to Japan's annexation of Korea.[3] In the first chapter, for example, we followed Yi Sangsŏl, Yi Jun, and Yi Ŭijong, who were dispatched in vain to The Hague in 1907 as part of an effort to reclaim Korea's independence from Japanese protection. In the entire process of Japan's annexation of Korea, the censored appeal of these emissaries offers perhaps the clearest illustration of the success of the dominator within the limits of international terms: not only were the Koreans physically expelled from The Hague, but their presence at the conference was expunged from the official record. Though less well known, other examples offer an even more nuanced understanding of the complicated power of these terms. In 1908, for example, a Korean high-court judge demanded that the world recognize his anti-Japanese rebellion as a legitimate war under the terms of international law. The same international arena that ignored the Koreans at The Hague, however, ignored Justice Hŏ Wi's appeal, and he was tortured to death in a Japanese prison in Seoul. That same year, two Korean immigrants in San Francisco, Chang Inhwan and Chŏn Myŏngun, shot to death an American diplomat to protest Korea's right to exist. One of the men fled to Russia to escape the police, while the other rotted in jail after his lawyer failed to sway juries with a plea of "patriotic insanity."

Examples from within Japan further reveal the inadequacy of defining power as the sole purview of the dominating nation's people. That is, Japan colonized Korea, but the Meiji government also colonized Japan from within. The few Japanese who tried to define Japan's relations with Korea in the same terms that the state used, but with different meaning, posed as great a threat to the government as the Koreans outside Japan. Anarchists and socialists remain the best-known of protesters at the time. With too few exceptions— Yosano Akiko and Ōsugi Sakae in particular—many of these thinkers paid virtually no critical attention to Japan's Korea policy until *after* annexation. Kōtoku Shūsui, Japan's most famous anarchist, questioned Japan's involvement in Korea earlier than most, and his critique was prophetic in many ways.

In contrast to such a famous dissenter as Kōtoku, however, a very different and almost wholly obscure voice also arose. In the 1870s, Tarui Tōkichi, a poor and unsuccessful politician from Nara, began to envision a new nation he called "Great East" *(Daitō)*, which would be formed by blending together Japan and Korea. The Meiji government censored Tarui's plan, until it effected its own version of *Daitō* by annexing Korea in 1910, whereupon Japanese officials celebrated Tarui's book, and nationalists ultimately co-opted his legacy into their glorious history of Asianist expansion. In all these examples, police, statesmen, and censors judged alternate definitions of international terms inadmissible or illegal vis-à-vis the state's encoded limits for them, erasing the proposed meanings and often the people themselves from the record of legitimate Japan.

## HŎ WI AND THE ŬIBYŎNG

Ill-equipped, poorly trained, and sporadically organized Korean men and women formed troops that fought armed, uniformed, and quartered Japanese troops throughout the hills of central and southern Korea between 1906 and 1914. Canadian reporter Frederick McKenzie described the first group of Righteous Army *(Ŭibyŏng)* fighters he encountered near Wŏnju in the autumn of 1907:

> [H]alf a dozen of them entered the garden, formed in line in front of me and saluted. They were bright lads, from eighteen to twenty-six. One, a bright-faced, handsome youth, still wore the old uniform of the regular Korean Army. Another had a pair of military trousers. Two of them were in slight, ragged Korean dress. Not one had leather boots. Around their waists were homemade cotton cartridge belts, half-full. One wore a kind of tarboosh on his head, and the others had bits of rag twisted round their hair.[4]

McKenzie's photograph (Fig. 3) of this group of fighters or a similar one is one of the best-known images of Korea from the period.

The *Ŭibyŏng* were anti-Japanese fighters, arising from a tradition whose leaders proclaimed violent uprisings against Japan as their sole patriotic recourse. Most often their leaders relied on an orthodox school of Confucian thought to describe their actions. One commander, however, declared the Righteous War legal in terms of international law. Hŏ Wi (also known by his nom de guerre, Wang San) argued that the Koreans fought a just war and demanded that they be allowed to effect changes within Korea that would regain the country's sovereignty. As a judge on Korea's high court, he knew that the complete eradication of Japan's privileges was critical in order for the Korean government to rule itself.

In the late spring of 1908, the commanders of several *Ŭibyŏng* brigades made a large-scale push to recapture Seoul from the Japanese colonial regime. According to the Japanese Resident General's official figures, the "rioters" (*bōto*, as they were belittled in Japanese) numbered 11,400 people at the time.[5] Though he was unsuccessful, Hŏ argued that the Korean government must define itself in terms of independence and sovereignty, and he issued a list of thirty demands to Resident General Itō Hirobumi calling for the full rectification of Korea as a nation.[6] His first three demands included the restoration *(yusin)* of Emperor Kojong, the reinstatement of control over diplomatic rights, and the abolishment of the Japanese colonial office. The Japanese tried to prevent the list of demands from being made public, but the most daring newspaper remaining in operation in Seoul, the *TaeHan Maeil Sinbo*, alluded to it shortly after its publication: "Rumor abounds that the *Ŭibyŏng* . . . submitted a list of thirty demands, including the abolition of the Resident General, the expulsion of Japanese officials, the restoration of diplomatic rights, and other things."[7]

The previous summer, the Japanese government had forced the Korean Emperor Kojong to abdicate and installed his son as a puppet ruler. The Japanese-backed succession delegitimated the new emperor's rule within Korea. In Hŏ's thinking, "restoring" Kojong would relegitimate the line. Only when Korea could articulate a condition of self-rule would Koreans be able to describe the nation as sovereign in international terms. Meanwhile, according

**FIGURE 3.** Korean resistance fighters, 1907

to the Japanese colonial records, fierce battles on the outskirts of Seoul continued through June.[8] In the end, the superior numbers, munitions, and organization of Japanese troops prevailed, and Hŏ was captured and tortured in jail. Hŏ's attempt to resuscitate the place of Korea in foreign consciousness resulted in his death.

Earlier bands of righteous fighters waved reactionary banners proclaiming their uprisings in terms quite different from the ones Hŏ Wi and his comrades used a decade later. In 1895 the antiprogressivist scholar Mun Sŏkbong led the first in a five-month-long series of armed uprisings against the Japanese in Korea and also against fellow Koreans he believed to be sympathetic to Japan. One of his comrades, Yu Insŏk, wrote a manifesto steeped in typical anti-Japanese rhetoric ("Japan has forced us to cut our top-knots") and described the Japanese as "Western bandits."[9] The scholars and fighters of this 1895 "righteous uprising" despised Japan and the Japanese, and they believed that all recently imported intellectual and material elements in Korean society were evil. The movement disbanded in part because the king rescinded the inflammatory top-knot decree that required adult males to adopt the so-called civilized, short haircut of the West. Despite the rebels' outrage toward him, the king named them "loyal" and pardoned them.[10]

Hŏ Wi, Yi Sangch'on, Pak Kyubyŏng, and others shared a similar hatred of Japan when they revived the idea of a Righteous Army in the summer of 1904. Departing from the tactics of their predecessors, however, the men used international terms to make their appeal.[11] Hŏ Wi had participated in earlier uprisings, and he never rejected outright his old principles. He did not, for example, condemn Confucian thought and become a member of Sŏ Chaep'il's Independence Movement.[12] In 1894 the first progressive reforms, the Kabo Reforms, wholly reorganized the Korean judicial structure.[13] Furthermore, although the political upheaval following the Sino-Japanese war reversed many of the reforms, the Independence Movement thinkers as well as the "reform Confucianists," as they were known, endeavored to keep the changes to Korea's legal system in place. After all, Hŏ passed an exam to enter government service in an independent Korea—the Empire of Great Korea—a political condition that did not exist when he participated in the first round of anti-Japanese fighting. As his biographer Cho Tonggŏl wrote, while preserving "the façade of a righteous fighter," Hŏ became an enlightenment thinker.[14]

Hŏ moved to Seoul in the late 1890s, and he determined to "shed" the provincial doctrine guiding his thinking.[15] He studied at the national Confucian academy, the *Sŏnggyungwan*, and passed the government's civil service exam. In 1904 he became a judge on Korea's high court. That summer, as a newly minted arbiter of law, Hŏ made every attempt to explain the new Righteous Army's cause in terms of national sovereignty and international law. On July 1, the *Hwangsŏng Sinmun* printed the group's manifesto, a proclamation that the Japanese Foreign Ministry promptly catalogued as a "declaration of independence from Japan."[16] Hŏ and his comrades announced that Japan was deceiving the Koreans and called for a national "armed uprising" in protest: "Japanese will emigrate in droves to our country and pillage it. . . . We are morally obligated to redeem ourselves and preserve the territorial integrity of our country. . . . Compatriots, we appeal to you to join us in our bloody struggle. We must cover the countryside and make banners from old cloth and weapons from farm implements to overwhelm the enemy. . . . Heaven supports our just cause."[17]

Although resonant with older, "righteous" rhetoric, in this proclamation Hŏ used the new international terms with which he had become familiar. He knew the expression "territorial integrity" from the agreement signed the previous February between Japan and Korea. The concept determined a basis for national independence, and Hŏ used it in an effort to rally Koreans to the cause. Andre Schmid has described how ideas of "territory" and "sovereignty" were becoming linked at the time as a means to define Korea's historical existence and place claims on the past. Schmid argues that "building on a number of late Chosŏn spatial discourses while supplanting others, the Korean state together with leading nationalist writers sought to define spatial conceptions of the nation within the vocabulary and practices of territorial sovereignty."[18] Hŏ was different from the thinkers discussed by Schmid; he was not concerned with redrawing Korean maps to aggrandize an originary Korea. Rather, he sought to ascribe the internationally sanctioned terms of national definition to his Righteous Movement.

Throughout his campaigns, Hŏ appealed his cause to the nations that sustained Japan's erasure of Korea, because they constituted the international audience. In the summer of 1904, a year *before* Japan declared Korea its protectorate, Hŏ wrote:

> According to their terms . . . Japan may "take the necessary measures if the welfare of the Imperial House of Korea or the territorial integrity of Korea are endangered." This provision does not ensure the welfare of our country. It is a trick to assert Japanese supremacy in Korea.[19]

Earlier in 1904, the Korean government formally declared its "neutrality" when Russian and Japanese troop movements indicated that war would soon break out. In February, the Japanese envoy to Seoul, Hayashi Gonosuke, signed a protocol with the Korean Minister of Foreign Affairs, Yi Jiyong, assuring that "the Imperial Government of Japan guarantees the independence and territorial integrity [*ryōdo hozen/yongo pochŏn*] of the Empire of Great Korea."[20] The protocol's subsequent article promised Japanese assistance should a "third country or internal uprising endanger the territorial integrity of Korea." Finding the agreement vacuous, Hŏ challenged the provision that granted Japan the privilege of "occupy[ing] strategic points when necessary":

> Fisheries and railways are now open to Japanese control . . . Japan will occupy strategic points all over the countryside . . . revealing Japan's desire to swallow Korea.[21]

He viewed the "strategic points" clause as evidence of "the inconsistency of Japan's words and actions." As a result, he judged that "this agreement violates the basic principles of international law."[22]

Expressing his cause in international terms not only enabled Hŏ Wi to elicit sympathetic support but also permitted him to define his war as a legal response to Japan's actions. Unfortunately for Hŏ at the time, his condemnation of Japanese "inconsistency" was undermined by Japan's repeated assurances to Korea that Korean independence would be fully restored after the war with Russia (promises publicized in the popular press to the Korean people).

In the wake of the protectorate, Hŏ Wi left Seoul to plan an uprising that would amount to a legally declarable war. As luck would have it for Hŏ, the Japanese disbanded the Korean army in 1907. The soldiers, angry and often taking their weapons with them, scattered around the country. Hŏ did not intend to be a lone martyr, and in order to mount the war he wanted to declare, he formed an alliance with another Righteous leader, Yi Inyŏng, and together they began to collect troops. Like Hŏ, Yi knew the importance of making their cause intelligible to the world. In September 1907, Yi Inyŏng distributed an ultimatum throughout Korea, demanding the "restoration of [Korea's] independence," which he also sent to each of the foreign consulates in Seoul. He even mailed the proclamation to Korean groups in Honolulu and San Francisco, so their members could publicize his message abroad.[23]

Together, as the self-proclaimed National High Command of the Righteous Army, Hŏ Wi and Yi Inyŏng issued a new declaration of their combined legitimacy: "The Righteous Army is a patriotic society. The Great Powers must acknowledge that Japan violated international law in waging war on us. We appeal in the name of justice and humanity."[24] Their plan to recapture Seoul in November 1907 aimed at "eradicating the treacherous new treaty" Japan had imposed in order to "reestablish the conditions of a nation."[25] From its inception, Hŏ defined his war as the legitimate means to prevent Japan from erasing Korean sovereignty—a just response to a breach of the international standard to which the Powers subscribed.

Hŏ's attempt to legally declare war failed. At the time, he was not a true representative of Korea any more than the three envoys to The Hague, and no foreign country recognized his appeal. The Powers maintained their nations' commercial privileges in Korea through treaties with Japan, the outward guardian of the peninsula. A foreign representative's sanction of Hŏ's war as just would have challenged Japan's classification in international law as Korea's protector, at a time when the imperializing nations of the world granted Japan "paramount supremacy" in Korea. Recognizing what Japan called a "rebellion" in Korea as a "war" would have legitimated "rebellions" around the world—in the Philippines, Hawaii, Vietnam, Malaysia, Algeria, Egypt, Madagascar, and Morocco, to name just a few. Japanese troops captured and imprisoned Hŏ Wi early in 1908, and the Japanese government labeled him a "rioter." He died in jail that summer.

## CHANG INHWAN AND CHŎN MYŎNGUN

On 23 March 1908, Chang Inhwan and Chŏn Myŏngun, two young Korean immigrants in San Francisco, shot Durham White Stevens, an American diplomat, in front of the San Francisco ferry terminal as he prepared to embark for Washington, D.C. Stevens, who worked for the Japanese government as an advisor to the Korean court, had returned to the United States on official duty and to visit his family. Two days after the shooting, Stevens died. Just before his death, the Meiji emperor conferred on Stevens the highest honor any individual could receive for service to the Japanese nation, the Grand Cordon of the Rising Sun. Stevens was buried on April 8, after a funeral service at St. John's Episcopal Church in Washington, D.C., which included among the honorary pallbearers Secretary of State Elihu Root. Large and impressive memorial services followed in Seoul and Tokyo, with the entire office of the Japanese Foreign Ministry in attendance at the latter.[26]

Chŏn fired the first shots at Stevens, but when he missed, he charged forward and began striking Stevens on the face with his revolver. In the frenzy that ensued, Chang accidentally shot Chŏn as he fired the two fatal bullets into Stevens's back. While the gathering crowd cried, "Lynch the murderer!" police arrested Chang and imprisoned him without bail.[27] Police Judge C. T. Conlan ordered Chang to appear before San Francisco's Superior Court on a charge of murder. Chŏn, who was hospitalized for his gunshot wound, was unable to appear for arraignment until May 1. At his preliminary hearing, on May 8, Chŏn was ordered to stand trial as an accessory to murder. San Francisco attorney Nathan Coughlan defended Chŏn and Chang, pursuing an insanity defense for both men based on Arthur Schopenhauer's theory of patriotic insanity. The Koreans' was a "nobler kind of insanity," Coughlan argued, defining their condition as "excessive patriotism."[28] In mid-June Chŏn was temporarily freed and fled to Siberia.[29] The following winter, Chang was sentenced to serve twenty-five years at San Quentin for second-degree manslaughter. He served ten. In 1930, impoverished and disaffected, Chang committed suicide in San Francisco. He remained buried there until 1975, when South Korean President Pak Chŏnghŭi ordered his body reinterred in Seoul in the Korean National Cemetery, with full hero's honors.[30]

When Chang and Chŏn found themselves in jail for shooting an American citizen in the United States, the Japanese government found itself taking center stage, and also in a precarious legal position. The first article of the 1905 protectorate agreement declared that, concurrent with Japan's usurpation of Korea's foreign affairs, "Japanese diplomats and consular representatives [would] protect [*hogo*] Korean subjects and their interests in foreign countries."[31] The Japanese government and immigration-company recruiters enjoyed the power this provision guaranteed in thwarting competitive Korean emigration to Hawaii, but in this instance, the potential this clause opened for Japanese legal responsibility panicked the Japanese government.[32] Chang and Chŏn, however, never sought Japanese legal protection. Quite the opposite. The Korean men's cause diametrically opposed protection by any representative of Japan. They believed that what they did and what they said would elicit sympathy for their cause from Americans, and would also convince the world that an independent nation called Korea continued to exist. When Chang and Chŏn gave statements to the press directly after shooting Stevens, each openly admitted his culpability. "Yes, me shoot him," Chang reportedly stated. "Me sorry? No, Him no good. Him help Japan."[33] Both Koreans described their action as the patriotic means of sustaining the independence of their country:

> Stevens is a bad man. . . . He is a traitor to Corea and with smooth words has deceived the heads of my country. . . . Soon all Coreans will be dead and the Japanese will fill the country. . . . I am a patriot and I

shot Stevens because I think he is a traitor. . . . Corea is as good a country as Japan and Corea does not want the Japanese to come and take the
power as Stevens said . . . I do not care what happens to me. I hope I
killed Stevens.[34]

Though reported in fractured English—perhaps verbatim but also possibly
exaggerated to affect a further foreignness of the subject—Chang's point was
clear: "Corea is as good . . . as Japan and Corea does not want the Japanese to
come and take the power." While not invoking any nominal legal doctrine,
Chang's statement succinctly embodied his position in recognizable international terms: Japan's erasure of Korea's external sovereignty was insupportable
because internally a country continued to exist.

    In further statements to the police and court, Chang again justified his
actions as necessary to maintain the integrity of his homeland:

> Why would I not kill him? Thousands of thousands of people have been
> killed through his plans. . . . So I shot him for the sake of my country.[35]

> I prefer martyrdom by death rather [than] by imprisonment. I did my
> duty to the country and I don't care what the law does to me.[36]

Chŏn Myŏngun more plaintively demanded recognition of Korea's existence:

> My name is M.W. Chun [sic]. I am 25 years of age. . . . All the world looks
> on Corea as a low country and I was very sorry for it. I left my home for
> studying to help our country as other nations, but since I left the con-
> dition of Corea became worse. Japan thinks might is right, and would
> force our government to make treaties. And after that the great trouble
> started in our country. My brothers and relatives have been killed by
> Japanese, but I have no power to do anything here, and so I have always
> had to stand around helpless. . . . After I saw what Mr. Stevens said I
> decided to kill him and to kill myself too.[37]

Chŏn explained why, for him, murdering Stevens was the rational choice to
avenge the deaths of his family members and also to try to prevent the death
of his country.

    The Shufeldt Treaty between the United States and Korea (1882) legally
promised American assistance to Korea and also established the practice of an
American advisor at the Korean court. Serving under Emperor Kojong in

1883, Lucius Foote personally inaugurated this policy. Foote and subsequent advisors—Owen Denny (1886–1890), Charles LeGendre (1890–1894), Clarence Greathouse (1894–1900), and William Franklin Sands (1900–1904)—often warned the Korean court about Japan's increasing powers but did not encourage any formal U.S. protest.[38] Twenty years later, this practice ended when the second article of the August 1904 agreement between Japan and Korea transferred the Korean government's ability to select its foreign advisor to the Japanese government.[39] The Japanese Foreign Ministry appointed someone from within its own ranks to assume the role of the American advisor: Durham White Stevens. Despite the difference in the structuring of his appointment, the legacy of earlier American advisors had, for right or wrong, helped to engender a vaguely popular consciousness in Korea that abstract entities called "America" and "Americans" were on Korea's side against the Japanese. This consciousness prevailed to the extent that the Korean, Japanese, and American press all mentioned it at the time of Stevens's assassination.

Beginning in 1883, the Japanese Ministry of Foreign Affairs employed Stevens in a variety of jobs in both Tokyo and Washington. During his tenure as a lobbyist for Japan in America, Stevens became good friends with Japan boosters such as George Trumbull Ladd and George Kennan, members of what Bruce Cumings has described as "the usual retinue of cheerleading American scholars."[40] These men often wrote for Progressive-era journals such as *North American Review, Outlook,* and *World's Work,* and in general they praised the Japanese government's efforts with what they routinely described as the "degenerate" Koreans.[41] The ruse of Stevens' new appointment in 1904 as the "neutral" foreign advisor to the Korean emperor did not fool many people. Nonetheless, American businessmen who were increasingly involved in railroad, mining, lumber, patent, and immigration contracts in Korea with both Korean and Japanese firms assumed that the American Stevens would always favor their concerns.[42]

In March 1908, a reporter from the *San Francisco Chronicle* interviewed Stevens when he arrived. Stevens is quoted as saying, "The peasants have welcomed the Japanese, while the official class has not, but even the officials are beginning to see that the only hope for the country lies in a reorganization of the old institutions."[43] Stevens naturalized Japan's protection of Korea and defined the country's internal structures as unsound. The reporter summarized, "Stevens says the Corean people have been greatly benefited by Japanese protection and that they are beginning to look more favorably on it."[44]

In a coincidence that proved fateful for Stevens, the Righteous Army leader

Yi Inyŏng issued a proclamation to Koreans residing abroad, which arrived on the same ship carrying Stevens to San Francisco: "Compatriots, we must unite and consecrate ourselves to our land and restore our independence. You must appeal to the whole world about grievous wrongs and outrages of barbarous Japanese. They are cunning and cruel and are enemies of progress and humanity. We must do our best to kill all Japanese, their spies, allies, and barbarous soldiers."[45] The leaders of the San Francisco immigrant community ruminated over these fiery words after church on the Sunday following the ship's arrival. At the same meeting, they also discussed the statements Stevens had made to the press several days before.[46] According to subsequent newspaper headlines, members of the Korean community in San Francisco furiously responded to Stevens' words. Under the headline, "PLAN ASSAULT OVER PRAYERS," a *San Francisco Chronicle* reporter explained how members of two Korean immigrant organizations (the *Kongnip-hwae* and the *Taedong-hwae*) met on early Sunday evening with "hatred for Japan and the man who approved of Nipponese rule . . . strong in the breasts of them all."[47] An article in the California Korean paper, the *Kongnip Sinmun,* reported that the Sunday gathering had "turned into a meeting for the discussion of adequate measures to be taken against Stevens."[48]

There were two attacks on Stevens. The first occurred in the lobby of the Fairmont Hotel on the evening of March 22. Encouraged by Yi Inyŏng's call to arms, representatives from the immigrant societies—Yi Hakhyŏn, Mun Yang-mok, Chŏng Ch'aekwan, and Ch'oe Yusŏp—went to the hotel to question Stevens about his statements to the *Chronicle*.[49] A desk clerk called Stevens down from his room to inform him that a delegation of "Japanese men" had come to welcome him to the city. The Koreans greeted Stevens and asked whether the words reported in the paper were his. When he said yes, they began hurling large rattan chairs at him.[50] Although the mayhem was no more than a minor scuffle—the Koreans were quickly thrown out of the hotel, and Stevens received only a few cuts on his face—the printed report, "COREANS ATTACK A DIPLOMAT," touched off a narrative describing the "bloodthirsty" Koreans.[51] Worse still for Koreans trying to attract sympathetic attention from the Americans against the Japanese, the next day Chang and Chŏn shot the diplomat, imbuing whatever any other Korean said in the press at the time with a violent hue.

Japan's colonial aspirations for Korea had strengthened under the gaze of the international press the previous summer, in the wake of the Korean mission to The Hague, and the reporting surrounding the Stevens shooting only compounded these opinions. Yale Professor George Trumbull Ladd assumed the prosecutor's role in the editorial pages of the *New York Times*. In one article, Ladd declared the Koreans a "bloody race," adding in another that "the really significant thing is that such assassination is no new, and no rare occurrence in Korean history."[52] Although several columnists tried to avoid condemning the Koreans as murderers before their trial, reporters on both coasts of the United States infantilized and dehumanized the Korean men:

> The Korean Chang who shot Mr. Stevens to-day is about as large as a 12-year-old boy, but he says he is 30 years old.[53]

> The tiny Corean stood stoically in the corner of the room [suppressing] . . . the fanatic zeal of the Corean "schoolboys."[54]

Even the weapons involved in the assassination did not meet standards of manhood:

> The revolver which Chon used to strike Stevens . . . is a cheap weapon that looks more like a boy's toy pistol than a revolver. The barrel of the gun is only an inch and a half in length . . . Chang's weapon [was] also a .32 but possessing little penetrating power.[55]

An earlier, sustained discourse of the "degenerate" Koreans foreshadowed and was interwoven with the discussion of "the bloodthirsty" and "childlike" Koreans at this time. Despite the Korean men's efforts to explain that they resorted to their actions as patriotic men fighting for their country—"Corea is as good a country as Japan"—the colonial ordering of peoples classified the Koreans as incapable of governing themselves.

On the one hand, the Japanese consul in San Francisco, Koike Chūzō, worried that Japan's legal control of Korea under its protectorate arrangement would hold Japan legally responsible for the Korean men. On the other hand, the consul also worried that the protectorate arrangement was still not perceived as legitimate in the international arena. As soon as Stevens was shot, Koike urgently requested printed materials from the Colonial Administration Records Office in Tokyo, in case he found it necessary to display Japan's "enlightened" administration to United States officials.[56] As American press attention increasingly focused on the Koreans, Koike sent a cable to Foreign Minister Hayashi Tadasu in Tokyo, warning that "lies" the Koreans were printing in their local papers would spread into the American press, contaminating American opinion of Japan: "[The Koreans] are trying to shock American public opinion about Korea by deceiving [Americans] with this opportunity. They are playing with language that is becoming extremely dangerous, praising the murderers as righteous patriots and crying that the Japanese are barbaric thieves [*wazoku*]."[57]

In keeping with the larger policy of lexically demeaning Korean resistance —a policy that belittled the Righteous Army soldiers who protested the Japanese regime as rioters and declared their war a rebellion—Koike and other Japanese officials had to prevent the Koreans in America from being perceived as "patriots." Koike's concern over the eruptive potential of the terms is revealing. In her examination of what she calls "excitable speech," Judith Butler asks readers to "consider the situation in which one is named without knowing that one is named. . . . The name constitutes one socially, but one's consideration takes place without one's knowing."[58] Butler's point is key here, as Koike's determination to prevent the "language" from eluding his direct control points to how a "named" object acquires its name in the first place. For Koike, in a position of power, the Koreans were "playing with language," which, if countered properly, he could control. The Japanese consul could officially "name" the Koreans "without their knowing," as it were, or in a way that was beyond their control.

Meiji officials foreclosed the question of Japanese legal entanglement with the Korean men, not only by expressing grief for Stevens' death on behalf of a civilized nation but also by naming him a hero of both Japan and America. Instead of "protecting" the Koreans abroad as Japanese near-subjects, the Japanese government made every quasi-official effort to "protect" Stevens, its American employee. The Japanese government opportunely encouraged the perception that the Koreans were "bloody assassins" who had slaughtered a great statesman.[59] Foreign Minister Hayashi cabled Stevens in the hospital, and the cable was reprinted publicly in the *San Francisco Chronicle*: "I am profoundly shocked to learn of the dastardly attempts on your life. I am anxiously awaiting for speedy news of your recovery. In the meantime the Consul-General of San Francisco has been instructed to offer you all the assistance and aid in his power."[60] The same *Chronicle* article also reprinted Itō Hirobumi's personal note to Stevens: "Deeply grieved to hear of dreadful attack. Sincere hope for speedy recovery."[61] After Stevens died, Itō eulogized him to reporters: "I regard the death of Mr. Stevens as a national disaster and a personal loss."[62] While bemoaning the "disaster," Itō took special care to quote the American ambassador to Japan, who praised Stevens as a "loyal American."[63] In claiming Stevens' death as a "national disaster" for Japan (and according him the Grand Cordon of the Rising Sun), the Japanese government elevated itself on a par with the United States, and far above the "childlike" Korea. The "bloody race" of Koreans did not consist of equal human beings. The appeals that Chang and Chŏn made for Americans to pay attention to the violence the Japanese regime perpetrated in Korea evaporated with the death of the "loyal American," who was revered by the nation of Japan.

In a final plea for understanding, Chang Inhwan wrote a letter from his prison cell to the *San Francisco Chronicle* on 24 March 1908. The following morning, the front page of the paper featured a facsimile of his handwritten note as background to a photograph of a silhouette of Chang's head (Fig. 4). The paper offered a sketchy translation on an inside page, but in fact only the already sympathetic could read the visible part of the letter. The simplicity of Chang's final line provided a sharp closure to the Koreans' effort to maintain their country: "What other words could I say?" [*Tarun mal hal kŏt ŏp no ra?*] [64]

**FIGURE 4.** The letter from Chang Inhwan that appeared in a photograph on the front of the *San Francisco Chronicle*, 25 March 1908

In 1905, the Korean emperor's aide-de-camp, Min Yŏnghwan, committed suicide to protest the Japanese protectorate. Min's suicide, followed by several others, embodied the desperation of official attempts to preserve Korea's sovereignty, as those Koreans who remained in power—most noticeably Yi Wanyong—transferred Korean sovereignty to Japan. In the summer of 1907, when Prime Minister Yi made Emperor Kojong abdicate in favor of his son, he and his supporters brought about the end of Korea's independence for forty years. Chang, an unknown immigrant to San Francisco, tried with others to present the existence of their country to the world. Their words found no audience, and like Hŏ Wi, Chang and Chŏn resorted to violence.

## KŌTOKU SHŪSUI

Throughout the year 1910—before police arrested Kōtoku Shūsui in connection with a plot to assassinate the Meiji emperor—inspectors gathered materials loosely related to Kōtoku, concerning a plot to build bombs that would be thrown at an imperial procession. The government's desire to make Kōtoku the central figure in what became known as the Great Treason Incident stemmed primarily from his career of subverting the terms with which the Meiji government ruled Japan. It is, therefore, no new insight to argue that Kōtoku contested the terms of sovereignty in Japan.

At the turn of the last century, Kōtoku's disaffection with European liberalism and his turn to socialism intersected with his increasing disdain for Japan's foreign policy.[65] Unlike several of his contemporaries, however, Kōtoku was less concerned with a particular group or nation exploited by Japan than with imperialism in general.[66] In this vein, although Kōtoku continues to claim top billing in the history of early-twentieth-century resistance, his practical sympathies for those being dominated seemed almost nonexistent at times and often made him sound a bit like the government he criticized. Writing in his diary toward the end of June 1905, for example, Kōtoku mentioned that he wanted to retreat from the world "to buy some land in Hokkaido or Korea . . . [to] lead an ideal life."[67] Kōtoku's blank and therefore colonizable Korea gives precedence to Louise Young's insight about Japanese depictions of Manchuria in the 1930s as an "empty, flat space—a vast frontier awaiting Japanese settlement. This depopulation of the imaginary landscapes of the region was an expression of the imbalance of power between the Japanese and their others."[68] The great rebel likewise envisioned "empty" places where his personal settlement would cause no particular dislocation.

Although it is useful to know that Kōtoku had no great love for Korea, his scathing assessments of Japan's efforts to lead Korea to enlightenment allowed him to redefine the object of international terms. In short, in his analysis of Japan's Korea policy, Kōtoku demanded that international terms allow the people of a nation—not the state itself or its aggrandizers—to benefit from international exchange. Kōtoku derived his new international order from an awareness of how the system's terms worked in the world around him: "We once favored the expression 'fostering independence.'. . . Over the course of a decade, however, the term has lost all meaning. The problem for now is not whether we should foster independence in Korea. . . . In Hawaii independence was not fostered. In the Philippines independence was not fostered, nor in the Ryukyu islands nor in Taiwan. What reason could there be to foster independence in Korea?"[69] Elsewhere he elaborated, "Isn't Japan trying to make Korea its protectorate [*purotekutoreto*] just as America has made of Hawaii and England of Egypt?"[70] Kōtoku's disillusionment with Meiji's domestic settlement meshed with his sense of the emptiness of how the state employed international terms.[71] Similar to hollow promises of freedom and equality within the Meiji system, Kōtoku determined that independence was arbitrary as an international form.

In the months before Japan went to war with Russia over Korea, Kōtoku wrote several articles for the *Yorozu Chōhō* explaining his position on Japan's policies in Korea.[72] At first glance, his views appear to support a power-politics equation of strong over weak, but deeper inspection reveals Kōtoku's argument to be more subtle. He contended that the thrust of international terms should be reconfigured so that the inhabitants of a state—"the Korean people," *not* Korea—benefited from the exchange. In short, Kōtoku's formula convulsed the underlying assumptions of international law.[73] An August 1903 article, "To Withdraw or To Annex?" *(Hōki ka Heidon ka),* challenged Japan's policy as it then stood:[74]

> Will the Korean race [*Chōsen no jinrui*] be able to look one morning into the bright light of constitutional politics or will they forever be enslaved by writhing barbarians? Shouldn't the development of Korea's heavenly endowed natural resources benefit the people's livelihood? Will they be forever left in the midst of wild desolation? Heaven has presented us with this stark dilemma, put it on the shoulders of the Japanese people, and now the time has come for the Japanese people to resolve this matter.[75]

Citing Mutsu Munemitsu's stark treatise of state sovereignty to explain that it was Japan's duty to "annex" Korea, Kōtoku then subverted the meaning of "annexation" by declaring that the state must *not* benefit at the expense of the people:

> The standard for solving the Korean problem is not [predicated on] gain or loss for Korea's aristocracy or its governing officials. It exists only for the peace and welfare of mankind [*jinrui*]. When all is said and done, shouldn't Korea's political affairs, Korea's economy, Korea's natural resources [exist] for the happiness of the Korean people [*Chōsen jinmin*]? Should they do anything but profit the civilization of the Oriental races [*Tōyō jinrui*]? Or mankind throughout the world [*Sekai jinrui*]? Mencius said that things must benefit the people first and their ruler second. Withdrawal. If it should benefit mankind, then withdraw! Annexation. If it should benefit mankind, then annex! If it benefits mankind then it is not concerned with the gain or loss of the aristocracy or officials.[76]

Kōtoku demanded that a nation's people should become the subjects of international terms. He did not suggest that the masses carry out international relations, but rather contended that the promotion of their existence (both material and otherwise) should become the goal of policies in the international arena. He wrote, "I loathe those who take pleasure in the glory of the flag or in the expansion of national territory. I loathe those who want fame. It goes without saying that such a foreign policy is utterly despicable."[77]

## TARUI TŌKICHI AND *DAITŌ*

In the late 1870s, a minor furor arose in Japan's Foreign Ministry over an "uninhabited island" *(mujintō)* that lay between Japan and Korea. Both the Japanese and Korean governments claimed the piece of rock as their country's territory, and formal diplomatic exchange revolved around procedures for shipwrecks and castaways.[78] Fishing-industry entrepreneurs along the western coastal areas of Japan and in the northern territories under Russian jurisdiction beseeched their government to define the disputed islands as Japanese. For example, Toda Takayoshi of Shimane prefecture wrote a series of letters to the governor of Tokyo, Kusumoto Masashi, to urge "expanding the imperial lands to promote national interests [*kōchi wo kakuchō shi kokueki wo okoshi*]."[79] The Matsushima Islands, as they are known in Japanese (and *Ulle-*

*ungdo* in Korean), and the Takeshima/Tokdo group—known collectively on late-nineteenth-century European maps as the Hornet and Liancourt Rocks—formed the basis of this dispute. One fisherman wrote home from a Russian-occupied port and encouraged his government to "develop" *(kaishaku)* Matsu-shima. "Although the island is small," he wrote, "it is very profitable."[80] These men and others spoke about the rich and vast quantities of fish around the islands, and they formulated their arguments in terms of national interest and prestige. They argued for new, expanded borders for Japan.

Unlike Kōtoku's studied subversion of the meaning of "annexation," Tarui Tōkichi's chance involvement in the dispute over these "uninhabited islands" reveals that Tarui—a less educated but equally politically inclined individual—also conceived of reformulating national borders in the same terms used by Meiji state aggrandizers, but with a wholly different object in mind. In 1878, Tarui visited friends in Tokyo for a few days, after he failed to join soldiers in northern Japan who were raising a rebellion against the new regime.[81] Five years later, Tarui wrote about his trip and mentioned a conversation he had in Tokyo about an "uninhabited island" located off the western coast of Japan and toward Korea.[82] Several scholars have drawn attention to Tarui's meeting in Tokyo, but none that I am aware of has connected his conversation with the Japanese-Korean island dispute occurring at the time, a conflict that appeared daily in the Japanese papers. The location of the island Tarui discussed with his friends almost matched the location of the fishermen's descriptions, which is important to understand in light of the new nation that Tarui decided to found several years later.[83] Rather unimaginatively named "Great East" *(Daitō)*, it is possible that Tarui intended at first to establish his country on this disputed speck of land, or, possibly, on an island near the one that today bears the name *Daitō*.

Whoever his informant was, and whatever the actual location of the island that he sought, Tarui made creative use of the rocks he was thinking about. He returned to Kyushu, and between 1878 and 1881, while teaching part-time at a Chinese studies school and working as a reporter for the *Saga Shinbun*, he sailed off into the waters between southern Japan and southern Korea four separate times in an effort to locate the site for his *Daitō*. Each time, he and his crew failed to find it.

On their first adventure, in December 1879, they were confused by the large number of tiny islands off the southern coast of Korea around Tongyung, and they decided to beach their boat.[84] Korean villagers recognized the spruced-up raft as a foreign vessel and took its sailors to the local officials. Emphasizing heroics in his account, Tarui described how he and his crew used their motley guns and swords to escape and set sail again. This time, weather confused them, and when they sought refuge in a port on western Korea's Chŏlla Coast, officials seized them and their boat as they entered the harbor. Tarui told one of the officials that he "was on [his] way to see a friend in Shanghai." To another one, he said that he was from Tsushima and that he had intended to sail to the Ryukyu islands."[85] The Koreans consulted their manuals and determined what course of action to follow, agreeing finally to escort Tarui and his crew to Pusan and then send them back to Japan. Soon, however, the officials decided to free their catch, and Tarui retreated toward Kyushu in early January 1880.

Failure to locate the island dampened his spirits. Throughout the 1880s, Tarui's frustration with the world around him deepened as he watched the Meiji state co-opt supposedly egalitarian ideals into repressive instruments of its rule. His desire to find the "uninhabited island" had, I believe, nothing to do with fishing rights or national aggrandizement. Instead, as becomes clear from Tarui's writings about his imaginary nation, Tarui wanted to create a utopian, egalitarian state there. Back at home in northern Kyushu, Tarui involved himself in a variety of self-described progressive political movements that opposed the Meiji terms of rule. He attended meetings for months and remained unconvinced that even Itagaki Taisuke's Liberal Party *(Jiyūtō)* was morally committed to an equal redistribution of wealth. And so, in May 1882, vowing a "morality of spirit," Tarui and Akamatsu Taisuke established the Oriental Society Party *(Tōyō Shakaitō)*.[86] Tarui and Akamatsu gathered followers at the Kotoji Temple near Nagasaki. About one hundred people came from Shimabara, where the temple was located, three came from Nagasaki, and one each came from Tokyo, Osaka, Niigata, and Saga. One of the few historians of modern Japan to note Tarui's party, historian E. H. Norman, described it as "one of the most interesting examples of [a] left-wing derivative of the liberal movement."[87] Norman pointed to the significance of choosing Shimabara, "since one of the last great uprisings against Tokugawa domination took place there in the early seventeenth century."[88] The founders inscribed the principles of "morality" *(dōtoku)* and "equality" *(byōdō)* in the party's charter and promised to strive for "the greater welfare of society's masses" *(shakai kōshū no saidai fukuri)*.[89] Tarui's concern for other societies in the region manifested itself in article five of the party's charter, which urged party members to publish Chinese-style *(kanbun)* versions of their publications and distribute them in China and Korea. The following month, when the

Meiji regime's home minister Yamada Akiyoshi learned of the group's existence, he disbanded it on grounds that it disturbed the peace. Early the next winter, a Nagasaki court imprisoned Tarui for a month for printing copies of the organization's charter.

Tarui's sympathetic understanding of inequality within Japan led him naturally to understand the inequality in the ways that Europe and the United States grabbed at Asia. That being said, Tarui never seems to have made the critical connection between what Meiji aggrandizers ultimately wanted to do in Asia and what Americans and Europeans were also doing. Despite his lack of formal instruction in theories of social justice, Tarui encountered sufficient economic and political dislocation growing up in rural Nara, and later experiencing poverty when he moved to Tokyo in the year of the *Ishin* (1868), to inform his sensibilities to the extremes of wealth and power around him. A telling example of the precarious nature of his home life can be understood by considering the fact that, when he finally ran for parliament in 1892, he did so under the pseudonym of Morimoto Tōkichi because his family was known in his home region for its constant state of bankruptcy. Tarui even published the first edition of his famous treatise—which I elaborate upon shortly—under the name Morimoto.[90] Unlike thinkers such as Nakae Chōmin and Ōi Kentarō, who are remembered for their antigovernment positions, Tarui never received an education that might have rendered the use of his terms of opposition referential or summoned the authority of European knowledge.[91] Nakae and Ōi, for example, used the term "equality" with clear quotation or invocation of John Locke and John Stuart Mill. Tarui, on the other hand, used "equality" as if the concept in its Lockean sense had always been part of Japanese language and thought, a tendency that has left him subject to extremely different historiographic claims.

Adherents and detractors alike have labeled Tarui's thought eclectic and unsophisticated. This sentiment was best articulated by the famous social critic Tanaka Sōgorō, who suggested that the influences on Tarui's thought resembled "a cocktail of Confucian and Buddhist teachings and contemporary European and American thought."[92] Despite the hodgepodge nature of Tarui's ideas, Tanaka placed Tarui at the center of his genealogical pantheon of thinkers who envisioned egalitarian possibilities for modern Japan. Oddly enough, however, Tanaka scarcely mentioned his protagonist's lifelong concern for Asia, paying scant attention in his 1930 biography to Tarui's renowned essay proposing the unification of Japan and Korea. The book's frontispiece (Fig. 5) did afford some reference to Tarui's zeal for Asia by reprinting a photograph of him, centered against the background of a copy of a letter he wrote to the Korean king appealing for assistance in the unification of Japan and Korea.

On the other hand, the in-house historians of the notorious Pan-Asianist Black Dragon Society *(Kokuryūkai)* accorded Tarui the honor of having formulated the "first policy that strove for the general safety and well-being of East Asia."[93] The stench of Pan-Asianism from this group's affection for Tarui continues to render his legacy highly suspicious, and several historians have denounced him as the progenitor of Japan's "invasionistic" thought.[94]

In 1884, when several French navy ships opened fire on the Chinese port

**FIGURE 5.**   Photograph of Tarui Tōkichi on the frontis of a
1930 biography.

city of Fuzhou, Tarui's sense of Asia as a victim of Euro-American conquest intensified into a commitment to revolt. After the French bombardment, Tarui went to Fuzhou to participate in the resistance. From there, he moved to Shanghai, where he helped establish a school—the East Asia Academy *(Tōa Gakkan)*—sponsored by the Tokyo-based Asian Development Society *(Kōa-kai)*. Under the direction of the self-described nationalist/Asianist Suehiro Tetchō, Tarui worked at the school for a year with colleagues who included Baba Tatsui, Nakae Chōmin, Sugita Teiichi, and Hiraoka Kotarō, until financial problems forced the school's closure. In 1885, Tarui returned to Osaka, where he made new friends such as Ōi Kentarō through his Shanghai acquaintance with the Korean reformer Kim Okkyun, who had just returned to Japan after fleeing a recently failed coup attempt in Seoul.[95] Tarui soon joined Ōi Kentarō's scheme to sail from Osaka and invade Korea, winning over the Korean government by distributing translations of Rousseau and Mill—a plan that could not have been more different from the Meiji government's Conquer Korea debates a decade earlier. Osaka police discovered the plot before the ship left port and imprisoned the group's organizers. Tarui served only a few months in jail, but while there he drafted what remains the original plans for his imaginary state, *Daitō*. In at least the rewritten version of the essay that he later published, he crystallized his efforts to create an Asia-centered, socially egalitarian political body at this time.

That Tarui celebrated Japan's annexation of Korea in 1910 should in no way be effaced. In his younger days, he appears to have been ignorant of, or blind to, the obstacles posed by the already unequal relationship between Japan and Korea, or perhaps he believed that these obstacles represented an insignificant threat to the formation of an egalitarian nation. His preoccupation with designating a legal term for the nation he wanted to establish points to the shortcomings of simply weighing Tarui's thought according to where it fell on the political spectrum. Osaka police destroyed the initial draft of Tarui Tōkichi's *Treatise on the Unification of Great East (Daitō Gappōron)* when he was released from jail in 1885, but he rewrote and published the essay several years later in the form that has become known to many readers.[96] Tarui's vision of *Daitō* incorporated a variety of positions, but fundamentally he blended a profound concern for creating egalitarian politics with an abstract empathy for other Asian nations. Furthermore, he insisted that his vision of society meshed legally with international law.

Although the incidents were not at all connected, the negotiations between Itō Hirobumi and Li Hongzhang discussed in the previous chapter were occurring in Tianjin at the same time that Tarui was in jail writing his treatise. Considering the events together, however, brings into greater clarity Tarui Tōkichi's unusual contribution to Meiji political discourse. At the arms reduction talks in Tianjin, Itō emphasized to the Chinese diplomats that the government of Japan intended to conduct diplomatic intercourse with all nations— including Britain and China—in the terminology of international law. In his treatise, Tarui stressed that his *Daitō* belonged to the same discourse. For Tarui, by invoking the same terms of law, it was possible to envision an ordering of relations among Japan, Korea, and China that was radically different from what Itō proposed as "Japanese policy." Itō understood "equality," for example, as the term that officially—and, therefore, untouchably—governed relations among sovereign independent states and only those defined as such. In contrast, Tarui saw potential in these same terms as the genesis for the harmonious interdependence of all political bodies.

Because Tarui's proposal would have eradicated Japan itself, he posed no small threat to how the government defined the country, but it is clear from his essay that Tarui's goal was possible within the limits of international terms as he defined them. His political reconfiguration of Japan and Korea would first have extinguished the separately perceived sovereignty of both Japan and Korea. Together as *Daitō*, the nations would have assumed a unitary existence. Unlike the terms of the 1905 protectorate agreement the Meiji government later established over Korea, Tarui saw the ultimate (though not immediate) erasure of a hierarchical distinction between the two components of his new country. He envisaged "Great East" as a utopian place of equality, not only within its geographic borders but also as a state that would join equally in federated alliances with China to stave off the acquisitive desires of the Europeans and Americans. Tarui imagined his nation as an egalitarian state in which the countries would need to overcome the unequal social and economic conditions that prevailed in Japan and Korea at the time. He described the merger as initially "unprofitable" for Japan, but, believing in his utopia, he proclaimed, "that which profits Korea profits Japan, and that which profits Japan profits Korea." Unfortunately for Tarui's dreams, the book did not sway hordes of followers. In fact, not until twenty years later—*after* Japan's official annexation of Korea in 1910—did the book even attract a measurable readership.

The desired audience of Tarui's book was clear: he published the text in *kanbun* with the express intent of making it more accessible to Korean readers. Relying on the reputation he had gained as a parliamentary representative from the short-lived Oriental Liberal Party *(Tōyō Jiyūtō)* in the early 1890s,

Tarui published his treatise in 1893. Naming the new nation profoundly concerned him, and he devoted the second section of his essay to the problem. Quoting *The Analects,* he wrote:

> It is said that, "If the name is not correct, words lose their order." It is also said that, "a name is the guest of its substance." . . . First, I will clarify the name, and then examine how the substance accords with the name."[98]

He elaborated:

> My main point is to cause Japan and Korea to form a single, unified country. There would be nothing misleading about calling my plan "the Union of Japan and Korea." However, if we want to create a unified substance, we must resolutely turn away from this method. In both past and present times, disputes have arisen from heated disagreements over the placement and hierarchy of names [in a title]. For example, the Adriatics and the Romans formed an alliance and conquered Macedonia. A poet celebrated [the victory] with a triumphal song, but in the verses of this poem he placed the Adriatics ahead of the Romans. Discord developed between the two countries, and they began fighting. This deserves consideration, especially in the case of the name for a newly established nation.

More important, it was fundamental to Tarui that his national project be understood internationally. He was adamant that *Daitō* accord to the terms of international law:

> Equality for both sides is truly the principle of exchange. International law does not posit [national] hierarchies based on territorial size or the size of populations. I will not rely on the old names for the countries, and [in] the hope of avoiding any discrimination, I will designate the two countries under a [new] unified name: *Daitō*. In the federated countries of Europe as well, the name of each state [continues to] exist while a general name overarches [all]. Should the two countries unify now and use *Daitō* to name them both while also continuing to use their respective old names, they will avoid discord amongst themselves.[99]

In light of the fact that men such as Uchida Ryōhei, leader of the Black Dragon Society, wrote paeans to him, it is difficult even to want to see Tarui in a different light. His spastic attempts to form alliances with Korean progressives (such as Kim Okkyun) in the 1880s, however, embodied his concern for creating a viable resistance to what he saw as the wholly racist and destructive imperialist policies that the United States and the European countries were perpetrating in Asia. Tarui believed that he could overcome borders and create a better political body by choosing "the correct name" for the amalgamation of Korea and Japan. Moreover, he evoked the "teachings of international law" as the legitimating means with which to effect the "harmonious unity" he envisioned. *Daitō* negated both Japan and Korea. Although the government first discarded and then shelved Tarui's ideas, they resurrected and praised his foresight after Japan officially erased Korea in its own terms.

The process of bringing together these disparate voices is difficult because they are rife with incompatibility. Class difference alone, for example, likely would have prevented the Korean immigrants from sharing a meal with the Righteous leader whose cause they espoused. Together, however, these individuals all encountered an impasse, which bonded their actions. The inability to use international terms for purposes that differed from the limits that Japan ascribed to them underscores the historical condition that only authentically recognized regimes registered in international law at the beginning of the twentieth century. At the beginning of the twenty-first century, the international arena brims with examples of disconnected voices using international terms in ways not defined by the world's recognized authentic regimes. From former sex slaves of the Japanese Imperial Army to the unknown leaders of the recognized twenty-two million refugees in motion on the planet, it is undeniable that terms such as equality, independence, and sovereignty continue to inspire hope to those who rail against perceived injustice.[100] The problem remains of who is able—or who is recognized as able—to define meaning for these terms. The next chapter does not answer this problem, but in a related way it examines how modern Japan's internal reordering of law interacted with the nation's ability to display its empire as legitimate.

# CHAPTER 5

# MISSION LÉGISLATRICE

*T*he international politics of imperialism taught Meiji state aggrandizers that, if they were to gain full legitimacy in Korea as an enlightened exploiter, they should establish new legal codes in their protectorate. Before annexing Korea in 1910, in the absence of formalizing a Japanese code of law for Korea, Japanese colonial rulers realized that they ought to at least convey a desire and a plan to do so in international terms.[1] In short, Japan needed to demonstrate that it had embarked on a legislating mission—a *mission législatrice*—to Korea.[2] Japan's endeavor to make Korea *legal* in the eyes of the international community at the time brings into relief a forgotten, yet highly revealing, component of the process of the annexation. Although the Powers declared Korea illegal in 1907, the same group declared Japan's Korea fully legal in 1913, when Japan abrogated extraterritorial privileges in Korea and submitted its nationals to the terms it established there.

At the turn of the last century, the few remaining threads of Western extraterritoriality in Japan pertained to civil codes, particularly business practices. The demand to implement and sustain extensive extraterritorial privileges originated from what can best be understood as an "imperialist gaze" that was focused on Japan's criminal and penal codes.[3] Western heads turned at the sight of heads of executed criminals on stakes.[4] In their horror at this spectacle, so-called enlightened merchants and travelers from Europe and the United States often failed to remember that their safety was maintained by the constant threat from their countries' cannon-laden ships.

In the 1850s, it was always easier for American and European imperialists to judge the "uncivilized" as "barbaric," "unchristian," or "cannibalistic" and forget the large-scale violence that accompanied and privileged their own adventures. Half-a-century later, Japan was participating fully in the terms and practices of this discourse. As we have seen in other examples, the international arena's failure to credit Korea as more than a pawn of China, Russia, and finally Japan routinely benefited Japan's actions there. The world, for example, paid no appreciable attention to King Kojong's declaration of Korean sovereignty in 1897 or renaming himself as Korea's emperor. Conversely, in 1907, when the world paid attention to Korea in the wake of the incident at The Hague, it was only to applaud Japan's actions there.

Most important, with respect to the discussion that follows, the world paid no measurable attention to the Korean judicial restructuring in the 1890s, which, among other things, enabled Hŏ Wi to serve on Seoul's new high court and begin making decisions in international terms in the first place.[5] The world's failing thus kept Korea in a state of suspension in the imperialist's gaze. For many, Japan's well-known, newly achieved levels of civilization could only benefit the Koreans. Stories concerning Korea's "barbaric" ways of dealing with criminals—burying some murderers alive up to their necks, then kicked in the head and devoured by insects—compounded this logic.[6] The international arena's collective belief that "civilized" legal codes would uplift the world's "heathen," or at least make them manageable, comprised, therefore, an additional element of how Japan could display its control of Korea, and this chapter describes how Japan demonstrated its legislating mission to Korea in such terms. The process ultimately led the world to confirm full status on Japan among the world's legitimate imperialists when the Powers abrogated their own privileges of extraterritoriality in Korea and subjected their nationals to Japan's laws there. In addition, however, Japanese colonizers simultaneously justified the need to maintain less than "civilized" procedures—specifically, flogging—to control their charges, the Koreans.[7] Seen in a different light, an observation made by *The Times* of London when Japan overthrew the Korean emperor in 1907 bespoke the self-satisfied international sentiment of the day with respect to this seeming paradox: "We can easily appreciate the position of the Japanese in Korea."[8]

In 1907 the Koreans' disastrous mission to The Hague only encouraged further Japanese control of Korea. In particular, the international community praised Japan's new legislating mission.[9] As mentioned earlier, reports from London explained Japan's co-option of the Korean judiciary by writing, "Marquis Ito's first measure aims at securing life and property in Korea by substituting pure and competent tribunals of justice for the present and unskilled law Courts."[10] A hurdle arose, however. With Japan now legally legislating Korea, the question of whether what were sometimes awkwardly called "foreign foreigners" in Korea—Americans, English, French, and so forth—would recognize Japan as *their* "pure and competent" ruler, too, or whether they would continue to demand their long-standing privileges of extraterritoriality. Japanese legal and state theorists knew that, if the "foreign foreigners" maintained such restrictions in Korea, the Powers would not fully recognize Japan's rule. In 1882, the United States promised Korea that, once Korean judicial procedure and codes "conformed to the laws of the United States," it would eradicate special privileges for its nationals there.[11] The United States, therefore, held a particularly important role in judging Japan's sovereignty over its colonial prize. Ultimately, Japan's performative display of why the Powers should abandon extraterritoriality in Korea cemented Japan's control of Korea in international terms.

Before analyzing the terms of Japan's legislating mission to Korea, it is helpful to consider two photographs the Meiji government distributed in the period prior to the annexation in 1910, which elucidates the larger, discursive strategy at play. The Japanese colonial regime's *1907 Report on Reforms* included glossy pictures that illustrated the legitimacy of its rule in Korea to readers around the world. Some photos (Fig. 6) featured the new law courts—such as the new "Court of Cassation" (High Court of Appeal) in Seoul—in order to display the fruits of Japan's zeal.[12]

**FIGURE 6.**   Court of Cassation, Seoul, 1907

The visual "Europeanness" of the building challenged the viewer to imagine anything identifiably "Japanese" about Japanese rule in Korea. For a reader familiar with Tokyo at the time, though, the structure would not have been surprising. Architecture inspired by Euro-American influences had become standard for major government buildings in Tokyo by the turn of the century.[13] In Seoul at the time, as well, Korean progressives—both for and against Japan—sponsored a number of very un-Korean structures in the city. The Independence Movement's own 1898 Arc de Triomphe, built to commemorate Korea's independence from China, dominated the city's skyline to the northwest, where today it seems small. To visually convey their power, governments that maintained extraterritorial privileges in Seoul—the United States, France, Britain, Russia, and others—spent huge sums on lavish, non-Korean-style consulates.[14] And in the southern section of the city, the Japanese Resident General's headquarters rose high on a hill within a large European-style building, towering over the single-story Korean houses below.

Despite these non-Korean buildings in Seoul, however, the new, massive, French-influenced Japanese Court of Cassation, in neo-Renaissance style, did not merge quietly into the landscape when it was built near a palace in downtown Seoul. As philosopher Gilles Deleuze might have phrased it, the building's "assemblage" invaded all prevailing proportions and attracted the kind of attention needed by a dominator to simultaneously secure and display its controlling position.[15] The photograph published in the Japanese regime's *Report*, however, would have obscured any possible concern that the Japanese were "invading" the landscape, because the photograph was cropped to block out any surrounding buildings. However, whether the Japanese colonial regime intended this photograph to obfuscate the "noticeability" of the structure is not the point. The producers of this *Report*—and subsequent ones as well—conveyed a sense of the colonial, "anywhere" quality of this building through such photographs, confirming the universality of the Japanese endeavor.

The following year's *Report* included a page of smaller pictures, which went right to the heart of the universal terms of Japan's legislating mission to Korea.[16] An updated photograph (Fig. 7) of the now-opened Court of Cassation and one of the newly built, Japanese-run prisons in Seoul sandwich "before" and "after" photographs depicting trial proceedings. The "before" picture—in pre-Japanese Korea—features a magistrate flanked by advisors and seated in front of closed doors, listening to someone read charges from a scroll at his feet. Eight officials beneath him surround the two offenders/plain-

**FIGURE 7.** Photographs illustrating Japan's *Mission Législatrice* in Korea, 1909

tiffs, who squat on the dirt with their heads bowed. Most of the men wear long, white robes and hats that define their rank.[17]

The image against which this scene is juxtaposed—the "after" picture—shows a sun-filled, white room. "Scientifically sanitized rule has come to Korea," the picture seems to shout. The judges, six men in dark Western suits, sit behind a long wooden bench. Their nationality is difficult to ascertain because no names are listed, and Japan's judicial rules permitted qualified Koreans to serve. The "Koreanness" of the defendants, however, is clear. Five men stand directly in front of the judges and wear the typical white shirts and pants of Korean commoners. All but one wears his long hair in the traditional top-knot. By contrast, a supposedly neutral, universal dress code of modernity costumes the judges. Three policemen sit near the Koreans, and the court clerk sits sideways between the judges and the offenders, recording the words spoken over his head. The sprawling new prison pictured at the bottom of the page confirms that the colonial regime was already sentencing people. Two years before annexation brought the issue of extraterritoriality to the fore, such images conveyed Japan's position to fellow imperialist nations in the confluent terms of colonial control.

## THE "FATHER OF MODERN JAPANESE LAW"

In the 1870s and 1880s, the Meiji government's French legal advisor in Tokyo concocted the formula that ultimately released Japan from extraterritorial restrictions. Examining how he did so sheds light on often-overlooked connections between legal terms and international power. In keeping with the early Meiji passion to "seek enlightened knowledge from throughout the world," in 1873 Justice Minister Etō Shinpei dispatched a group of young bureaucrats to Paris, where they listened to Gustave Boissonade lecture on criminal and civil codes. The group was so impressed—or so confused—by what Boissonade told them that he was immediately offered a job as a consultant to draft Japan's new legal codes. Initially hired for three years, Boissonade remained in Tokyo for the next two decades, securing his place in legal history as the "father of modern Japanese law."[18] He began his work on criminal codes and, during the late 1870s, drew up a system of laws and procedures based largely on his country's 1810 Napoleonic Code. As described earlier, legal scholar Mitsukuri Rinshō remembered his frustrations at trying to render these same codes into Japanese before Boissonade came to Japan—in the pre-Meiji days of "no annotations, no glossaries, no instructors." Once Boissonade was in Tokyo, however, Mitsukuri and others at the Ministry of Justice readily sought his advice. The young legal scholars translated Boissonade's final product as Japan's new criminal codes, which were promulgated in 1880 and put into force in 1882.

His 1870 resume reveals that, although Boissonade was a scholar of modern comparative law, he was not a gifted linguist. He had the ability to read English but not speak it (*"Lit l'anglais, le parle peu"*).[19] Boissonade would have known Latin and possibly Greek (his father was one of the most famous clas-

**FIGURE 8.**    Gustave Boissonade, the Father of Japanese Law

sicists in France), because the entrance examinations to the legal profession in France at the time demanded competency in the classics. The breadth and depth of his language skills is more than just a petty detail, because during the twenty years Boissonade spent advising and instructing the Meiji government in the uses and meanings of European legal terminology, the "father of modern Japanese law" did not know Japanese well. Rather than seeing this as a defect on Boissonade's part, however, it is more useful to consider it as a measure of how foreign language study had expanded in Japan. Only ten years after the overthrow of the Tokugawa regime, foreign advisors such as Boissonade taught young Meiji students and politicians arcane legal concepts in their native tongues, because the formerly hidden European languages—once even heretical—had become useful elements of modern practical knowledge.

Both the Ministry of Justice and the Ministry of Foreign Affairs employed Boissonade for different purposes, but he did not simply sit at his desk waiting for orders. Meiji politicians, bureaucrats, and students consulted him widely on contemporary and historical issues of European legal and political thought, and he responded with highly opinionated and often unsolicited evaluations. Almost immediately on his arrival in Japan in 1874, for example, Minister of Foreign Affairs Ōkubo Toshimichi sought Boissonade's advice over a dispute with China, whereupon Boissonade joined the official entourage to Beijing to give shipboard lectures on international law.[20] In the wake of the Conquer Korea debates at the time, Itō Hirobumi sought his advice concerning the course of Japan's Korean policy. With the encouragement of students of French law, Boissonade began teaching classes at the Ministry of Justice's Legal Academy, courses that eventually formed the basic curriculum at the Law School of Tokyo Imperial University.

In the freedom of this atmosphere, Boissonade issued his most critical mandate to the Japanese government: if the Meiji regime did not immediately abolish the practice of torturing prisoners in Japan, the "Western Powers" would not begin to abolish their privileges of extraterritoriality in Japan. Young legal scholars embraced Boissonade's formula, determining that Japan needed to eradicate its practice of torture-on-display to be considered a fully "independent" nation. Boissonade could not have been more axiomatic in his explanation. On 15 April 1875, he wrote a blunt letter to Minister of Justice Ōki Takato: "Mortifying scenes occur every day [in the prison] without any attempt to conceal them. This takes place next to a school of law, opposite the offices of the Ministry of Justice—as if these acts were not contrary to law and justice itself. . . . Should I not be apprised of some Imperial Act to amend this outrage against humanity and slight to reason, I shall have to leave the Ministry of Justice."[21] A month later, Boissonade presented the unresponsive Ōki with an ultimatum: that the Japanese government end the use of torture against prisoners in the country's jails, or he would leave Japan at once.[22] Boissonade emphasized that continuing the practice of torture was contrary to Japan's interests because, as he wrote, the Meiji regime had "promised [the European ministers] it would abolish torture. Until this is accomplished, Japan cannot pretend to begin serious negotiations about obtaining jurisdiction over foreigners."[23] The emperor responded and limited the randomness with which torture could be used, and in 1879 Japan formally abolished the practice of torturing prisoners. Like other advisors, Boissonade viewed Japan as a promising student but made it clear that some bodies were still more civilized—less colonizable—than others. France's citizens would not succumb to Japanese law until it could be measured as civilized by their terms. Meiji politicians and legal theorists understood that as long as extraterritorial spaces existed for foreigners within Japan, the country was not a full sovereign state according to international law.

Boissonade contributed mightily to Japanese conceptualization of these issues, and his success as the "father of modern Japanese law"—the reason he is so fondly remembered to this day—comes from his having integrated himself as an element of Meiji modernization. He confidently claimed his role as the bearer of civilization to Japan, the civilizer who provided the terms of legal modernity. Earlier Tokugawa-era "expel the barbarian" rhetoric, for example, underscored how extraterritorial privileges restricted what nativists described as an inviolable national entity.[24] Meiji nationalists subsequently learned, however, to argue for the eradication of these privileges in international terms. Increasing knowledge of what the new terms entailed afforded the ability to debate the extraterritorials (as it were) in their own terms. They protested extraterritoriality as an infringement on the sovereignty of their independent nation, and Boissonade encouraged their actions. In 1882, Boissonade published a thousand-page commentary on Japanese criminal procedure under the new laws, and in the forward to this mammoth tome, he described what he saw as the logical evolution of Japan's course of self-civilizing: "For our purposes, in drafting this Schemata for the criminal Codes and also for the civil Codes, we have preserved and held in view as our main objective the preparation of the complete independence of Japan with respect to Jurisdiction. By introducing these Laws, we have accomplished this. At the same time, under our Tutelage, we have instilled principles of justice and natural reason which are the honor of modern times and which remove all plausible grounds, even pretexts, for Extraterritoriality."[25] Should Boissonade's efforts bear fruit as he thought they would, he conceded that even civilized bodies could be confident that they would be treated with the "honor of modern times." Extraterritoriality would be unnecessary.

Boissonade's vision of himself as a vital but objective participant in the modernization of Japan was entwined with a belief that he imported universal knowledge. Like the terms of international law, the French criminal codes that Boissonade explicated to Meiji jurists and students presumed their own universality, and he himself made a point of diminishing the "Frenchness" of Japan's new codes: "Whatever legitimates our national pride with regards to the French Codes, which have so often been imitated in Europe and America, we must recognize that, in many respects, today they are no longer on a level with modern science and practical, daily needs. . . . We have modified what was recognized to be defective, although we have guarded against rash innovation, we have avoided blindly following routine."[26]

For Boissonade, a universal norm that required no elaboration inscribed what linguist Roland Barthes might have described as a naturalized "horizon" line, and under Boissonade's "tutelage," Japan's new codes blended seamlessly into that line.[27] He elaborated this point to justify why the existence of the new codes in Japan necessitated the eradication of extraterritoriality: "Moreover, if these new Codes are destined one day to be applied to foreigners residing in Japan, it is good that they are not of an overly particular national character. It is good that they offer, above all, a sort of common international law, sheltered from traditional prejudices and systematical criticism and from which nations, except on occasion, are no longer exempt."[28] Boissonade postulated that the Meiji regime could display its participation in a thoroughly universal mean to the nations of the world. His own pomposity aside, Boissonade arguably wanted to bring about the end of degrading restrictions in Japan. His reasoning suggested to readers in Europe or America—in terms they understood—that the Powers would be safe to dissolve their extralegal zones in Japan, because terms that were familiar to them now prevailed.

## LAWLESS AND LEGAL KOREA

Japanese officials worked to ensure that their legalizing mission was perceived as a success before the annexation took place. As Japan increasingly extended its rule in Korea, Japanese opinion makers sought to depict pre-Japanese

Korea to both international and domestic audiences as a place entirely devoid of law. At the same time—and also following international practice—such descriptions allowed that, although Korea did have some criminal codes, they were random and exceedingly dangerous, worse than no law at all. Once Japan secured the 1905 protectorate agreement, however, legal theorists swiftly began to suggest that foreign foreigners should soon be at ease because Japanese law would prevail in Korea. When Japan took over the judiciary, in 1907, promoters of Japan's enlightening role explained that legal codes there would be consistent with those in Japan. According to the logic of colonization, Japan's Korea could then be declared legal like Japan, a place the Powers could determine to be "civilized" by erasing their extraterritorial privileges there.

Japanese colonial boosters explained the progress made by their legal missionaries to assuage any civilized concern about conducting business or affairs in Korea now that the enlightened exploiters were making progress. In addition to photographs, the 1907 *Report on Reforms on Progress in Korea* offered a brief summary of recent events. The authors of the *Report* allowed that "the historical conditions which existed at the time [in Korea] when the [initial] treaties [between Korea and other nations] were concluded [meant that] it was quite natural that civilized nations should have wished to make their consular jurisdiction as extensive as possible."[29] They now pointed, however, to "the progressive tide of reforms" Japan's legal messengers sponsored as reason for a "greatly diminished" need for apprehension. Anthropologist Bernard Cohn's assessment of late-eighteenth-century British views of India is instructive for placing Japanese descriptions of Korea a century later:

> Although it was recognized that there was "law" in India, that "law" was believed to be different from the European kind . . . the model of the Mughal-Indian political system was absolute and arbitrary power, unchecked by any institution, social or political, and resting in the person of the emperor, with property and honors derived solely from the will of the despotic ruler. . . . Justice was dependent not on the rule of law but on the rule of men, who could be influenced by money, status, and exercise in their office of judge. The idea that "despots" had ruled India was revalorized in the nineteenth and twentieth centuries as one of several ruling paradigms that formed the ideological infrastructure of British rule in India. In its cleaned-up version it was expressed thus: Indians are best ruled by a "strong-hand," who could administer justice in a rough-and-ready fashion unfettered by rules and regulations. Their

courts, their procedures, their regulations, and the propensity of Indians to perjury and the suborning of witnesses only served to delay justice.[30]

According to the Japanese colonial regime in Seoul, Japan shared England's difficulties. Civil procedures, the colonizers believed, existed minimally at best, and criminal codes were unmentionable:

> The Koreans had little or no conception of private rights as were understood elsewhere in the Orient. Thus, when such maladministration existed for so long a time that public officials were accustomed to pay only scant respect to the private rights of the people, and the latter, on their side, dared not complain against official extortion. In short, civil law guaranteeing private rights had practically no existence. . . . [J]udges and procurators, being utterly deficient in legal knowledge and training, often delivered wrong judgments. . . . Prison administration as heretofore carried out in Korea is a matter almost too unsavory to describe. The most common form[s] of punishment were beating, imprisonment, and confinement in the stocks. The Penal Code is full of directions for administering floggings, which were often so severe as to render the victim crippled for life, if he did not die under the infliction.[31]

Paralleling Cohn's ventriloquized British colonizer denouncing "*their* courts, *their* procedures, *their* regulations," the Japanese removed themselves to a position that mandated that the Koreans were eminently colonizable in Japan's new "pure and competent tribunals of justice." More important, the *Report* implied, non-Koreans could now be sure of their safety.

The English-language *Report* thus reflected what had been taking place in Japanese descriptions of the situation in Korea for quite some time, particularly in the legal profession's newspaper, the *Hōritsu Shinbun*.[32] In 1900, editor Takagi Masutarō first published the *Hōritsu Shinbun* as a weekly paper but soon increased its printing to six times a month, and it remained in circulation until 1945.[33] Called the "Edoko Defender," Takagi represented the Nihonbashi section of Tokyo in parliament. The subject matter of his newspaper was often too specialized for the mass-circulation presses, and so he secured an important niche as well as a constant readership. Articles regularly followed Justice Ministry proclamations and reforms. Moreover, and of particular importance to Japan's annexation of Korea, the paper routinely reported the activities of Japanese lawyers, judges, and professors who embarked on legislating missions throughout Japan's growing empire. Thus, part of this newspaper's value to history is that it described the human element involved in writing Japan's laws abroad—for our concerns, Japan's laws in Korea. Like the Foreign Ministry documents that record the names of translators involved in explaining Japan's new diplomatic techniques, the *Hōritsu Shinbun* gave personality to an otherwise impersonal transformation of international relations. In May and June 1908, for example, the paper printed the names of judges hired by the new Japanese-run Korean Supreme Court.[34] Chief Justices from Wakayama, Matsue, Akita, and Naha were among those who served. Although not famous in most histories of modern Japan, those who also went off to Korea to spread the word of modern law included Sasaki Genosuke, a judge from Yamagata; Fujiwara Saburō, a Nagano prosecutor; and Ishikawa Tadashi, from the Osaka appellate court.[35]

Notably, various articles make it clear that Japan started to reorder Korea's judiciary even prior to the July 1907 agreement, when it became official. In the spring of 1906, the Ministry of Justice in Tokyo dispatched Ume Kenjirō to Korea to write new civil codes and Kuratomi Yuzaburō to work on the criminal codes. The ministry appointed Ume with confidence. Born in 1860 in Matsue, he embodied the archetypal early-Meiji-era student depicted in stories such as Tokutomi Kenjirō's *Omoide no Ki*.[36] Poor and brilliant, he advanced rapidly through his French-language studies at the Tokyo Foreign Language School and then at the Justice Ministry's Law School, where Boissonade taught. Before joining the law faculty of Tokyo Imperial University, the Ministry of Education sent him to Lyon, where, to the overwhelming pride of the Ministries of Justice and Education in Tokyo, he won the university's Vermeil Prize for an outstanding doctoral dissertation.[37] Ume rose to the occasion of his mission to Korea and, in good Napoleonic fashion, compiled reams of customary procedures as he traveled throughout the country.[38]

On the other hand, the Ministry's appointment of Kuratomi Yuzaburō reveals another international imperialist practice that Tokyo put to use in its new colonies: Kuratomi was an upper-class disciplinary problem. Two months before he was sent to Korea, the Tokyo Lawyers' Association and the Japan Lawyers' Association had jointly reprimanded him for gross mishandling of the Hibiya Riots trial in his role as chief prosecutor.[39] These groups may have seen the task of creating a new criminal justice system in Korea in and of itself as the perfect punishment.

The overall tone of the *Hōritsu Shinbun*'s articles concerning criminal justice in Korea ascribed a sense of maturity to the late-Meiji-era legal system by routine, yet subtle, comparisons to Korean forms of criminal jurisprudence.

Reporters described Korean practices as "barbaric" and "uncivilized" and relied on the international discourse of enlightened exploitation to imply why such conditions necessitated some sort of "civilization" process. In the 1870s, for example, Boissonade made it clear that contemporary European criminal theory overwhelmingly condemned the practice of beheading, explaining—albeit perversely—that hanging was the accepted civilized means of execution. Articles in the *Hōritsu Shinbun* in the spring of 1905, for example, described at length Korea's barbaric execution practices: "In Korea, a country with which we have friendly and close relations, even now in the civilized twentieth century people are beheaded like pigs."[40] By the time of the article's publication, in May 1905, hanging had been standard procedure in Japan for three decades.[41] The article describing the apparently barbaric Koreans also conceded that there were occasional hangings in Korea, but this was conveyed in an aside that recounted the events of a recent evening in which thirty-six criminals were hanged en masse while another prisoner was beheaded in front of them all.[42] According to articles of this ilk, prisoners lived in wretched tiny cells, and "according to Korean law repeated theft [meant] the death penalty."[43] Reporters of conditions in Korea—as well as those in Taiwan and Mainland China—apparently had no interest in reminding readers of not-so-old practices in Japan, because its current methods were accepted as common sense. According to the *Hōritsu Shinbun,* Japan's legal professionals were working manifestations of Fukuzawa Yukichi's 1885 mandate to "leave Asia," only at the beginning of the twentieth century they had come to full circle to bear civilization there.[44]

Articles in the *Hōritsu Shinbun* point to how Japanese legal theorists incorporated European notions of criminal anthropology—particularly phrenology—into their new conceptions of criminal law. In Europe, around the time Boissonade left for Tokyo, reports flourished of savage behavior among "natives" in places that Europeans related to through an imperialist gaze. In those places, reports of such savage behavior intersected with other discussions of degeneracy among the poor masses spawned by industrialization in urban areas. Social thinkers advocated for what French social philosopher H. A. Frégier termed the "dangerous classes."[45] So-called experts, particularly medical ones, came to be involved in "repairing" criminals.[46] In France in particular, society "moved towards the practice . . . of calculating punishment not in terms of the crime, but the psychology and circumstances of the individual criminal."[47] Discussions of criminal deviance widely appeared in newspapers, and criminal legal proceedings drew large crowds of spectators. Simultaneously defining oneself as not criminal as well as someone who participated in the reform of a criminal marked a person as civilized—that is, *not* native, *not* colonizable. Reforming criminals in terms of "the psychology and circumstances of the individual criminal" rendered civilized societies distinct from the far-flung colonial places where "dangerous" people lived.[48]

A 1906 article in the *Hōritsu Shinbun,* for example, featured a sketch of a man's head partitioned and labeled with *"iroha"* characters (alphabet letters).[49] Next to the drawing, a key explains what each letter designates, descriptive human traits such as "secrecy," "sexual instinct," and "temporal sense," and the accompanying article underscores the importance of knowing the passionate composition of the human brain in relation to criminal law. Historians Umemori Naoyuki and Daniel Botsman have separately argued that Tokugawa philosopher Nakai Riken's late-eighteenth-century proposal for a "long-term jail" foreshadowed Meiji criminal theory by advocating the need to reform criminals individually.[50] Meiji European-inspired theories of knowing the criminal mind built on this process by blending the so-called truths of contemporary racial and gender typology with psychological sciences, adding distinctively new elements to Meiji prescriptions for reforming criminals. Reforming a "primitive type," for example, now required colonizing knowledge.[51] Japan's legislating missionaries to Korea brought codes with them that enabled these lawyers and scholars to preserve themselves and Japan as discrete from the places to which they bore their civilization. And this particular aspect of Japanese imperialism must always be reiterated, because it enabled Japan to colonize what much of the world looked upon as the same types of peoples.

Japanese legal missionaries to Korea increasingly began to publicize the wide range of their efforts to readers at home. Articles reported, for example, how "the judicial reform advance party [*senpatsu*]" in Korea worked to establish 125 courts and 9 prisons (8 to accord with 8 local courts and 1 for exiles on a remote island)—all *before* annexation. Moreover, as occasional reports described, Japanese worked together with Koreans to rewrite Korean codes and even convened a Korean Judiciary Friendship Association *(Kankoku Hōsō Konwakai)* in the process.[52] In August 1909—a full year before the official colonization—criminal-code reformer Kuratomi Yuzaburō sent a long article back to Japan providing his "Summary of the Korean Judicial System."[53] In respectful fashion, he emphasized that Japanese and Korean officials had worked in harmony to reform and build on the Korean system established in the "third year of the Kwangmu reign" (1899). He described the current transformation as a matter of course within Korean history and criticized the "fail-ure" of earlier Korean "judicial efforts to protect individual rights," making it clear that this was Japan's primary cause.[54]

Notably, however, Kuratomi's report also stressed that several differences would have to be maintained between codes that applied to Japanese and those that applied to Koreans. In particular, Kuratomi explained that the law would sustain the practice of flogging Korean prisoners, a decision that had very obvious benefits for the colonizers. Kuratomi assured readers that there was nothing alarming in this discrepancy and announced that the general struc-tural apparatus of the new Korean judicial system meshed seamlessly with Japan's. At the time, of course, it was not at all unusual for colonizing regimes to make useful exemptions in their colonies—such as sustaining the practice of torture—to empower their dominance. Historian Yoshimi Yoshiaki calls these exemptions "giant loopholes."[55] Yoshimi has himself most famously examined the "giant loopholes" that allowed Japan (and other imperialist nations) to exempt their colonial populations from the international laws prohibiting the trafficking of women and children.[56] Like flogging, enslaving Koreans as so-called comfort women, for example, was legally provided for in international terms according to Japan's standard civilized procedure. And the imperialists made these provisions openly among themselves.

In 1909, therefore, Korea made legal sense both in Japan and abroad. Korean courts now operated according to the European-defined "three-tiered trial system" *(sanshin seidō).*[57] The composition of the new judiciary is shown in Table 1. Not surprisingly, the proportion of Japanese legal missionaries to that of Korean practitioners of law favored the colonizers. The predictably weighted ratio reveals, however, that Japan intended Korea to make sense with

**Table I.  Korean Judiciary, 1908**

| Position | Number of Personnel, by Nationality | | |
| --- | --- | --- | --- |
| | Japanese | Korean | Total |
| Judges | 116 | 66 | 182 |
| Prosecutors | 46 | 12 | 58 |
| Chief Clerks | 4 | 0 | 4 |
| Clerks | 153 | 141 | 294 |
| Translation Department | 4 | 0 | 4 |
| Interpreters | 18 | 49 | 67 |

*Source: Hōritsu Shinbun,* 5 August 1909.

Japanese law but also that Koreans would practice these laws themselves. Under the workings of the new system, a third of the men working as judges were Korean.[58]

Japan's legal mission is also displayed in the structure of its prisons (see Table 2). In light of the number of wardens listed, the exile penal colony perhaps vanished from the published record. Also of note, the number of Korean jailers exceeded Japanese, and it was the Korean jailers who could be ordered to flog their fellow Koreans. Although Japanese censorship laws severely restricted information, Edward Baker has demonstrated that torturing Korean prisoners in Japanese-run jails not only remained a practice throughout the colonial period, but became, as he archly phrased it, a "policy objective."[59]

According to Baker, "Flogging was an extremely cruel form of punishment. Victims suffered as many as ninety strokes on the buttocks with a bamboo rod while tied in a prone position. . . . In a number of cases, death resulted. The total number of people flogged between 1913 and 1920 has been estimated to be as high as 600,000. According to official figures (Japanese printed), of the 83,128 people (Korean) subjected to summary judgment proceedings in 1912 and 1913, 38,397 were flogged."[60]

Compounding Baker's findings, in an emotional attack against Japanese colonial rule written in 1921, Korean immigrant to San Francisco Henry Chung argued that the Japanese continually justified the use of flogging "by claiming it was an 'old Korean custom.'"[61] With such a healthy ratio of Koreans working in the jails, a Japanese warden would always have had a Korean

**Table 2.   Korean Prisons, 1908**

| Position | Number of Personnel, by Nationality | | |
| --- | --- | --- | --- |
| | Japanese | Korean | Total |
| Wardens | 8 | 0 | 8 |
| Head Jailers | 31 | 8 | 39 |
| Interpreters | 0 | 8 | 8 |
| Prison Doctors | 3 | 0 | 3 |
| Part-time Doctors | 5 | 0 | 5 |
| Part-time Priests | 1 | 0 | 1 |
| Part-time Pharmacists | 1 | 0 | 1 |
| Jailers | 151 | 160 | 311 |
| Superintendents, Women's Jail | 2 | 0 | 2 |
| Part-time Superintendent, Women's Jail | 1 | 0 | 1 |

*Source: Hōritsu Shinbun, 5 August 1909.*

jailer available to flog a Korean inmate, ingraining the claim that flogging was an "old Korean custom" as demonstrable fact and memory. It is worth mentioning also that those who maintain an elitist reverence for Itō Hirobumi, subscribing to notions of his benevolent hand (i.e., that Itō would *never* have annexed Korea), overlook the fact that he authorized torture in the Korean penal codes under his rule, and that such legacies endured throughout the colonial period and arguably beyond.

At the time, readers of such reports in Japan would not have worried about themselves in reference to the practice of flogging because Japan had not yet officially annexed Korea, so Japanese and foreign foreigners continued to be judged outside the new laws in Korea. However, an editorialist for the *Hōritsu Shinbun* suggested that the time had come that "if [Japan] took the initiative and repealed [extraterritorial] rights the United States and the others would not be able to countermand."[62] The author of this article summed up the pride of his profession when he defined the success of Japan's *mission législatrice* in Korea as a process of "making them assimilate to us" *(waga ni dōka seshimuru no michi).*[63] The belief that extraterritoriality should and could be abandoned in Korea even before the annexation took place expressed a general opinion that Japan's Korea was legitimate in international terms.

## LEGALITY ON TRIAL

It is useful to jump ahead here and consider international response to Japan's first decade of colonial control in Korea. Only in the wake of the March 1, 1919 Independence Movement did the world once again pay measurable attention to Korea as it had in 1907. In response to the Japanese colonial regime's very violent response to the Independence Movement, Canadian journalist Frederick McKenzie criticized Japan's rule there:

> Between the annexation in 1910 and the uprising of the people in 1919, much material progress was made. . . . And yet this period of the Japanese administration in Korea ranks among the greatest failures of history, a failure greater than that of Russia in Finland or Poland or Austria-Hungary in Bosnia. . . . Good administration is impossible without the part of sympathy on the part of the administrators; with a blind and foolish contempt, it is impossible. They started out to assimilate the Koreans, to destroy their national ideals, to root out their ancient ways, to make them over again as Japanese, but Japanese of an inferior brand, subject to disabilities from which their overlords were free.[64]

Measuring one colonial experience against another is odious because the very nature of comparison renders one experience less than the other. Whether Korea's experience was worse than that of the Hawaiians or Chechens or Algerians is not the point, but it is important to draw attention to this first decade of Japanese colonial rule—especially its first few years, 1910–1914—because it appears to have been an exceptionally brutal period.[65]

The international condemnation of the severity of Japan's 1919 actions in Korea greatly embarrassed Taisho-era (1912–1926) politicians and diplomats who were, at the time, testing their international muscle by clamoring for inclusion of a racial-equality clause into the League of Nations charter. Although Japanese officials in Tokyo almost assuredly did not read the Canadian journalist's account, some might have agreed with his description, at least in part. Following a series of Japan's crackdowns on the Korean protesters, Prime Minister Hara Kei (Takashi) altered the formal structure of the Japanese colonial regime in Korea for the first time since the 1905 protectorate. In August 1919, Hara changed the provision that the Japanese ruler of Korea was answerable only to the Japanese emperor, making him more responsible to Parliament; he ordered the colonial governor, Hasegawa Yoshimichi, back to Japan; and he proclaimed a revised set of laws. Hara's cabinet in Tokyo had succeeded the cabinet of former Korean Governor General Terauchi Masatake the previous autumn. The new, self-avowed "liberal" prime minister sensed that the prevailing method of rule in Korea contradicted both the post–World War I international mood and the particular style of governance—the "Taishō democracy"—he advocated in the empire's mainland. Despite a new clause allowing nonmilitary persons to serve as governors general, however, Hara chose former Naval Minister Saitō Makoto to launch a new era of colonial rule in Korea, an era of "cultural rule" *(bunka seiji)*.[66]

After the mass uprisings throughout Korea, it became commonplace in Japan to condemn the excesses of Governors General Terauchi's and Hasegawa's reigns (1910–1916 and 1916–1919, respectively). It was widely held that their iron fists and "military rule" *(budan seiji)* had fomented angry mass rebellion against Japan, the March First Movement. Before the outburst, however, even Japanese journalists of McKenzie's ilk, such as Yoshino Sakuzō, only rarely criticized Japan's rule of Korea. *After* the March First Movement, Yoshino freely condemned the policies that the "former Government General" had pursued. Following the changes, Yoshino hopefully proclaimed, "The new Government General has been placed under the command of the Prime Minister, which is the single biggest improvement for everything connected with the rule of Korea."[67]

In 1905, Itō Hirobumi, who viewed political parties as methods of social control rather than conduits of democratic discussion, established the provision that the Resident General of Korea would be answerable only to the Japanese emperor. Almost fifteen years later, Yoshino Sakuzō, democratic advocate of the party process, espoused the shift in the rules for governing colonial Korea as the best of all possible changes. The approach each man advocated, however, arguably had more to do with what each saw as detrimental to Japan's domestic politics and was not specifically related to Korea. Opinion in a variety of Japanese newspapers and on the floor of Parliament held that it was not Japan's fault that circumstances had become so extreme in Korea as to cause Koreans to "riot."[68] The fault lay with extreme individuals. Now that Japanese law prevented the new Governor General from running his own country within the Japanese empire, all would be for the best.[69]

I mention this 1919 moment because critics found it easy to lambaste a decade of horrendous violence *after* the 1919 outburst. Earlier, around 1910, when provisions legitimating the random terror that ensued were put into motion, even the Powers judged Japan's rule of Korea lawful and consented to Japan's desire to end extraterritorial privileges there. This process is eerily similar to the contemporary CIA's expression, "blowback," which Chalmers Johnson has effectively co-opted for the title of his recent book.[70] "'[B]lowback,'" Johnson writes, "refers to the unintended consequences of policies that were kept secret from the American people. What the daily presses report as the malign acts of 'terrorists' or 'drug lords' or 'rogue states' or 'illegal arms merchants' often turn out to be blowback from earlier American operations." In 1910, without *official* exception, the international arena applauded Japan for taking up what it perceived—and with all the racist implications intended for how it was perceived—as the "yellow man's burden," in a whitish sort of way. Along with renaming the country (*Kankoku* became *Chōsen* in the *kanji* world but usefully remained "Korea" in other international documents), the Japanese renamed their presence there to the elevated stature of Governor General *(Sōtokufu)*. In international terms, a "Governor Generalship" (extant in India, Algeria, and the Philippines at the time, for example) declared full colonization. On 1 September 1910, Terauchi sponsored elaborate ceremonies in Seoul for "de-emperoring" Sunjong and remaking him into a king. Although the Ministry of Finance in Tokyo continued to reckon Japanese trade with and investment in Korea as "foreign," the Governor General changed the Korean calendar to accord with Japanese imperial reign-years. On 1 January 1912, Japan even aligned Korea to its time zone, where it remains today.

After August 1910, Japanese and Koreans were theoretically ruled by the same laws in Korea—with useful "giant loopholes," of course—but in order for Japan to be recognized as the legal ruler of Korea, Japan needed to incorporate the other foreigners there into their terms of law.[71] In the early years of the annexation, the Japanese press and popular literature often referred to Koreans as "cousins" and "half-siblings" (lit., children of a different womb). The Japanese in Korea remained "Japanese" or "mainlanders." Japanese were not "foreigners," but foreign foreigners still were.

On 29 August 1910, a week after Terauchi Masatake and Yi Wanyong sealed the Treaty of Annexation between Japan and Korea, the Japanese government issued a full explanation of the treaty's provisions.[72] The physical space of the peninsula was now a part of Japan, and any agreements that Korea had made with the Powers were "invalid" *(mukō)*. Moreover, "all foreigners residing in Korea [were now] subject to Japanese jurisdiction." Although the Koreans were not redefined as "Japanese," legally the Japanese were no longer "foreign." The American ambassador to Japan, Thomas J. O'Brien, requested a more detailed explanation concerning the meaning of the note generated by the 29 August meeting. On 6 October 1910, Foreign Minister Komura Jutarō wrote the ambassador a lengthy response, emphasizing that "the modern judiciary system of Japan has been put into actual operation in Korea to the extent that in all cases in which foreigners are interested as plaintiffs, defendants, or accused, the organization of the competent Courts and the qualifications of the sitting Judges, are essentially the same as in Japan Proper."[73] At this, no foreign Power formally approved of Japan's assertion of legal control over foreign subjects or citizens, but none issued any protest.

The ultimate decision to recognize Japanese law as legal in Korea was tightly interwoven with international perceptions of criminal due process and the eradication of the practice of torture, true to Boissonade's ultimatum in the 1870s. The so-called conspiracy to assassinate Governor General Terauchi—known in Korean history as the "105 Persons Incident"—forced the question of extraterritoriality onto center and world stage.

In the autumn of 1911, the Governor General began an all-out effort to "round up the usual suspects," investigating an alleged (or wholly fabricated) attempt to kill him the previous December. At the time, Terauchi was on tour of the northern area of Korea to display himself as the new ruler of Korea.

In the wake of Itō Hirobumi's much-publicized assassination in Harbin by Korean nationalist An Chŭnggun in October 1909, it was not a difficult leap to describe the country as full of anti-Japanese conspirators and spies. In 1909, however, photographers caught An on film with his smoking revolver. Two years later the only weapon ever found in relation to Terauchi's supposed near-death experience was a two-inch-long penknife in a ten-year-old's backpack. Hundreds of Koreans were imprisoned, tortured, and in some cases beaten to death, yet the whole affair would probably have remained unnoticed—as similar events most likely did—if Terauchi's investigation had not implicated a number of American Presbyterian missionaries. The "foreign foreignness"— and specifically, the *white* foreignness—of some of the suspects exploded the affair into an international incident.[74]

Quite a few of those arrested were Korean Christian converts and ministers working in Christian missionary schools in the northern part of the country, viewed uneasily by the Japanese regime as potential obstacles to their rule. Between September 1911 and the early winter of 1912, Terauchi's police examined several hundred Koreans, ranging from randomly selected schoolboys and local thugs to Yun Ch'iho (1865–1946)—the vice-president of the YMCA in Seoul, a graduate of Vanderbilt University, and a Nitobe Inazō–like internationalist. Eventually the police arrested and imprisoned more than a hundred Korean men. At least four died in prison. Japanese colonial police also arrested many non-Christians, however. They were men who had at some time or in some way criticized Japanese rule of Korea. Notable "conspirators" of this type included Yang Git'ak (1871–1938), publisher of the *Korean Daily Mail (TaeHan Maeil Sinbo);* Chang Ungchin, publisher of the nationalist journal *Taegŭk hakpo (Taegŭk* is the name for the Korean flag); Cha Isŏk (1881–1945), a leader of the progressive New People's Movement *(Sinminhwae);* An Taegŭk, a member of a self-strengthening agronomy group; and, perhaps most notably, Major Yu Dongyŏl. Yu actively protested the Japanese colonial regime and was repeatedly thrown in jail throughout the colonial era for his criticisms of Japanese imperialism. Yu vanished to what is now North Korea early in the Korean War, and though it is likely that he joined with Kim Il Sung after having become disgusted with Syngman Rhee, much South Korean historiography laments his martyrdom as a "6-25 abductee," a person "stolen" north by the communists.[75]

Reports of the so-called conspiracy emerged murkily. It is important to note at the outset that, as the supposed plot against Terauchi became public, the American consul in Seoul, George Skidmore—an American *ambassador* who served in Tokyo—made it clear that the United States had already begun to acquiesce to complete Japanese control of Korea. From the moment the affair began to unfold, Skidmore dissociated the U.S. government from official obligation. Japanese and foreign reporters at the *Japan Weekly Chronicle* in Kobe learned that the Japanese colonial regime in Korea had interrogated several American Presbyterian missionaries as "accomplices to the conspiracy." The *Chronicle*'s editor, Robert Young, noticed in an article in the *Osaka Mainichi* that a missionary named George McCune had been arrested and he surmised:

> [I]t is evident that the United States Government will have to make a protest against the arrest of an American citizen or in default recognize the abolition of extra-territoriality. This would mean Japan was justified in abolishing extra-territoriality without prior consultation with the Governments which exercised such rights in Korea. . . . At the time the first arrests were made the American Government had not recognized the abolition of extra-territoriality by the Japanese Government. Since then it has been reported that the annexation and its concomitants have been recognized by the United States Government, though no formal announcement has yet to be published to this effect.[76]

The United States consul "in default" recognized Japan's claims, in part by preventing the Americans from claiming extraterritorial privileges.

Skidmore also made it clear that the official American position was that the Government General of Korea acted in accordance with the law. Several entries in Governor General Terauchi's journal at the time reinforce the idea that the U.S. representative in Seoul wanted the missionaries to resolve the matter without official intervention. Terauchi kept a sparse diary, and he briefly mentioned conferring with the American consul in October 1911.[77] In early 1912, he noted meeting with "foreign" missionaries without any official representation, indicating that the U.S. government's preferred method was at work. Several weeks later, he wrote that he "promised to meet with foreign missionaries," which he did by sending them a letter guaranteeing the legality of the investigation:[78]

> Since the introduction of the new regime, the old procedure has been done away with, the persons under examination are now treated in the modern way. . . . If you take into consideration the hours required of each person for careful examination, especially for interpretation, you

will easily understand that the process is not at all unusual. Meanwhile, I may assure you that the authorities concerned under my provision would faithfully perform their duties entrusted to them by law, so that justice may be done to everybody. You may rest assured therefore that if anyone is punished, it is only after he has been proven guilty of a crime by a fair trial.[79]

Though he never manifested a proclivity for diplomatic euphemisms or flourishes, Terauchi knew that the missionaries did not represent U.S. policy, but he did elaborate on the legal means with which his regime was proceeding.

Terauchi's police were, however, not as polite to the missionaries as Terauchi was, and they ransacked the missionaries' houses. On 15 January 1912, local police escorted the Chief Prosecutors from Seoul and Pyongyang to George McCune's house outside of Pyongyang. The Governor General's Private Secretary (and future Governor General of Taiwan), General Akashi Motojirō, accompanied the entourage and ordered the police to rummage through McCune's possessions.[80] The following day, investigators began digging up their yards, and the missionaries again appealed to Skidmore, protesting now for the first time as citizens: "We feel that you are responsible for this searching of houses, and as American citizens our lives are in your hands for anything that may come from imprisonment."[81]

The consul responded that in his estimation Terauchi's men had acted legally in their searches because the missionaries lived in the so-called interior of the country, outside extraterritorial protection. And, as far as he knew, the police had acted according to the law in their conduct with the Korean prisoners because there was no direct evidence to the contrary. Clearly, the United States government did not regard the investigation of a missionary or two—on sedition charges against a foreign regime, nonetheless—worth risking any of its commercial privileges, and it prevented them from seeking legal protection under consular jurisdiction.[82] By 1912, the United States had sanctioned Japan's full takeover of Korea, and the American diplomat in colonized Seoul worked not to criticize the colonizing regime but to secure remaining American privileges there.

Although Skidmore hoped to resolve the incident quietly and locally, the American missionaries wrote and cabled friends and colleagues at home to tell them of their own and their Korean coworkers' plight. No less than Charles Eliot, Harvard's famous president (and himself once Governor General of Kenya), traveled to Seoul as a concerned observer to witness the trial. Appalled by the Japanese judges' and prosecutors' disregard for the Korean defendants and their lawyers, Eliot went to Tokyo to express his dismay to the Japanese government and emperor. In early September, Eliot wrote his friend, Arthur Judson Brown, Secretary of the Presbyterian Board of Foreign Missions in New York:

> After I got to Tokio, and while the preliminary investigation was still going on, I had several conversations with eminent Japanese about the treatment of the accused Christian Koreans. The two points I have endeavored to make were, first, that no American would believe on any Korean evidence that a single American missionary was in the slightest degree concerned with the alleged conspiracy; and, secondly, that the Japanese preliminary police investigation ought to be modified, and particularly, that the counsel for the defense ought always to be present during all stages of the preliminary investigation. Counsel for the defense might or might not take part in the proceeding, but should be invariably present. *I represented that the standing of Japan among Western nations might be improved by judicious modifications of her preliminary proceedings against alleged criminals.*[83]

Eliot explained the significance of legal due process. Speaking on behalf of the "Western nations" in favor of the Christian Koreans, he made it clear that perceptions of Japan as a legal nation critically extended to activity in its empire.

In America during the summer of 1912, as reports of the Seoul district court proceedings reached New York, Brown decided to voice the Presbyterian Board of Foreign Mission's concerns at official levels. He and four other religious leaders went to Washington to meet with the Japanese ambassador to the United States, Chinda Sutemi, President Taft, and Secretary of State Philander Knox. Brown described their position: "We did not go to Washington to ask for the intervention of our Government. The trial of the accused Koreans is still in progress and no proof has been furnished that the treaty rights of our missionaries as American citizens have been denied, although missionary work there has been seriously embarrassed. Officially, therefore, the question at its present stage concerns the dealings of the Japanese Government with its own subjects, and, of course, our Government would not feel that this called for interference through diplomatic channels."[84]

The sentencing of the 105 "conspirators" in late September, however, propelled the board's leaders to act with more resolve, and they called an emergency meeting on 11 October 1912. Brown invited men like Eliot, who had returned to the United States and wanted to share his opinions. The list of guests at the "Confidential Conference on the Situation in Korea," held at a men's club in New York, included powerful and well-connected men whom the United States government would not ignore:

> *The Honorable Seth Low, LL.D.*, formerly Mayor of New York and Chairman of the American Section of the Edinburgh World Conference Commission on the Relations of Missions and Governments
> *The Honorable John W. Foster, D.D., LL.D.*, formerly Secretary of State
> *Charles W. Eliot, LL.D.*, formerly President of Harvard University
> *Arthur T. Hadley, LL.D.*, President of Yale University
> *The Reverend Lyman Abbott, D.D., LL.D.*, Editor of *The Outlook*
> *The Honorable James Brown Scott*, Advisor on International Law to the United States at The Hague Peace Conference[85]
> *Jeremiah W. Jenks, LL.D.*, Professor of Political Economy, New York University
> (*Admiral Alfred Mahan* absent due to illness)[86]

The group resolved to negotiate directly with the Japanese ambassador, to assert that "the course of the Japanese police and the first trial of the accused Koreans did not do justice to the real spirit and purpose of the Japanese Government and people in dealing with their subjects in Korea."[87] The men registered their displeasure over what appeared to all as a lawless trial. They acknowledged, however, that Japan had legally gained control of Korea. Similar to the American consul who did not want to risk commercial privileges, the religious coalition wanted to guarantee its proselytizing privileges. Despite their challenge to the Japanese colonial regime's desire to police its new territory, the men purposefully implied that, after cordoning off those privileges, the missionaries would work quietly within the prevailing system.

The following month, Arthur Brown published a strongly worded essay concerning the Terauchi affair, ironically coining what would become the Japanese historiographical appellation of the event, the "Korean Conspiracy Case."[88] Similar to Boissonade in his *Commentaire* and Itō Hirobumi's scribes in their *Reports*, Brown asserted that he spoke for "the civilized world." In the opening lines, he wrote:

> The interest of the civilized world has been aroused by the difficulties that have developed in Korea (Japanese Chosen) and which have culminated in the arrest, trial and conviction of a large number of Korean

> Christians on a charge of conspiring to assassinate Count Terauchi, the
> Governor General. The circumstances raise some grave questions in
> which western peoples are deeply concerned.[89]

Sanctimoniously inserting a specific moral gravity to the situation, Brown
continued:

> It is true that from the viewpoint of international law and diplomatic
> intercourse, these questions primarily relate to Japan's treatment of her
> own subjects; but it is also true that it may be said of nations, as of indi-
> viduals, that "none of us liveth to himself." Mankind has passed the
> stage where it is indifferent to what any Government does to a subject
> race.[90]

Regardless of the fact that international law presumed its own legality because
its terms were practiced under God, in this activist missionary's estimation,
the voice of the apostle Paul overruled this particular mundane theory. Brown
ended up defining Japan as a full practitioner of international terms, terms he
considered the lesser standard than Christian law.

Like Boissonade, Brown prescribed a method by which Japan could escape
international denigration. Quoting and commenting on Eliot's letter, Brown
took up the suggestion that "judicious modifications of [Japan's] preliminary
proceedings against alleged criminals" would raise "the standing of Japan
among Western nations." Brown elaborated, "Japan wishes to be considered
one of the most advanced nations of the world, and if it expects to be regarded
as such, it should so amend its criminal law that it can withstand criticism that
is based not on a technical difference of method but on that essential justice
which mankind has come to demand even from the lowest of men."[91] In effect,
the American secretary of the Presbyterian Board of Foreign Missions challenged the Japanese Governor General of Korea to display "essential justice" to
"the civilized world" to secure Japan's status as one among the "most advanced
nations of the world."

Before the 1910 annexation, Itō's legal scions laid the foundations for
Japan's display of its "pure and competent" rule of Korea. Many in Japan and
abroad had discerned a mishandling of justice at the first trial in the Seoul
District Court, in 1912, but the display of justice performed at the subsequent
appeals trials in Seoul and Taegu legitimated Japan's rule of Korea. Moreover,
observers came away from the trials convinced that the Japanese regime had

stopped the practice of torture—despite the overwhelming evidence to the contrary. The "civilized world" judged Japan's rule of Korea legal.

Japanese judges, prosecutors, and defense lawyers presented Japan's lawful rule of Korea to courtrooms full of spectators at the appeals proceedings. Only a few American missionaries had observed the first trial in 1912, but interest in the appeals hearings brought crowds of spectators to the new, brightly lit witness gallery. Defense lawyers had complained in the first trial about lack of Korean translation, but for the appeals proceedings the Governor General's office supplied ample interpretation of the proceedings. What observers judged, however, was not the good English that the interpreters could provide, but how the legal terminology they uttered accorded to civilized practice. Similar to Itō Hirobumi's negotiations of the Treaty of Tianjin in English, in 1885, the significance of the legal terminology at the hearings surpassed the particular language in which it was spoken. In the eyes and ears of both the Japanese defense lawyers and the foreign spectators in the courtroom gallery, the reflexively understood proceedings proclaimed the legitimate universality of Japan's rule in Korea.

The first appeals proceedings lasted until March 1913, when the court upheld lengthy sentences for six of the accused but acquitted the remaining ninety-nine. Even Robert Young's *Japan Weekly Chronicle,* which had so strongly condemned the Japanese Governor General and American complicity the year before, praised the results: "We are satisfied to congratulate the Seoul Court of Appeal on having wiped away a very large blot which threatened to discredit the Japanese judicial administration in the eyes of a world for a generation."[92]

Shortly thereafter, the Powers erased extraterritorial privileges they had not yet ceded. On 21 April 1913, diplomats from the United States, Great Britain, Germany, France, Italy, and Belgium formally abolished extraterritoriality in Korea and reverted all their official property to the Japanese Governor General.[93] During the appeals trial, Japan demonstrated justice to the world. Both the verdict and the Powers' assessment combined openly to declare Japan the legitimate ruler of Korea.

Oddly, however, the relationship between the external perception of internal justice in Japan's Korea and the enduring practice of torture there surfaced acutely during these appeals proceedings.[94] In view of international outrage at even the suggestion of torture, one might assume that witness testimony would have cautioned the Powers in their praise of Japan's Korea. On the contrary, the defense based its appeal on the violent manner in which Terauchi's police had obtained the prosecution's evidence. It sought to overturn all 105 sentences, because lawyers argued that the convicted men made their confessions under torture. Judges Suzuki Kumisaburo, Maruyama Etarō, and Hara Masakane opened the appeals proceedings on the first day by calling Yun Ch'iho before the bench. In response to their interrogation, Yun stated simply, in fluent Japanese, that he lied to police because he was "tortured" *(gōmon).*[95] The next "conspirator," Kim Ilchom, proclaimed through an interpreter that he told wild lies during the initial trial because torture had caused him to be "delirious."[96]

By the second day of the appeals trial (27 November 1912), the defense team's strategy was clear. When the judges questioned Yi Yonghwa, he graphically detailed how police procured their evidence. A reporter from the *Japan Weekly Chronicle* captured the scene: "Yi Yong-wha was called. He is a stout, good-looking man with a moustache. He is a great orator and is said to be more skillful in his own defence than any lawyer. He spoke so eagerly as to enlist the sympathy even of those who did not understand Korean."[97]

Countering the charges against him, Yi asserted that his jailers tortured him at length. They beat him, they starved him for days, they strung him up by his fingers, they burned him, and they injected unknown fluids into his body.[98] Yi's testimony set the stage for subsequent defendants to detail their experiences, which they did throughout the proceedings' fifty-one hearings. Unlike the first trial the previous summer, where defense lawyers often met the accused the moment they were expected to provide defense for them, at the appeals trials the prisoners' attorneys met with the defendants beforehand to discuss what they would say. Moreover, the defense fostered an environment in the courtroom that encouraged the accused to report, for example, having been "hung from a tree with a sword thrust at neckpoint" and to describe death threats issued to family members.[99] One prisoner, Yi Pyŏngje, gave a particularly vivid account. He described how Terauchi's police had suspended him by his thumbs, which were tied together behind his back. After further beatings and burnings with cigarettes, the police covered Yi's face with paper, poured freezing water over him, and left him to hang outdoors, occasionally beating his hips with a block of wood.[100]

The prisoners' testimony shocked trial spectators and newspaper readers, Japanese and foreign alike. And yet as they presided over a trial that displayed the "essential justice" of the colonial legal system in Korea to the "civilized world," the Japanese never mentioned that Terauchi's police actually were

within the bounds of the existing law, because the Koreans whom they tortured were legally defined as "native offenders." The previous March, the
Governor General's office had officially upheld certain torture practices in the
penal codes for use against Koreans. Anyone interested could read the rationale in English in the colonial regime's annual report: "Flogging being a form of
punishment practised in Korea for ages past, it seemed likely more effective
as a measure of punishment for trifling offences than short imprisonment or
small fines, provided it was done in a proper manner. Consequently it was
decided to retain it, but only for application to native offenders. . . . The
method of infliction was also improved so that, by observing greater humanity, unnecessary pain in carrying out a flogging could be avoided as far as possible."[101] Despite the far-reaching implications of the Japanese government's
action, the vast number of overturned convictions (ninety-nine) satisfied the
trial's international observers that their journeys had been worth the effort:
"pure and competent" justice had come to Korea.

The events bringing the so-called conspiracy proceedings to light—coupled with the missionaries' general satisfaction that the Japanese colonial
regime legitimately ruled Korea—underscore the partiality of external perceptions of a particular regime's internal execution of justice. Governor General
Terauchi legally encoded torture for Koreans. In an open courtroom, Korean
prisoners described the horrors they endured, horrors that bespoke the deeply
held beliefs of many Japanese colonizers: Koreans were refuse and merely the
objects of experimentation. In spite of the brutality of Japanese rule, the Powers recognized the legality of Japan's display and openly abrogated their privileges of consular jurisdiction a month after the first appeals trial ended. For
the legal nations of the world, Japan's rule of Korea was fully legal in international terms.

# *Coda*

## A Knowledgeable Empire

The Meiji state aggrandizers' mission to declare Japan a legitimate imperialist power came at enormous expense both to Japan and the countries Japan colonized. I mention this *not* to encourage us now to feel sorry, as it were, for the hardships the colonizers endured. Instead, it is important to recognize that by inscribing Japan in the early-twentieth-century world as a so-called first-rank nation, the country's leaders necessarily set about remaking Japan from within in ways that meshed with the nation's policies abroad. Japan's entire national self-definition became that of an imperialist power, a power that eventually met gruesome defeat at home, at Hiroshima and Nagasaki.

In the reflexive condition of modern politics, defining a nation as an imperialist power meant that certain practices circled back and forth between the country's colonies and the mainland, all displayable amidst similar practices around the world. Such policies were not mirror reflections of each other, but they were refracted and refined depending on location, budget, and personality, and also on international conditions such as war or anticolonial movements and moods. In all instances, however, colonizers exerted power by defining themselves against the colonized; while simultaneously defining the "other" as dependent, they embedded the relationship as practice and fact as it took shape. Such relationships revealed themselves within Japan as without in the various trappings of the modern state—Foucault's *dispositifs*—such as education, health care, religious organization, the military, telecommunications networks, museums, bureaucracy, fiscal policy, and, perhaps most tenaciously, in law courts, police, and jails. At the beginning of the twenty-first century, we may all even have come to accept this once radical notion—that the colonizing power also colonized itself—as fairly common sense. If not common sense, then, at least it is a compelling idea.

There are several excellent, recent studies describing various aspects of this recursive formation of modern Japan, a formation dependent on Japan's being a colonizing power.[1] One area that still deserves consideration, which dovetails with this book's discussion of how Meiji statesmen described Japan as a legitimate imperialist, is the development of colonial policy studies. Such studies were as much an element of the creation of modern Japan as the more visible components of power—the schools in which they were taught, for example—because this discipline confirmed by its logic that the Japanese knowledgeably controlled their colonies. Put differently, colonial policy studies explained to the Japanese how Japan's empire—defined as legitimate in international law—engaged with and also was upheld by the prevailing international political science of the day.

By way of conclusion, then, the pages that follow discuss the place of this new discipline and, in particular, its first imperial professor, Nitobe Inazō (1862–1933). Nitobe was Japan's leading internationalist of the era, a man who remains famous (like his own hero, Woodrow Wilson), yet the colonial policy studies that Nitobe espoused taught the Japanese that colonization and empire writ large defined informed knowledge at the time.[2] The discipline that he shaped for Japan became required study for young bureaucrats entering government service, as well as for Japanese subjects in general, who wished to maintain a sense of their nation's policies.[3] Such studies gave authoritative, academic explanation to the international terms that defined Japan's empire, such as "protectorate" and "annexation." By the time Japan annexed Korea in 1910, colonial policy studies at Tokyo's elite universities, vocational colleges, and high schools alike taught Japanese what this action meant in the larger global context of imperialist politics. The implementation of this new knowledge fostered a common sense that Japan controlled its expanding empire in terms similar to—but not necessarily the same as—U.S. rule of the Philippines and French control of Vietnam.[4] The international political atmosphere of the colonizing nations legitimated and sustained a mutually practiced science of domination.

The reason this matters now is, quite simply, that colonial policy studies makes its legacy known in our world in the contemporary form of the study of international relations. If we take seriously, then, this book's aim to offer a more complex understanding of how power functions, it is useful to conclude by examining how this historical discipline fits into the larger frame of Japan's early-twentieth-century empire, because many of its assumptions abound in our world today.

## KNOWING KOREA'S PLACE

At first glance, Nitobe Inazō appears only as a peripheral figure in Japan's annexation of Korea. His name does not appear in most Japanese procedural records concerning Korean colonization. Taiwan, where he is known as the "father of the sugar industry," is the remnant of Japan's once-colonized terrain where his legacy endures. As the father of colonial policy studies, however, Nitobe was, I believe, the most crucial theorist of the annexation of Korea in international terms.

Nitobe's science of "planting people"—as he defined it—would become an axiom of Japanese political thought and practice in the early decades of the twentieth century. Educated in the politics and mores of the Great Game at both its centers and peripheries, Nitobe's science of colonial policy was international in flavor. Only according to his own Japanese formulation, however, did Japan's colonies even enter into this supposedly international theory.[5] As his nation's preeminent specialist, Nitobe explained colonial politics writ large by calculating Japan's control of regions such as Hokkaido, Taiwan, Korea, and Manchuria into his explanations of Japan's place in the international world, in addition to examples of U.S. and British experience. By considering colonies as a component of international political thought, Nitobe introduced into Japan a new form of knowledge about the country's imperialist expansion as well as a new way of discussing the world.

As a young man in the early Meiji era, Nitobe resolved to thrust Japan into competition as an internationally recognized civilized nation, which for him meant a nation in full possession of colonial territories, itself uncolonizable by any other power. In the mid-1880s, during his graduate-school days at Johns Hopkins, Nitobe studied international politics under the famous Herbert Baxter Adams and became enthralled with the so-called civilizing missions of self-defined enlightened societies. As a result, he determined to locate Japan as such a society within the world.[6] In 1885, he wrote to a friend in Japan's northern outpost of Sapporo that he would dedicate his life to transforming their nation, beginning with its educational practices, much as his hero Thomas Arnold, the great educator of colonial functionaries, had in England: "Can't I be a doctor Arnold of Sapporo? . . . It is, indeed, my earnest desire and sincere prayer."[7]

Nitobe delighted in Japan's colonial acquisitions, and throughout his life he explained to students, politicians, and general reading audiences alike that a nation's positive control of colonial territory defined enlightened international political theory. His outlook was above all patriotic: "I recently saw an article in which a writer said that a certain person is an internationalist and that another is a nationalist. I wish I could see such a distinction clearly. . . . A good internationalist must be a good nationalist and vice versa. The very terms connote it."[8] For Nitobe, quite simply, Japan's budding existence as an imperialist power defined its politics as part of the greater—and morally good—international practice. As his students at the University of Tokyo later remembered, for example, he began each lecture of his colonial policy course in the 1910s by writing the following mantra on the blackboard: "Colonization is the spread of civilization" (植民は文明の伝播).[9]

As efforts were under way to establish for Nitobe the inaugural lectureship in colonial policy studies in the law school at the University of Tokyo, in the autumn of 1906 he traveled for the first and only time to Korea. It is likely that Nitobe's view of Japan's recently won protectorate was colored by the applied colonial arts he had studied and taught at the Sapporo Agricultural School in Hokkaido, coupled with his studies of international political theory in the United States and Germany and courses in Kyoto.[10] In short, Nitobe knew the Koreans before he actually saw them. Following the internationally accredited theories of the day, Nitobe saw that the Koreans awaited their Japanese colonizers to inscribe them in progressive history.[11] For example, Nitobe's journal entries from October and November 1906, "Thoughts on a Dying Country" and "Withering Korea," confirmed and simultaneously compounded the international order in which he had come to have full faith.[12] Nitobe's description of Korean laborers sounded like descriptions of Korea made by American travel diarist Isabella Bird Bishop, or the Korea of Yale political scientist and Japan enthusiast George Trumbull Ladd, or the Korea of progressive journalist George Kennan (the elder): "They have absolutely no will to work. The men squat in their white clothes smoking on their long pipes and dream of the past, never thinking of the present nor hoping for the future."[13] The trope of the "squatting" and "slothful" native meshed neatly into the prevalent international discourse with which Nitobe identified, one that upheld progress and vigor as the criteria that determined national survival. Nitobe's travels in Korea's southwestern Chŏlla region propelled him further to name his surroundings "Arcadian," and he judged that the Korean farmers he saw were "not of the twentieth century, nor [were] they of the tenth nor even the first. They [were] a people who predated history."[14] The soon-to-be fully colonized

Korean remained in a stagnant limbo, or, as Nitobe described them, clutching their "dead traditions [in a county] soon to be governed by death."[15]

For Nitobe, the great narrator of Japan's imperialist expansion, the official annexation of Korea in 1910 granted Japan's legitimate entry into the society of nations, the foothold he had been striving for since he first studied international political theory at Johns Hopkins. Throughout the international arena at the time, national aggrandizers described their respective countries' colonial acquisitions as *faits accomplis*. They defined these spaces and the inhabitants within them as the objects of national missions, sidestepping the messy issue of how these territories became newly shaded colors on world maps. In September 1910, several weeks after the annexation, as principal of the First Higher School in Tokyo—the University of Tokyo's feeder academy —Nitobe addressed the students at the opening assembly of the fall term:

> This past August was full of things that will be difficult for me to forget. . . . For example, the terrible floods throughout the country caused damages exceeding 30 million yen. . . . Another unforgettable event was the annexation of Korea. Such an occurrence takes place only once in a lifetime. Overnight, our country became bigger than Germany, France, and Spain. Many people will comment and make speeches, [but no matter how you look at it] all of a sudden we grew by ten million people.[16]

Smoothly incorporating Korea's population into Japan's numbers, Nitobe continued his speech with an image of concentric circles, which later in the 1930s became popular in Pan-Asianist Co-Prosperity Sphere propaganda illustrating the expanding dimensions of the nation:

> If one were to draw a circle with a radius of about 180 *ri* centered on the Noto peninsula at Hokutan point and include Hokkaido, Kyushu, and Korea inside the circle, it would extend right to the border at the Tumen River. If the circle's radius were increased to 320 *ri* and its center were shifted to 40 degrees north latitude and 135 degrees east longitude, southern Manchuria and the Liaotung peninsula would fit inside, and the circle would extend right to 50 degrees north latitude in Karafuto. And if the circle's radius were increased to 380 *ri* and its center moved just a little, naturally Harbin would fit inside as would Chichihar in northern Manchuria.[17]

In a few short phrases of his speech, Nitobe's description of Japan's annexation of Korea brought into relief the grammar of colonizing politics. He naturalized decades of land grabs, rapes, forced abdications, and other features of colonization into a statement of politics as usual. Nitobe explained that, "Although our nation has not had any thought of invading foreign countries, the reality is that we have become much larger. In fact, the first circle is already an actuality."[18] In this innocuous formula—as common to colonizing discourse at the time as it is to a large share of international relations theory today—the annexation of Korea happened without human involvement, but "we" (the Japanese) accrued new meaning in the ranks of the imperializing nations as a result.

In short, Nitobe described to the country's future leaders what he envisioned as Japan's logical and legitimate imperial development. After all, by the time Japan annexed Korea, the international arena had recognized Japan's "special interests" in Manchuria for several years, so thinking northward occurred naturally in his aggrandizing spheres. He emphasized the students' new status to them:

> Our nation has become more of a Great Power than many European countries, and you all [the students] have also become much more important. Japan of a month ago and Japan of today are completely different.[19]

Nitobe never dreamed that his concentric circles would ever be valued as anything but the outgrowth of enlightened political science.

Shortly after the annexation, in 1911 Nitobe published his inaugural statement as Japan's intellectual authority on colonial policy with an essay entitled, "On the Term 'Colony.'"[20] In Nitobe's estimation, Japan practiced international politics fluently, along with other colonizing nations, but still hesitated from fully declaring itself as such a power. In his understanding, by officially designating what Nitobe viewed as the correct rendering of the term "colony," Japan would make the necessary international declaration. He embraced as native practice concepts that had been, until recently, alien, taking special care to make Japanese usage of these concepts discrete from the Chinese. "So that there wouldn't be any doubt about whether this European word . . . had first been translated into Chinese [or Japanese]," he wrote, "I consulted many French-Chinese and English-Chinese dictionaries. The Chinese language lacked 'colony' as a meaningful term until very recently [and it] is not yet commonly used in our neighboring country."[21]

At the beginning of the twentieth century, the European term "colony" and the concept it described were still new in the *kanji* that were common throughout Asia. Nitobe's insistence that the Chinese did not understand a term that the Japanese now defined for the *kanji*-literate world at once placed Japan above China within that sphere and linked Japan to the imperializing nations whose society Nitobe sought. Throughout Japan, Nitobe maintained, people were familiar with the "idea of colonization." "As our countrymen continue to think about the word," he explained, "they become more enlightened about the concept of colonial enterprise. These days national prestige and national strength depend on overseas expansion, and the idea of colonization has reached our nation's people."[22]

Significantly, Nitobe used his essay to urge the Japanese government to adopt the rendering of the term "colony" that he believed best expressed its meaning in European languages:

> The word "colony" first reached our countrymen's ears from the English and the Dutch. . . . The *Doeff-Haruma Japanese-Dutch Glossary* was published between 1855 and 1858, and I have looked up the word in this dictionary and have found no Japanese translation for the Dutch *"zie Volkplanting."* Isn't it odd that the Japanese scholars helping Doeff could not come up with the term *"shokumin"* [planting people]? Did they lack sufficient knowledge? Did they simply avoid it . . . because it was a word that had not been used before? . . . Beginning in 1862, the word "colony" appeared in Hori Tatsunosuke's *English-Japanese Dictionary.*[23]

Two phonetically identical variants of "colony" *(shokumin)* existed—"to plant people" (植民) and "to increase people" (殖民)—and, as its chief policy promoter, Nitobe encouraged his government to select "planting people" as the standardized term:

> Regardless of its general use, however, the characters *shokumin* (植民) are used in the vernacular but not yet officially. . . . [Whenever] names of places like Korea, Taiwan or Karafuto are mentioned . . . they are referred to as "new additions to the empire." Does it suffice to name these newly occupied territories with old expressions? Wouldn't it be better to use the new term—*shokuminchi* (植民地)?[24]

Nitobe argued that "planting people" captured the contemporary European meaning and better translated Japanese policy abroad, defining the arena in which he hoped Japanese imperialist expansion would be understood: that of European languages. Form mattered, and now that Japan was a legitimate imperialist Nitobe wanted his nation to use the version of terms that made the most international sense.

## THE COLONY AS VOCATION

At the outset of the twentieth century, Japan's internationally minded policy-makers also realized that there was a need to teach the colonies, as it were, to students who would serve as functionaries there. In 1898, at a meeting of the recently established Taiwan Society in Tokyo, the society's president and for-mer Governor General of Taiwan Katsura Tarō discussed the importance of language training for dealings with Japan's newly acquired colony.[25] Members began at once to raise funds for a school attached to the society, but two years later one member spoke to a society gathering at the Imperial Hotel in Tokyo and lamented that both "government officials and people in general are [still] lacking in colonial knowledge."[26] He delineated concrete plans for a "colonial school" and proposed a curriculum of specialized language study (Chinese and Taiwanese dialects, English, Russian, and Korean), politics, economics, diplomatic history, colonial history, and law.

On 15 September 1900, one hundred high-school-aged students gathered in Tokyo's Fujimicho, and Katsura presided over the opening ceremony of the Taiwan Society School. Classes began two days later. The faculty included Ume Kenjirō, whose courses at the school helped earn his 1906 appointment to Korea, where he spent four years rewriting the civil codes under Itō Hiro-bumi.[27] And the University of Tokyo's famous war-boosting economist Kanai Noboru taught accounting and finance to future colonial bureaucrats and businessmen.[28]

Five years later, and shortly after the Japanese government declared Korea its protectorate, Katsura Tarō conferred with Nitobe Inazō and Gotō Shinpei and recognized the expansive directions the Japanese empire was taking. He decided to rename his Taiwan Society the Oriental Society. In a speech to soci-ety members including Nitobe and Gotō, as well as Itō Hirobumi, Terauchi Masatake, and Hara Kei (all current or future rulers of Japan's Korea), Katsura also asserted that the newly named Oriental Society would also include the Oriental Society Technical School. Several years later, however, its board mem-bers changed the name again, this time to Takushoku University (literally, Colonial Development University), and this name held when Nitobe taught there in the teens, and it holds to this day.[29]

At the time of renaming the society and school "Oriental," the society counted 1,855 members and had established branch offices in Osaka, Nagoya, Kobe, and Kyoto. The school enrolled 264 students in 1905, by which time 220 had already graduated.[30] Noticeably, therefore, and concurrent with Gotō Shinpei's efforts to establish Nitobe's lectureship at the University of Tokyo for the nation's elite, Gotō and other board members of the Oriental Society stressed the need for separate training for future colonial functionaries. A month after Katsura renamed the organization, Gotō summarized the significance of the school's graduates in the future Japanese empire. He proclaimed, "By the time our students graduate, they are able to converse well in the [necessary] languages, and they also know how to write well with a typewriter. They will have no difficulties taking charge of a trading company."[31] Whatever his ultimate motivation, Gotō's assertion about the connection between knowing something about the colonies and securing future employment indicated that working in the colonies was increasingly an accepted and integrated part of late Meiji society. Demonstrating some mastery of a skill needed to help the colonies function would enhance nonelite students' opportunities as well.[32]

In the spring of 1907, Katsura met with Itō to discuss opening a branch school in Seoul. Japan's Resident General of Korea provided a building and a little over half an acre of land to open the school, which received its first students on October 1 of that year. Classes and baseball practice started right away. Administrators in Tokyo designed the school in Seoul as a year-abroad program for third-year high school students who elected to concentrate on Korea as their special knowledge. The coursework reflected the Tokyo-approved curriculum—commercial law, public and private law, public finance, international law, and bookkeeping. Hiring Japanese scholars and specialists already in Seoul, the school also featured a class in Korean affairs and intensive Korean language. At the opening ceremony, Kadota Masanori, one of the Oriental Society's founding members, compared the students to the *bakumatsu*-era "men of purpose/men of action" (the *shishi*) who had toppled the former Tokugawa regime to found the Meiji state: "You, who come from Tokyo, cannot attain a thorough knowledge of Korean affairs or of the Korean language on your own—let alone the customs here or racial harmony. Together, in accord and without antagonism, you will become men of action in administration and business. Whether you are involved in public or private affairs is irrelevant."[33]

The Oriental Society's branch school in Seoul opened around the same time that the Japanese colonial regime secured the abdication of the Korean emperor and sealed an agreement with Korean officials granting Japanese control over Korea's internal legal affairs. These events were not causally linked. Plans for the school began before the colonial government realized its opportunity for further control. Nonetheless, the construction of the school in Seoul meaningfully conjoined with Japan's expansion. When Katsura arrived in late October 1907 to inspect the school, he brought a contribution from the future Taishō emperor, conveying the Japanese imperial household's appreciation of the school and also of the Oriental Society's purpose in institutionalizing colonizing knowledge on broader levels.

### "MISSION OF INTERPRETATION FOR HIS COUNTRY"

Although much of the historiography about Nitobe absolves him of involvement in Japan's push into northern China, in 1932 Japan's great internationalist offered a reasoned defense of Japan's invasion of Manchuria. During the summer after Japan's takeover of various cities and regions there, Nitobe traveled across the United States to explain Japan's actions, justifying them to widespread American audiences in CBS radio broadcasts.[34] It is useful here to close our discussion by considering Nitobe's mission to the United States in 1932 as an awkward but complementary counterpart to the Korean mission to The Hague in 1907. Nitobe, too, discovered that he told an "unthinkable story" to his listeners, yet he, like the Koreans, argued that his "story" was legitimate.

Repeatedly claiming to speak on behalf of "thinking" Japan—or, as he often identified himself, as one of Japan's "practical minds"—the terms with which Nitobe expressed the legitimacy of his nation's military and political actions in Manchuria resonated with theories and policies he had advocated throughout his life. Different from his previous tours of the United States, however, former colleagues and acquaintances viewed this final visit with suspicion and mistrust. Nitobe died the following year. Several years after his death, his wife Mary recalled that "those were, indeed, dark days for Japan and for us personally, when my husband and I set forth in 1932 on his mission of interpretation for his country. America was hostile in thought—even friends there often did not understand. Many thought that he had come as a propagandist and protagonist for what he could not endorse—a part that Nitobe never did and never would play."[35] A constant companion to her husband throughout his (and their) career, Mary Nitobe campaigned against the rumor that, as punishment for remarks that Nitobe made about the militarists in Tokyo, army generals forced the old man to travel to the United States against his will to defend Japan's image. On the contrary, his radio addresses, the lectures he delivered throughout the following autumn at the University of California, and his wife's posthumous defense suggest that Nitobe did not capitulate to anyone's desires but his own. Coupled with his wife's vindication, his resolve indicates that Nitobe traveled to the United States to explain how Japan's invasion of Manchuria accorded to international terms.

In his first nationwide broadcast across the United States, on 8 May 1932, Nitobe explained to American listeners that he was "afraid the League was not aware that China does not or cannot function as a sovereign state, in the modern sense of the term."[36] The United States, of course, had never joined the League of Nations, so Nitobe could invite listening Americans to join him in understanding what League members failed to grasp without thinking he would be heard as anti-American. He challenged the international organization's condemnation of Japan, allowing that the state of affairs had become clouded "due partly to the emotional aspect it assumed, and partly to the insufficiency of knowledge concerning the actual situation in the Far East."[37]

Declaring absurd the League's decision to criticize Japan, Nitobe elaborated on what he viewed as the informed legal principle in question. By 1932, the world's colonial powers—the United States very much included—had for several decades maintained special privileges, treaty ports, and spheres of influences throughout China. Nitobe did not delve into sticky questions of how foreign special interests interfered in China, but instead focused on the question of China's domestic turmoil. He explained, "The so-called national government, which is represented in Geneva, is the government at Nanking . . . which exercises control over a very small part of the geographical area known as China. Within that area are several states, independent of the Nanking government. The European or South American states-members of the League are not fully aware of this anomalous condition. They have little practical dealing with China. Not so with us. We have suffered from this situation for years."[38]

Shortly thereafter, and a month before Emperor Hirohito sanctioned Pu Yi as the "Last Emperor" of China when he ascended the throne in Manchuria under Japan's watchful gaze, Nitobe made remarks that echoed Itō Hirobumi's words from twenty-five years earlier concerning Korea. Nitobe described Manchuria as the perfected object of decades of Japan's careful concern, explaining that "the salvation of China lies in her co-operation with Japan. Japan's future is bound up with that of China. It is Manchuria that links the two peoples together."[39] He argued that the bond between Japan and Manchuria followed the standard political practice around the world, and he chose a particularly germane comparison to underscore his point to American listeners. "That Manchukuo was established with the help of Japan, no one denies," Nitobe explained. "It is common experience of new countries to be founded with the help of others. The example of Panama is far too recent to be forgotten."[40] Nitobe argued further that "Roosevelt's far-seeing statesmanship favored Japanese expansion in Manchuria," recalling the 1905 agreement that America's former president had brokered to justify his claim.[41] Also, the recent Lansing-Ishii Agreement (1917) guaranteed anew Japan's "special interests" in Manchuria because of Japan's proximity to the region, while assuring the United States of Japan's continuing support for America's "Open Door" policies.

Because nearby Manchuria was defined as Japan's "special interest," Nitobe ultimately challenged U.S. Secretary of State Henry Stimson's decision to urge the League to condemn Japan. Quoting John Bassett Moore, Nicholas Murray Butler, and William Shakespeare to justify Japan's actions, he abstracted his reasoning to a higher plane:

> Let us not look at Manchuria as merely a law case. . . . Lawyers may find to their satisfaction for their logic and idealists for their conscience, by adhering to the new interpretation of the Pact; but such intellectual satisfaction means the loss of millions of lives and hastens the disintegration of the mighty and venerable civilization which we call China. . . . In the name of humanity, then, let us exercise a little patience, study the Pact, implement it, make it practical and applicable to the realities—so that the new dispensation may bring lasting peace to the Far East and to the whole world.[42]

Just before returning to Japan, Nitobe delivered a final lecture—an "unthinkable story" to an unwelcoming audience in California—in which he tried to distinguish Japan's actions from the negative spin ascribed to them by American politicians and opinion makers.[43] "Because of unfortunate warlike developments in Manchuria," he said, "Japan's economic penetration there has been dubbed by the opprobrious term of imperialistic invasion. The latter term has another unsavory association. . . . This idea is very far removed from Japan's present position in Manchuria."[44]

In short, Nitobe described Japan's occupation of Manchuria in line with beliefs he had held throughout his career: the Japanese empire extended rationally, in accordance with the flow of civilization. He remained blind to the violence that attended this flow, arguably because its methods meshed with the international politics of planting people. Although Nitobe's appeals fell on deaf ears, on a different level his remarks evoked George Trumbull Ladd's 1908 counter to anyone who challenged Japan's designation of Korea as its protectorate, when Ladd urged upholding Japan's questionably secured agreement for the larger cause of "the peace of the world."[45] For Ladd, "the peace of the world" justified forged seals and overthrown emperors, and for Nitobe, "peace . . . to the whole world" sustained his faith in Japan's offer of "salvation" to China.

Throughout the twentieth century, however, "practical minds" such as Ladd and Nitobe and their inheritors continued to mollify takeover, exploitation, and genocide with international terms such as "peace" and, increasingly, "security." As if in judgment of the use of these terms, and also of the entire century, social critic Norma Field described "fiftieth-anniversary-end-of-the-war" 1995 Tokyo by writing, "Peace, peace, peace, peace, peace. The word has been beaten senseless from overuse."[46]

## CLOSING NOTES

The historiographic tendency to uphold men such as Nitobe Inazō—and Itō Hirobumi for that matter—in a separate chamber of history from Japan's acknowledged, imperialist Pan-Asianists of the 1930s has fostered rather deterministic distinctions between the political creation of Japan's colonies and the repression that occurred in them. Nitobe's and Itō's followers demanded faith in their reasoning, for example, that no blurring of lines existed between Japan's carving out of empire and its knowledgeable control of totalitarian policies and practices.[47]

It has, however, never been more important to understand how rendering Japan's early twentieth century so conceptually discrete from developments in the 1930s and 1940s thwarts our attempts to internationalize the history of Japanese imperialism.[48] The legal and epistemological reach of Japan's colonizing practices with reference to the nation's early colonies, then, affords a critical way in to the problem and continues to need more analysis.

Seen differently, Nitobe guided the early Japanese empire in a manner similar, for example, to how America's architect of containment theory, George Kennan (the younger), structured the foundation of the Cold War. In the second half of the twentieth century, the United States and the former Soviet Union might have brought us to the verge of global destruction all the same, but Kennan's 1946 articulation of containment theory continued to give meaning to the dangerous confrontation throughout the era.[49] In the first half of the twentieth century, Japan, China, Russia, England, and the United States likely would have vied over the territories that brought them to the wars they fought, but Nitobe defined Japan's imperialist expansion as informed political practice at its outset. Itō Hirobumi similarly expounded the legitimacy of the empire that he contracted into being in international terms.

In light of Japan's now recognized infamous practice of sexual slavery, for example, historian Yoshimi Yoshiaki has focused on the legal treaties Japan signed during the first few decades of the twentieth century concerning its colonized peoples. According to Yoshimi, the Japanese government not only organized a system of sexual slavery for its military and civilian personnel throughout the empire during the Asia-Pacific War, it made every effort to guarantee that the enslavement of the women was legally ensconced in international law. In keeping with the country's late-nineteenth-century commitment to engage in international law, in 1904, in 1910, and, most important, in 1921, Japan signed the "International Arrangement and Conventions for the Suppression of Traffic in Women and Children." Although there were possibly more exceptions than the rule, these laws specifically forbade the forcible selling of women and children as prostitutes.

In drastic contrast to the humanitarian ideals these agreements encoded, however, these same laws contained clauses that permitted signatory nations to exempt their respective colonial territories from jurisdiction. Clause eleven of the 1910 Agreement and clause fourteen of the 1921 Agreement—"giant loopholes," as Yoshimi calls them—subsequently enabled the Japanese government's hired representatives to force women and girls throughout the empire's exempted colonies into sexual service without breaking the law at the time.[50] Just as the international laws of colonization were not broken in 1910 when Japan erased Korea from the world map of nations, the international laws of trafficking certain human beings were not broken when Japanese "recruited" Koreans, Taiwanese, Chinese, Manchukuoans, South Sea Islanders, Indonesians, Malays, Filipinas, Singaporeans, and Burmese. Colonized bodies, defined as such in international law and upheld as such in knowledgeable political science at the time, were less than human.

There remains, then, a very real issue involved with this living element of Japan's former empire, as supporters of the former sex slaves and the women themselves today bring their claims before the United Nations to seek redress from the government of Japan. Yoshimi has suggested that should this case be tried in an international court and encounter difficulties with such "loop-holes," it might be possible to demonstrate with other laws or with technical infringements that Japan violated another international code at the time.[51] The recently instituted understanding of rape as a war crime in international law might also suffice to declare the comfort stations *illegal* and the Japanese government *guilty* of having operated them.[52] The problem arises, however, with how such legal judgments would confront the writing of history during a time when precisely the opposite conditions prevailed, when a different story was "thinkable."

As mentioned at the beginning of the book, many thoughtful Korean historians and their colleagues in Japan and elsewhere argue that the legal arrangements providing for Japan's annexation of Korea in 1910 were forged and forced and, therefore, invalid; thus, they say, the whole colonial period should be described in similar terms. By extension, in effect they are urging a definition of the past itself as illegal. Unfortunately, the position such scholars have taken derives from the same frustrations Yoshimi faces. Simply put, the standard parameters for describing Japan's empire—the predominant historical apologisms—continue to constrain the possibility of going beyond ex post facto reasoning that depends on having to find yet another document to demonstrate the already wretched reality.

In the wake of the First World War, historian Sidney Fay noticed the tremendous and instant power held by national narrative in enshrining good and evil as historical truth. Fay countered what he perceived as his fellow Americans' facile jubilation over having been on the conquering side of the war "to save civilization," apart from what were described as the wholly evil and guilty Germans. Fay was a respected professor in the less-than-radical Smith and then Harvard history departments. He found repugnant the Versailles Treaty's formula of condemning one nation with having lone responsibility for a multiple-sided, banal willingness to slaughter millions of people. As he dryly phrased it, "the present writer['s] ... historical sense told him that in this present case, as in the past, no one country or no one man was solely, or probably even mainly, to blame."[53] But in national history the politics of blame and exculpation—that is, guilty or not guilty reasoning—for the wars that resulted from expanding empires or the empires that resulted from rapacious wars only intensified as the twentieth century ran its course. Fay's challenge to muddy narrations of good and evil in warfare remained marginalized—to the extent that in 1995, intelligent newspapers such as the *Washington Post* and the *Wall Street Journal* ridiculed Gar Alperovitz's attempts to complicate the history of the atomic bombings of Hiroshima and Nagasaki. Thus, national narratives of good and evil are increasingly hardening their forms now, during renewed wars of "good" versus "evil."[54]

With those blind to the history of Japanese troops' massacre of hundreds of thousands of Chinese in Nanking in 1937 at the forefront, in recounting Japan's twentieth century, there are those who flatly deny that the Japanese people perpetrated the acts that archival evidence proves they or their parents did. In apologizing for the past, there are also scholars who do not, however, deny that Japan had an empire, but instead, they continue to explain away the horrors perpetrated in the colonies by describing the details of Japan's overseas acquisitions in so-called rational terms. With over half-a-century's remove from the collapse of Japan's territorial empire, however, the two methods now uncannily work in tandem to complement each other in vindicating history by compensating for the past. As the century rotates, the denier apologists commit violence by swallowing new evidence as fabrication or rewriting it to suit their mythmaking, while the commonsense apologists feed the larger alibi by quantifying colonial brutality into production charts and "thinkable" stories.

# *Notes*

## INTRODUCTION

1. Hilary Conroy, *The Japanese Seizure of Korea, 1868–1910: A Study of Realism and Idealism in International Relations* (Philadelphia: University of Pennsylvania Press, 1960); Peter Duus, *The Abacus and the Sword: The Japanese Penetration of Korea, 1895–1910* (Berkeley and Los Angeles: University of California Press, 1995); Yamabe Kentarō, *Nikkan Heigō Koshi* (1966; reprint, Tokyo: Iwanami Shinsho, 1995); Moriyama Shigenori, *Nikkan Heigō* (Tokyo: Yoshikawa Kokubunkan, 1992). A critical exception to the "Western normativity" problem remains E. H. Norman's undervalued article, "The Genyosha: A Study in the Origins of Japanese Imperialism," *Pacific Affairs* 17, no. 3 (1944): 261–284.

2. Although Michael Hardt and Antonio Negri's acclaimed new study of empire points to inherent hierarchies entrenched in the European history of sovereignty and imperial debate, it, too, fails to offer a historical entry for the non-West as active participant in the origins of globalism. Hardt and Negri, *Empire* (Durham, N.C.: Duke University Press, 2000). Also, see Patrick Wolfe's otherwise substantial review essay, "History and Imperialism: A Century of Theory, from Marx to Postcolonialism," which unhesitatingly acknowledges in the second footnote that "for reasons of space, Japanese imperialism will not be discussed" (Wolfe, *American Historical Review* 102, no. 2 [1997]: 388–420).

## CHAPTER 1   ILLEGAL KOREA

1. In 1993, Professor Kim Ki-Seok of Seoul National University, while conducting research in Columbia University's Rare Book and Manuscript Collection, unearthed a 1906 letter written by Kojong, the emperor of Korea. In the letter, the emperor regis-

tered his protest against Japan's "plundering" of his country to the heads of nine European countries and the president of the United States. In 1907, his envoys carried a similar letter to The Hague. See Kim Ki-Seok, "Kwang-Moo Emperor's Diplomatic Policies for the Protection of Sovereignty," in Tae-Jin Lee, ed., *Japanese Occupation of the Dae-Han Empire* (Seoul: Kachi, 1995); the Japanese version appears in Unno Fukuju, ed., *Nikkan Kyōyaku to Kankoku Heigō: Chōsen Shokuminchi Shihai no Gōhōsei o Tomonau* (Tokyo: Akashi Shoten, 1995). Homer Hulbert, an American advisor to the emperor, had encouraged him to protest Japan's protectorate to an international audience. See Hulbert, *The Passing of Korea* (New York: Doubleday Page, 1906); also, Hulbert, *History of Korea* (Seoul: Methodist Publishing House, 1905).

2. Gaimushō [The Japanese Foreign Ministry], ed., *Nihon Gaikō Monjo* (Tokyo: Nihon Kokusai Renmei Kyōkai, 1933–). There is a vast mural commemorating this moment in the entrance hall of the Museum of Natural History in New York City.

3. For a useful compendium of the early colonial treaties see Yamada Akira's convenient single volume, *Gaikō Shiryō: Kindai Nihon no Bōchō to Shinryaku* (Tokyo: Shin Nihon Shuppansha, 1997); also, for facing-page translations, including Japanese, Korean, and English, see Unno, *Nikkan Kyōyaku to Kankoku Heigō*.

4. Michel-Rolph Trouillot, *Silencing the Past: Power and the Production of History* (Boston: Beacon Press, 1995), 93–95.

5. For discussion of the international history of slavery, see Peter Linenbaugh and Michael Rediker, *The Many-Headed Hydra: Sailors, Slaves, Commoners, and the Hidden History of the Revolutionary Atlantic* (Boston: Beacon Press, 2000); see also Raymond A. Winbush, ed., *Should America Pay? Slavery and the Raging Debate on Reparations* (New York: Amistad Books, 2003).

6. The expression "enlightened exploitation" is intended to evoke the mood of President William McKinley's declaration of U.S. aims in the Philippines: "the mission of the United States is one of benevolent assimilation, substituting the mild sway of justice and right for arbitrary rule." Letter from McKinley to Secretary of War R. A. Alger, 21 December 1898, in *Correspondence Relating to the War with Spain and Conditions Growing Out of the Same* (1902; reprint, Washington, D.C.: Center of Military History, U.S. Army, 1993), 2:875. See also George Trumbull Ladd, "The Annexation of Korea: An Essay in 'Benevolent Assimilation,'" *Yale Review* 1 (1911–1912): n.p.

7. For much of the nineteenth century in Europe, the idea of protectorates was in play in legal and journalistic discussion of current events, but the proclamation at the Berlin Conference made the term a legal precedent.

8. Historian Tessa Morris-Suzuki has analyzed how the pre-Meiji *ka-i* (civilized/barbaric) spatial understanding of the world transformed to the late-nineteenth-century *bunmei* (civilization) temporal view in her compelling essay, "The Frontiers of Japanese Identity," in Stein Tønnesson and Hans Antlöv, eds., *Asian Forms of the Nation* (Surrey, UK: Curzon Press, 1996), 41–66; see also Morris-Suzuki, *Time, Space, Nation* (Armonk, N.Y.: M. E. Sharpe, 1997).

9. In early October 1996, a "mistakenly transmitted" cable escaped the confidential intentions of its author (a low-ranking diplomat at the U.S. embassy in Sarajevo) and ended up on a variety of desks in Washington. The author criticized the Clinton administration's predictions of early troop withdrawal, suggesting instead that Bosnia might have to become a "protectorate" of the West shielded by an American-led military contingent stationed in the country for five or more years. *New York Times,* 10 October 1996.

10. For example, see the text to the best-selling photographic record, compiled and edited by Yi Kyuhoon, *Sajin u ro Ponun Dongnip Undong* (Seoul: Sumundang, 1992).

11. For discussion of the need to complicate notions of "puppet sovereignty," see Han Sŭk-Jŭng, *Manchu'guk Kunguk ŭi Chehesŭk* (Busan: Busan Donga Taehakkyo, 1998); see also Han Sŭk-Jŭng, "Puppet Sovereignty: The State Effect of Manchukuo from 1932 to 1936," Ph.D. diss., University of Chicago, 1995. For the costumes, if not the history, see also Bernardo Bertolucci's 1987 film, *The Last Emperor.*

12. Quoted in the *New York Times,* 26 July 1907; Gaimushō, *Nihon Gaikō Monjo,* vol. 40, 492–493. Article 2 of the new agreement declared that the "Government of Korea shall not enact any law or ordinance without the prior assent of the Resident General," and Article 3 removed the judiciary from the "ordinary administration" of the Korean government and put it under Itō's care. See also Kim Chongmyŏng, *Nikkan Gaikō Shiryō Shusei* (Tokyo: Gannando, 1964), vol. 6b, 626–636; also Unno, *Nikkan Kyōyaku to Kankoku Heigō,* 390–391.

13. *The Times* (London), 20 July 1907. For a concise discussion of how the view of the international coinage of Korean people and their rulers as "barbaric" has persisted throughout the twentieth century, see Bruce Cumings, "Occurrence at Nogun-ri Bridge: An Inquiry into the History and Memory of a Civil War," in *Critical Asian Studies* 33, no. 4 (December 2001): 520–521.

14. Kim Kosin, professor of history at Kim Il Sung University, has declared this agreement invalid because Emperor Kojong did not sign it, and he considers Kojong the rightful ruler at the time. See the Japanese translation, Kim, "Subete no Kyū 'Jyōyaku' wa Fuhō, Mukō na koi Bunsho," in Unno, *Nikkan Kyōyaku to Kankoku Heigō,* 23–36.

15. *The Times* (London), 29 July 1907.

16. *Asahi Shinbun,* 26 July 1907; *New York Times,* 26 July 1907. The 1905 protectorate agreement, for example, was kept secret for a week after it had been signed, and the 1904 agreement concerning financial advisors was not disclosed until the time of the 1907 agreement.

17. One exception was the French legal scholar, Francis Rey, who published an article in 1906 questioning the procedural aspects of Japan's actions. I discuss this article in the next chapter.

18. Nishikawa Nagao, *Chikyū Jidai no Minzoku = Bunka Riron: Datsu "Kokumin Bunka" no tame ni* (Tokyo: Shinyōsha, 1995), 85.

19. William Hull, *The Two Hague Conferences and Their Contributions to International Law* (Boston: Ginn & Co., 1908), 27.

20. Hilary Conroy, *The Japanese Seizure of Korea, 1868–1910: A Study of Realism and Idealism in International Relations* (Philadelphia: University of Pennsylvania Press, 1960), 345–351; Peter Duus, *The Abacus and the Sword: The Japanese Penetration of Korea* (Berkeley and Los Angeles: University of California, 1995). See also Kinefuchi Nobuo, *Kaigai no Shinbun ni Miru Nikkan Heigō* (Tokyo: Sairyūsha, 1995), 213–220.

21. Netherlands Ministry of Foreign Affairs, *Conference de la Paix de la Haye 1899* (Amsterdam: n.p., 1899); F. W. Holls, *The Peace Conference at The Hague* (New York: n.p., 1900).

22. Hull, *The Two Hague Conferences,* 10.

23. *The Times* (London), 17 June 1907.

24. *The Times* (London), 17 June 1907; 29 June 1907.

25. *The Times* (London), 17 June 1907.

26. Ibid.

27. In French, these names are *Allemagne, Amérique,* and *Angleterre.* Hull, *The Two Hague Conferences,* 15. Hull commented on the choice of *"Amérique"* instead of *"Etats-Unis,"* wondering if at the first conference the recent war between Spain *(Éspagne)* and America had provoked a little alphabetical politesse on the organizers' part.

28. *New York Times,* 17 July 1907.

29. See Frederick Arthur McKenzie, *Korea's Fight for Freedom* (New York: Fleming H. Revell, 1920), chap. 7; see also Nagata Akifumi, *Seodoa Ru-zuberuto to Kankoku* (Tokyo: Miraisha, 1992), 190–194.

30. Gaimushō, *Nihon Gaikō Monjo,* vol. 38, no. 1, 450–452; Gaimushō, *Nihon Gaikō Monjo,* vol. 38, no. 1, 59–61.

31. Arguably, the coverage of The Hague conference was a Habermasian moment at its most easily understandable. Habermas, in describing how the logic of publicly disseminated opinion functions, wrote, "Caught in the vortex of publicity that is staged for show or manipulation the public of nonorganized private people is laid claim to not by public communication but by the communication of publicly manifested opinions." In Jürgen Habermas, *The Structural Transformation of the Public Sphere: An Inquiry into a Category of Bourgeois Society* (Cambridge, Mass.: MIT Press, 1992), 247–248. Reporters extended the conference's reach by disseminating information about how a seemingly international body enacted policies to secure the peace of the world, forming a "communication" between The Hague's delegates and newspaper readers that reinforced the legitimacy of the conference.

32. David Spurr, *The Rhetoric of Empire: Colonial Discourse in Journalism, Travel Writing, and Imperial Administration* (Durham, N.C.: Duke University Press, 1993), 1–2. Addressing the question of discourse in this manner, Spurr usefully preempted Robert Young's query: "Can we assume that colonial discourse operates identically not

only across all space but also throughout time?" See Young, *Colonial Desire: Hybridity in Theory, Culture, and Race* (London: Routledge, 1995), 164–165. Differing from Spurr's more flexible position, Young wants to locate a "general theoretical matrix . . . to provide an all-encompassing framework."

33. Several Russian examples are given in Kinefuchi, *Kaigai no Shinbun ni Miru Nikkan Heigō.*

34. *The Times* (London), 20 July 1907.

35. *The Times* (London), 29 July 1907.

36. *The Times* (London), 19 July 1907.

37. *Le Temps* (Paris), 21 July 1907.

38. *New York Times,* 20 July 1907.

39. From the *Frankfurt Gazette,* quoted in *Le Temps* (Paris), 22 July 1907.

40. Reported in the *New York Times,* 28 July 1907.

41. *Le Temps* (Paris), 29 July 1907. A week earlier another editorial claimed that "not only are Orientals timid, their timidity is such that it presents itself as a true disease, a disease which is ancient and hereditary." *Le Temps* (Paris), 21 July 1907.

42. *New York Times,* 28 July 1907.

43. *New York Tribune,* 26 July 1907; also quoted in Conroy, *Japanese Seizure of Korea,* 350.

44. *The Times* (London), 20 July 1907.

45. *Le Temps* (Paris), 29 July 1907.

46. From the *Cologne Gazette,* cited in *The Times* (London), 22 July 1907.

47. *New York Times,* 25 July 1907.

48. *South China Daily Journal* (Shanghai), 6 August 1907.

49. *The Times* (London), 29 July 1907.

50. *Asahi Shinbun* (Tokyo) and *Mainichi Shinbun,* July–August 1907.

51. *Asahi Shinbun* (Tokyo), 25 July 1907.

52. *Yorozu Chōhō* (Tokyo), 18 July 1907; 20 July 1907; 22 July 1907; 24–28 July 1907; 1–3 August 1907.

53. Kuroiwa Ruikō (1862–1920) founded the *Yorozu Chōhō* in 1892. Famous anarchists, socialists, and anti-state intellectuals such as Kōtoku Shūsui, Uchimura Kanson, and Sakai Toshihiko all wrote for the paper until 1903, when they resigned over the anti-Russian turn they felt the paper took. See Yamamoto Taketoshi, *"Yorozu Chōhō" no Hatten to Suitai* (Tokyo: Nihon Tosho Senta, 1984).

54. The cartoon on 28 July 1907 featured seven evil-faced white men with Medusa-like snakes coming out of their heads, biting at each other. All the men extend their hands to pat the back of a fat, white dove.

55. *Yorozu Chōhō,* 18 July 1907. After four nonconsecutive terms as prime minister between 1885 and 1901, Itō took charge of Japan's colonial rule of Korea as Resident General from 1905 until 1909, when An Chǔnggun assassinated him.

56. See Louise E. Virgin's excellent catalogue of the Jean S. and Frederic A. Sharf

Collection of Japanese war prints from the wars with China and Russia, in Louise E. Virgin, *Japan at the Dawn of the Modern Age: Woodblock Prints from the Meiji Era, 1868–1912* (Boston: MFA Publications, 2001), esp. 66–68. Kobayashi Kiyochika (1847–1915) was the most popular war-print artist of his time and was also a widely published cartoonist. In the early Meiji era, he studied with Charles Wigman, the special correspondent from the *London News* who produced the very popular series titled "The Japan Punch" in the 1860s and 1870s. The museum at Ryōsenji in Shimoda (where Perry signed the U.S. treaties with the shogunate in 1854) has a good collection of both Wigman's and Kobayashi's works. See also Shimizu Isao, *Nihon Kindai Manga no Tanjō* (Tokyo: Yamakawa Shuppan, 2001), 33–37, which describes Kobayashi's work as a cartoonist. For discussion of how the advent of photography impacted illustration, see Kono Keisuke, "Shashin no naka no 'sensō': Meiji sanjūdai 'Taiyō' no Kuchie o Megutte," in Narita Ryūichi, ed., *Kindai no Bunkashi Kindaishi no Seiritsu 1870–1910 nendai* (Tokyo: Iwanami Shoten, 2001), 233–264.

57. For discussion of the Hibiya Riots, see Andrew Gordon, *Labor and Imperial Democracy in Prewar Japan* (Berkeley and Los Angeles: University of California Press, 1992).

58. The famous philosopher Nishida Kitarō wrote in his diary about the mortification he felt when he learned of what he saw as Japan's meager gains: "A railroad concession to Changchun!? I cannot bear it." See Nishida, *Sunshin Nikki* (Tokyo: Kobundo, 1948).

59. H.I.J.M's Residency General, ed., *Annual Report for 1907 on Reforms and Progress in Korea* (Seoul: n.p., 1908). Andre Schmid compellingly discusses editorial decisions in later editions of the *Report* in Schmid, *Korea Between Empires, 1895–1919* (New York: Columbia University Press, 2002), 161–162.

60. Hishida Seiji, *The International Position of Japan as a Great Power* (New York: Columbia University Press, 1905).

61. Major universities in the United States and England, such as Columbia, Harvard, the University of Chicago, and Oxford, began receiving the *Report* in 1908. A contemporary example of this practice would include such publications as the Japanese Defense Agency's annual English edition of its white paper, *Defense of Japan*. See JDA, ed., *2001 Defense of Japan: Toward a More Vigorous and Professional SDF in the Twenty-First Century* (Tokyo: Urban Connections/Defense Agency, 2001).

62. H.I.J.M's Residency General, *Annual Report for 1907*, 2–3.

63. Ibid., 3.

64. For a pithy account of the prince's visit, see Onojima Sachiko, "Kankoku Heigō ni kansuru Hitotsu Kōsai: Kankoku Kōtaishi I Un no Nihon Ryūgaku," in *Hokudai Shigaku*, no. 28 (1988): 41–50; see also Kendō Shirosuke, *I Okyu Hishi* (Seoul: Chōsen Shinbunsha, 1926).

65. Kim Chŏngmyŏng, *Nikkan Gaikō Shiryō Shusei*, 10 vols. (Tokyo: Gannando Shoten, 1962–1967), vol. 6, no. 2, 646–647; also quoted in Onojima, "Kankoku Heigō ni kansuru Hitotsu Kōsai," 42.

66. *Asahi Shinbun,* 16 December 1907.

67. A better-remembered case is that of King Norodom Sihanouk of Cambodia, who spent his student years in Paris, partaking of "civilization."

68. Takashi Fujitani, *Splendid Monarchy* (Berkeley: University of California Press, 1996), 44.

69. Onojima, "Kankoku Heigō ni kansuru Hitotsu Kōsai," 45.

70. *New York Times,* 26 July 1907.

71. Even Alice L. Conklin's insightful questioning about colonialism's role in the creation of democracy politics assumes that only American and European historians would be concerned with the relationship between colonies and "advanced democracies." Contemporary Japanese studies would benefit greatly from such questioning. See Conklin, "Colonialism and Human Rights, A Contradiction in Terms? The Case of France in West Africa, 1895–1914," in *American Historical Review* 103, no. 2 (1998): 419–442.

72. Kōtoku Shūsui, *Teikokushugi: Nijū Seiki no Kaibutsu* (Imperialism: Monstrosity of the Twentieth Century). Collected in Meiji Bunken, ed., *Kōtoku Shūsui Zenshū* (Tokyo: Meiji Bunkensha, 1968), vol. 3, 107–196.

73. Partha Chatterjee has made a similar point about the history of nationalisms. See Chatterjee, *Nationalist Thought and the Colonial World: A Derivative Discourse* (Minneapolis: University of Minnesota Press, 1993), esp. 1–30; see also Dipesh Chakrabarty's eloquent observation that the non-West has been consigned to an "imaginary waiting room of history," in *Provincializing Europe: Postcolonial Thought and Historical Difference* (Princeton, N.J.: Princeton University Press, 2000), 8. Frantz Fanon makes similar points in *Black Skin, White Masks* (1952; reprint, New York: Grove Press, 1991), 147, 231.

74. For example, see Ronald Robinson and John Gallagher, "The Imperialism of Free Trade 1815–1914," in *Economic History Review* 6 (1953): n.p. See also Lewis H. Gann, "Western and Japanese Colonialism: Some Preliminary Comparisons," in Ramon H. Myers and Mark R. Peattie, eds., *The Japanese Colonial Empire, 1895–1945* (Princeton, N.J.: Princeton University Press, 1984), 497–525.

75. See, for example, Yamabe Kentarō, *Nikkan Heigō Kōshi* (Tokyo: Iwanami Shinsho, 1995); see also Yoshioka Yoshinori, *Nihon no Shinryaku to Bōchō* (Tokyo: Shin Nihon Shuppansha, 1995).

76. See the essays in Shibahara Takuji, Ikai Takaaki, and Ikeda Masahiro, eds., *Nihon Kindai Shisō Taikei,* vol. 12, *Taigaikan* (Tokyo: Iwanami Shoten, 1991); Moriyama Shigenori, *Kindai Nikkan Kankeishi Kenkyū* (Tokyo: Tokyo Daigaku Shuppankai, 1987); Duus, *The Abacus and the Sword.*

77. The Lansing-Ishii Agreement (1917) guaranteed Japan's "special interests" in Manchuria because of Japan's "propinquity" to the region. See *Congressional Record of Foreign Relations, 1922* (Washington, D.C.: Government Printing Office, 1938), vol. 2, 591. The Root-Takihara Declaration (1908) foreshadowed the terms of the 1917 Lansing-Ishii Agreement.

78. Mark Peattie, Introduction to Ramon Myers and Mark Peattie, eds., *The Japanese Colonial Empire, 1895–1945* (Princeton, N.J.: Princeton University Press, 1984), 6–7.

79. Nakae Chōmin, *Sansuijin Keirin Mondō* (1887; reprint, Tokyo: Iwanami Bunko, 1995), reprint ed. Kuwabara Takeo and Shimada Kenji (reprint edition includes their contemporary Japanese reading); see also Nobuko Tsukui's English translation of Kuwabara and Shimada's rendering, *A Discourse By Three Drunkards on Government* (New York: Weatherhill, 1992).

80. Nakae Chōmin, *Sansuijin Keirin Mondō*, 200–201. The "four nations" referred to were Prussia, France, England, and Russia.

81. Ibid.

## CHAPTER 2  INTERNATIONAL TERMS OF ENGAGEMENT

1. International Law Commission, ed., *International Law on the Eve of the Twenty-First Century: Views From the International Law Commission* (New York: United Nations, 1997), 37.

2. Commodore Matthew Perry's 1853 arrival off the coast of Kanagawa, with the firing of cannons and brandishing of swords, was in marked contrast to Captain James Biddle's 1846 peaceful overture. Needless to say, Biddle did not get the Japanese to sign any treaties.

3. Throughout, I quote from the Carnegie Endowment for International Peace's 1936 centenary reprint of Wheaton's book. Edited by George Grafton Wilson, this edition fully replicates the original and also includes the highly valued notes Richard Henry Dana added to the eighth edition in 1866. It is available in most university libraries. Wilson, ed., *Henry Wheaton, Elements of International Law* (New York: Carnegie Endowment for International Peace, 1936), 44.

4. See Carol Gluck, *Japan's Modern Myths: Ideology in the Late Meiji Period* (Princeton, N.J.: Princeton University Press, 1985); see also Steven Vlastos, ed., *Mirrors of Modernity: Invented Traditions of Modern Japan* (Berkeley and Los Angeles: University of California Press, 1998).

5. Prasenjit Duara, "The Regime of Authenticity: Timelessness, Gender, and National History in Modern China," in *History and Theory: Studies in the Philosophy of History* 37, no. 3 (1998): 287–309; see also Prasenjit Duara, *Rescuing History from the Nation* (Chicago: University of Chicago Press, 1996).

6. German and Japanese assertions of uniqueness, for example, made sense because each country proclaimed mutually intelligible qualities as state builders refashioned their national bodies in modernity's terms. See Takashi Fujitani, *Splendid Monarchy: Power and Pageantry in Modern Japan* (Berkeley: University of California Press, 1996); see also Eric Hobsbawm and Terence Ranger, eds., *The Invention of Tradition* (Cambridge: Cambridge University Press, 1983).

7. Fukuzawa Yukichi, *Bunmeiron no Gairyaku* (Tokyo: Iwanami Bunko, 1995); see also, Norio Tamaki, *Yukichi Fukuzawa 1835–1901: The Spirit of Enterprise in Modern Japan* (New York: Palgrave, 2001).

8. Tetsuo Najita, *Visions of Virtue in Tokugawa Japan: The Kaitokudo Merchant Academy of Osaka* (Chicago: University of Chicago Press, 1987); James McClain and Wakita Osamu, eds., *Osaka, the Merchant's Capital of Early Modern Japan* (Ithaca, N.Y.: Cornell University Press, 1999); Tessa Morris-Suzuki, *The Technological Transformation of Japan: From the Seventeenth to the Twenty-First Century* (New York: Cambridge University Press, 1994); David Howell, *Capitalism from Within: Economy, Society, and the State in a Japanese Fishery* (Berkeley and Los Angeles: University of California Press, 1995).

9. See Moishe Postone, *Time, Labour, and Social Domination: A Reinterpretation of Marx's Critical Theory* (New York: Cambridge University Press, 1993), esp. 366–367.

10. Karl Marx, *Capital: A Critique of Political Economy*, vol. 1 (New York: Penguin, 1990), 876.

11. Ordinance No. 98, 17 February 1868. Collected in Naikaku Kanpōkyoku, ed., *Hōrei Zensho*, vol. 1 (reprint; Tokyo: Harushobō, 1974), 45.

12. "Instruction concerning Harmonious Relations with Foreign Countries" [Gaikoku to no Washin ni Kan suru Yūkoku] (17 February 1868), collected in Gaimushō [The Japanese Foreign Ministry], ed., *Nihon Gaikō Nenpyō oyobi Juyō Monjo*, vol. 1 (Tokyo: Gaimushō, 1955), 33–34.

13. "The Charter Oath" [Gokajyō no Seimon], 14 March 1868. Collected in Naikaku Kanpōkyoku, ed., *Hōrei Zensho*, vol. 1, 64.

14. See Lydia Liu, "Legislating the Universal: The Circulation of International Law in the Nineteenth Century," in Liu, ed., *Tokens of Exchange: The Problem of Translation in Global Circulations* (Durham, N.C.: Duke University Press, 1999), 127–164.

15. William Martin, *A Cycle of Cathay* (New York: Fleming H. Revell, 1897), 233–234. See Yamamuro Shinichi's discussion, in *Shisō Kadai Toshite no Ajia* (Tokyo: Iwanami Shoten, 2001), 222–232, which reprints the great picture of Martin holding a shotgun (231) originally published in William Martin, *The Siege of Peking* (n.p.: 1900). See also Ralph Covell, *W. A. P. Martin, Pioneer of Progress in China* (Washington, D.C.: Christian College Consortium, 1978).

16. See Liu, "Legislating the Universal," 148–150.

17. See Ronald Toby, *State and Diplomacy in Early Modern Japan: Asia in the Development of the Tokugawa Bakufu* (Stanford, Calif.: Stanford University Press, 1991), esp. chap. 5, "Through the Looking-Glass of World Protocol: Mirror to an Ideal World," 168–230; see also Etsuko Hae-Jin Kang, *Diplomacy and Ideology in Japanese-Korean Relations* (New York: St. Martin's Press, 1997).

18. See Douglas Howland's discussion of "brush talking" in *Borders of Chinese Civilization: Geography and History at Empire's End* (Durham, N.C.: Duke University Press, 1996).

19. There is an enormous compilation of Chosön dynasty records, entitled the *Tongmun Hwigo,* which archives the exchanges between Korean rulers and their counterparts in Japan and China in the early modern era. The expression *"tongmun"* emphasizes the notion of a shared writing system and the mutuality of comprehension among the three realms.

20. *Nihon Gaikō Monjo,* vol. 38, no.1, 371.

21. Ibid., 371–372.

22. Honda Toshiaki, "Kaiho Seiryō," in Tsukatani Akihiro, ed., *Nihon shisō taikei,* vol. 44; see also Honda Toshiaki, "Keisei Hisaku," in *Nihon Keizai Sōsho,* vol. 12. See also Donald Keene, *The Japanese Discovery of Europe, 1720–1830* (Stanford, Calif.: Stanford University Press, 1969). Keene discusses Honda's desire to use the Western alphabet for dealing in "international trade" with the Europeans (72).

23. See, for example, Osatake Takeki, *Kinsei Nihon no Kokusai Kannen no Hattatsu* (Tokyo: Kyōritsusha, 1932); and Chang Cha Nin's recent essay in *Nihon Kindai Shisō Taikei,* vol. 15. See also Katō Shūichi and Maruyama Masao's discussion in *Honyaku no Shisō: Nihon Kindai Shisō Taikei* (Tokyo: Iwanami Shinsho, 1995), which follows these lines.

24. Osatake, *Kinsei Nihon no Kokusai Kannen no Hattatsu,* 40–41.

25. John Peter Stern addressed related discussions concerning "law of nations" and "natural law." See his published bachelor's thesis, *The Japanese Interpretation of the "Law of Nations," 1854–1874* (Princeton, N.J.: Princeton University Press, 1979), esp. chap. 3, "Bankoku Kōhō."

26. For example, see Yanabu Akira, *Honyakugo Seiritsu Jijō* (Tokyo: Iwanami Shinsho, 1995) and *Honyaku no Shisō: Shizen to Nature* (Tokyo: Chikuma Gakuei Bunko, 1995). See also Kobori Keiichi's interesting discussion of the derivation of the term *"sakoku"* (secluded country) through mistranslation, *Sakoku no Shisō* (Tokyo: Chūō Koronsha, 1974).

27. Pierre Bourdieu, *Language and Symbolic Power,* trans. Gino Raymond and Matthew Adamson (Cambridge, Mass.: Harvard University Press, 1991), 109.

28. This view also fosters reactionary responses in the Asia-Pacific region, such as the Singaporean/Malay/Taiwanese–sponsored notion of "Asian democracy."

29. Jeremy Bentham, *An Introduction to the Principles of Morals and Legislation* (New York: Hafner Press, 1948), 326, n. 1. Emphasis in the original.

30. For a discussion of the genealogy of European diplomacy of which the creation of international law plays a vital part, see James Der Derian, *On Diplomacy* (Cambridge: Blackwell, 1991); see also Douglas Howland's discussion specific to Japan, *Translating the West: Language and Political Reason in Nineteenth Century Japan* (Honolulu: University of Hawai'i Press, 2001).

31. Wilson, ed., *Henry Wheaton, Elements of International Law,* 20.

32. Ibid., 3.

33. For a compelling discussion of the implicit Christian god in European diplo-

macy's use of the term "Nature," see James Hevia, *Cherishing Men from Afar: Qing Guest Ritual and the Macartney Exhibition of 1793* (Durham, N.C.: Duke University Press, 1995).

34. Wilson, ed., *Henry Wheaton, Elements of International Law,* 19.

35. For the effect of international law on internally colonized people in the United States at the time, see Herman J. Viola, *Diplomats in Buckskins: A History of Indian Delegations in Washington City* (Bluffton, S.C.: Rivilo Books, 1995).

36. See Richard Henry Dana, ed., *Elements of International Law: With a Sketch of the History of the Science,* 8th ed. (Boston: Little, Brown, and Company, 1866), 19, n. 8.

37. Francois Guizot, *General History of the Outline of Civilization in Europe* (New York: D. Appleton & Co., 1840), 15. I used this American-English translation of Guizot because Fukuzawa Yukichi relied on American-English translations to write his *Outline of the Theory of Civilization.*

38. For a powerful exposition on how the concept of sovereignty functioned in the first decades of the Meiji period, see Foreign Minister Mutsu Munemitsu, *Kenkenroku* (Tokyo: n.p., 1895). See also Gordon Mark Berger's complete translation, *Kenkenroku: The Diplomatic Record of the Sino-Japanese War, 1894–1895* (Tokyo: University of Tokyo Press, 1982); and Hagihara Nobutoshi, *Mutsu Munemitsu* (Tokyo: Asahi Shinbunsha, 1997).

39. Political scientist Timothy Mitchell has argued that colonizing politics fashioned a "world where political power . . . operates always so as to appear as something set apart from the real world, effacing a certain, metaphysical authority." See Mitchell, *Colonising Egypt* (Berkeley: University of California Press, 1991), 160.

40. See Sōgō Masa'aki and Hida Yoshifumi, *Meiji no Kotoba Jiten* (Tokyo: Tōkyōdō, 1989).

41. Mori Arinori letter to William Whitney, 21 May 1872, collected in Katō Shūichi and Maruyama Masao, eds., *Honyaku no Shisō: Nihon Kindai Shisō Taikei,* vol. 15 (Tokyo: Iwanami Shoten, 1991), 317.

42. Nishi Amane, "Yōji wo motte Kokugo o Kaku Suru Ron," in *Meiroku Zasshi,* no. 1 (1874): n.p.

43. See Kurokawa Mayori's grade-school primer *Yokobunji Hyakujin Isshū* (Tokyo: Bunnendō, 1873). For a lavishly photographed and detailed—albeit cultural essentialist view *(Nihonjinron)*—of these issues, see Kida Junichirō, *Nihongo Daihaku Butsukan, Akuma no Bunji to Tatakatta Hitobito* (Tokyo: Jyasuto Shisutemu, 1994).

44. Mitsukuri Rinshō quoted in Katō Shūichi and Maruyama Masao, eds., *Honyaku no Shisō: Nihon Kindai Shisō Taikei,* 304.

45. In Katō Shūichi and Maruyama Masao, eds., *Honyaku no Shisō: Nihon Kindai Shisō Taikei,* 304–305. See also Miyanaga Kiyoshi, *Nihonshi no naka no Furansugo: Bakumatsu Meiji no Nichifu Bunka Kōryu* (Tokyo: Hakusuisha, 2000).

46. See Najita, "Ambiguous Encounters: Ogata Koan and International Studies in Late Tokugawa Osaka," in James McClain and Wakita Osamu, eds., Osaka, *The Mer-*

*chants' Capital of Early Modern Japan* (Ithaca, N.Y.: Cornell University Press, 1999). Najita demonstrates that thinker Dazai Shundai's 1729 discussion of Chinese writing made Sugita and Maeno's groundbreaking autopsy possible fifty years later. Literature scholar Sugimoto Tsutomu has also demonstrated that the compiler of the first official Japanese-Dutch word list, Aoki Konyō, believed that scholarship began with studying words, something he learned in the late 1720s when he studied under Itō Tōgai (Jinsai's son). His lifelong work yielded the Tokugawa shogunate's first official glossary of Japanese with a European language. See Sugimoto Tsutomu, *Edo no Honyakukatachi* (Tokyo: Waseda University Press, 1995), 9.

47. Sugimoto, *Edo no Honyakukatachi,* 2. Raymond Schwab's discussion of the significance of translators in his *Oriental Renaissance* is analogous. Schwab discussed French, British, and German translators of Sanskrit and other "exotic" languages whose work entwined with European overseas trade in the late eighteenth and early nineteenth centuries. He traced how their efforts eventually yielded the discipline of "Oriental Studies" and insisted on the vital importance of deciphering the words and then codifying "studies." See Schwab, *The Oriental Renaissance* (New York: Columbia University Press, 1986).

48. The men referred to Gerard Dicten's *Ontleekundige tafelen* (1734), a Dutch rendering of Johan Adam Kulmus's *Anatomiche tabellen* (1722).

49. Sugimoto describes *Rangaku* beginning "symbolically" with the publication of the *Kaitai Shinsho.* See Sugimoto, *Edo no Honyakukatachi,* 1; see also Grant Goodman's book chronicling *Rangaku* publications, *Japan: The Dutch Experience* (London: Athlone Press, 1986).

50. Bakumatsu/Meiji Shoki ni Okeru Seiyō Bunmei no Yunyū ni Kan Suru Kenkyūkai, eds., *Yōgaku Jishi* (Tokyo: Bunka Shobō, 1993), 57–64.

51. Nitobe Inazō Zenshū Henshū Iinkai, eds., *Nitobe Inazō Zenshū* (Tokyo: Kyōbunkan, 1960–1982), vol. 15, 499.

52. See Wada Haruki, *Hoppō Ryōchi Mondai: Rekishi to Mirai* (Tokyo: Asahi Shinbunsha, 1999); see also Brett Walker, *The Conquest of Ainu Lands: Ecology and Culture in Japanese Expansion, 1590–1800* (Berkeley and Los Angeles: University of California Press, 2001).

53. Inō Tadataka made a copy of the map before he began his travels to Ezo, and his version paints Great Japan in orange and Ezo in bright yellow. The map is housed in the Setagaya Ino House Collection and is reprinted in Watanabe Ichirō, ed., *Tadataka to Inozu* (Tokyo: Gendai Shokan, 1998), 52; see also Watanabe, *Inō Tadataka Aruita Nihon* (Tokyo: Chikuma Shinsho, 1999).

54. The Inō Tadataka Museum in Sawara near Narita International Airport displays Inō's maps as well as the tools developed by his teacher, Takahashi Yoshitoki, while working as the shogunate's chief astronomer.

55. In 1995, stamps celebrating Inō and Siebold were issued simultaneously in Japan.

56. Hugh Cortazzi reproduced these maps as well as numerous others in his *Isles of Gold: Antique Maps of Japan* (New York: Weatherhill, 1983).

57. Ōtsuki Fumihiko, *Mitsukuri Rinshōkun den* (Tokyo: Maruzen, 1907), 32. Like Mitsukuri, Ōtsuki was also a direct descendant of a great Dutch studies scholar, Ōtsuki Gentaku, who compiled extensive journals of his contacts with Russians in the late eighteenth and early nineteenth centuries.

58. Sawa Ōmi, in Bakumatsu/Meiji Shoki ni Okeru Seiyō Bunmei no Yunyū ni Kan Suru Kenkyūkai, eds., *Yōgaku Jishi*, 65.

59. Ōkubo Toshiaki, ed., *Nishi Amane Zenshū*, vol. 2 (Tokyo: Shuko Shobō, 1961), 3–102. Thomas Havens mentions Nishi Amane's *Bankoku Kōhō* in his biography of Nishi Amane, *Nishi Amane and Modern Japanese Thought* (Princeton, N.J.: Princeton University Press, 1970), 51–52.

60. Tsutsumi Kokushishi, *Bankoku Kōhō Yakugi* (n.p.: 1868), collected at the University of Tokyo.

61. Ibid., prefatory notes.

62. Harry Harootunian has evoked the confusion in writing, "Not even John Wayne, in that now long-forgotten classic movie *The Barbarian and the Geisha*, was able to convey the sense of perplexity Harris must have experienced when greeted by the puzzled Shimoda officials who had not expected the American's arrival. The confusion may have been compounded by the problem of translation, if Sam Jaffe's portrayal of Harris translator Harry Heuskins is accurate, since both his Dutch-accented English and his English-accented Japanese sounded like the same unintelligible language." In Harootunian, "America's Japan/Japan's Japan," in Masao Miyoshi and H. D. Harootunian, eds., *Japan in the World* (Durham, N.C.: Duke University Press, 1993), 197.

63. Shigeno Yasutsugu, *Bankoku Kōhō* (Kagoshima: n.p., 1869). A short segment of the second section is included in Katō and Maruyama, eds., *Honyaku no Shisō: Nihon Kindai Shisō Taike*. See also Yasuoka Akio, *Nihon Kindaishi*, 52–53; Numata Jirō comments briefly on this, too, in "Shigeno Yasutsugu and the Modern Tokyo Tradition of Historical Writing," in W. G. Beasley and E. G. Pulleybank, eds., *Historians of China and Japan* (London: Oxford University Press, 1962), 264–287.

64. In Katō and Maruyama, *Honyaku no Shisō*, 305–306.

65. See Hōsei Daigaku Daigakushi Shiryōiinkai, ed., *Hōritsugaku no Yoake to Hōsei Daigaku* (Tokyo: Hōsei Daigaku Shuppankyoku, 1993).

66. Michel Foucault beautifully described "existing discourses" as "slumbering in a sleep towards which they have never ceased to glide since the day they were pronounced," in Michel Foucault, *The Archaeology of Knowledge and the Discourse on Language* (New York: Pantheon, 1972), 123.

67. The Foreign Office, *Treaties and Conventions between the Empire of Japan and Other Powers* (Tokyo: Z. P. Maruya, 1899). Italics mine.

## CHAPTER 3    THE VOCABULARY OF POWER

1. 1 For recent examples, see various essays in Chūō Kōron's new Modern Japanese History series *(Nihon no Kindai)* such as Matsumoto Kenichi's discussion in the first volume, *Kaikō/Ishin,* 68–80, 134–165; and also Sakamoto Takaō's examination in the second volume, *Meiji Kokka no Kensetsu,* 294–310 (Tokyo: Chūō Kōron, 1998). See also E. H. Norman, "Japan's Emergence as a Modern State," in John Dower, ed., *Origins of the Modern Japanese State—Selected Writings of E. H. Norman* (New York: Pantheon Books, 1975). An instructive parallel to this condition is the postwar security treaty with the United States.

2. Wilson, *Wheaton's Elements of International Law,* 45.

3. Itō Hirobumi and Hiratsuka Atsushi, eds., *Hisho Ruisan: Chōsen Kōshō Shiryō* (Tokyo: Hara Shobō, 1969), vol. 2, 182–241.

4. Ōkubo Yasuo, *Nihon Kindaihō no Chichi—Bowasonado* (Tokyo: Iwanami Shinsho, 1977), 77.

5. Itō and Hiratsuka, *Hisho Ruisan: Chōsen Kōshō Shiryō,* vol. 2, esp. 213–220.

6. *Nihon Gaikō Monjo,* vol. 38, n. 1, 486–491. Translator Kokubo Shotarō recorded this moment for the Foreign Ministry, and he continued to work for the colonial regime in Seoul throughout the annexation. A picture of him wearing a government police uniform appears in a photograph of Terauchi Masatake's central staff taken right after Japan's annexation of Korea. See Gurahikku Tokubetsu Soken, ed., *Nippon no Chōsen* (Tokyo: Yūrakusho, 1911), 100.

7. A useful analysis remains Marlene Mayo, "The Korean Crisis of 1873 and Early Meiji Foreign Policy," in *Journal of Asian Studies* 31, no. 4 (August 1972): 793–819.

8. For the Iwakura mission, see the official materials collected in *Nihon Gaikō Monjo,* vol. 4, 67–128; in addition, see also Ōkubo Toshiaki, ed., *Iwakura Shisetsu no Kenkyū* (Tokyo: n.p., 1976).

9. Shibahara Takuji, Ikai Takaaki, and Ikeda Masahiro, eds., *Taigaikan: Nihon Kindai Shisō Taikei,* vol. 12, *Nihon Kindai Shisō Taikei* (Tokyo: Iwanami Shoten, 1991), 5–11.

10. In Shibahara, Ikai, and Ikeda, *Taigaikan,* 9. *"Kokken"* (*kuni* and *kenri no ken*) was, at the time one of the numerous terms being used for the concept of "sovereignty." *"Jishu"*—often used for "independent"—was another. Ultimately, *"shuken"* became the common term.

11. Ibid., 40–41.

12. See Kim Gi'ung, ed., *Kan-Nichi Kōryō Nisennen* (Seoul: Yulhwado, 1984), 78–79. This view appears generally accepted in Korea as well.

13. Shibahara, Ikai, and Ikeda, *Taigaikan,* 40.

14. Yoshioka Yoshinori, *Nihon no Shinryaku to Bōchō* (Tokyo: Shin Nihon Shuppansha, 1995), 55.

15. See Vipan Chandra's assessment in his essay, "Korea Human-Rights Conscious-

ness in an Era of Transition: A Survey of Late-Nineteenth-Century Developments," in William Shaw, ed., *Human Rights in Korea—Historical and Policy Perspectives* (Cambridge: Harvard Council on East Asian Studies, 1991), 25–79.

16. Itō and Hiratsuka eds., *Hisho Ruisan: Chōsen Kōshō Shiryō,* vol. 1, 113. The issue of apology occupies a critical place in contemporary Japanese diplomacy with Korea. Although journalists and scholars often describe apology as a peculiarly "Asian" dimension of international relations, the concept took root in translating the discourse of international law into Japanese practice. As international terms permeated the *kanji* world, apology as a technique of power also became an element of newly modern state interaction.

17. Ibid., 90–94. In keeping with the importance of nationally identifiable decorations, point six stressed that the "State flag of Korea should be different from the State flag of China *(Shina)*" (93).

18. Ibid., 95.

19. Ibid., 107. The Sō family ruled Tsushima.

20. *Nihon Gaikō Monjo,* vol. 9, 1–5.

21. Photographs off Kanghwa appear in Yi Kyuhoon, ed., *Sajin u ro Ponun Dongnip Undong,* vol. 1 (Seoul: Sumundang, 1992), 18. Sketches of the U.S. ships appear in *Beikoku Shisetsu Perii Torai Ezu Shaseichō,* 1854 (catalogued in the main library of the University of Tokyo, rare book collection). Photographs taken a decade later by Felix Beatto of the British, American, French, and Dutch ships anchored, waiting to bombard Shimonoseki, fall into a similar category. Beatto's pictures are reprinted in Ozawa Tsuyoshi, ed., *Bakumatsu—Shashin no Jidai* (Tokyo: Chikuma Shobō, 1993), 114–123.

22. *"Kaitakushi"* literally translates as "Ministry of Development," but the Meiji government created it from the English expression "Colonial Ministry" and often published its papers under the English name.

23. *Nihon Gaikō Monjo,* vol. 9, 44–49.

24. Ibid., 7. On 14 January 1876, Kuroda mentioned three Korean-language students from the Foreign Ministry who accompanied the mission: Urase Hiroshi, Arakawa Norimasu, and Nakano Kyōtarō.

25. Ibid., 47.

26. Ibid., 48.

27. Ibid.

28. Wilson, *Wheaton's Elements of International Law,* 44.

29. *Nihon Gaikō Monjo,* vol. 9, 87–92. Inoue's comments mentioned here are on 89.

30. Ibid., 90.

31. Ibid.

32. Ibid., 91. This comment suggests that the Korean government did not consider China as a "foreign country."

33. Ibid., 114–120. See also Gaimushō [The Japanese Foreign Ministry], ed., *Nihon Gaikō Nenpyō oyobi Juyō Monjo 1840–1945* (Tokyo: Gaimushō, 1955), 67–68.

34. *Nihon Gaikō Monjo,* vol. 9, 115; see also Foreign Office, ed., *Treaties and Conventions between the Empire of Japan and Other Powers* (Tokyo: Z. P. Maruya & Co., 1899), 1. A variety of terms for "independence" and "sovereignty" were used until the vocabulary became more standardized. Since the early twentieth century, *"dokuritsu"* and *"shuken"* have been the preferred terms.

35. My thanks to Andre Schmid for elaborating on this point. The June 2000 South/North Korean Joint Declaration used the term *"chaju"* to explain how both sides desire an "independently" achieved unification. Officially both the South and the North desire unification for Koreans, by Koreans, and in Korea—that is, not orchestrated by the United States or China, let alone Japan—and this term allows the South to stress the importance of "international cooperation and support" for unification without openly losing its autonomy. The question of U.S. bases, therefore, can remain at bay. See Kosuge Kōichi's analysis of various points of the agreement in *Asahi Shinbun,* 20 June, 2000.

36. They settled finally on *dokuritsu,* the term used today.

37. This moment is a good example of how thinker Fukuzawa Yukichi's famous conceptual demand for Japan to "leave Asia" could be given immediate and practical dimensions as well.

38. *Nihon Gaikō Monjo,* vol. 18, 196–200.

39. Itō Hirobumi, *Report of Count Itō Hirobumi, Ambassador Extraordinary to His Imperial Majesty the Emperor of Japan of His Mission to the Court of China, Eighteenth Year of Meiji/Itō Tokuha Zenken Taishi, Fuku Meisho* (Tokyo: Gaimushō, 1885).

40. Itō Hirobumi, *Fuku Meisho* (Tokyo: Gaimushō, 1885), 3 April 1885, 1.

41. Ibid., 1–2.

42. Ibid., 5–6, 12.

43. Enomoto Takeaki dispatched an English-language telegram to the Foreign Ministry detailing the proceedings of the first day's meeting: "Negotiation was commenced yesterday at Li's office. On our side, Ambassador, myself and interpreter. On Chinese side, Li-Hung-Chang, Gotaicho and Zokusho." Enomoto also did not call attention to the technique, mentioning only an "interpreter." *Nihon Gaikō Monjo,* vol. 18, 237.

44. Hirobumi, *Fuku Meisho,* 12 April 1885, 3.

45. Ibid., 4; the Japanese translation here when Li speaks is *wagakuni* (our country) for "China." Also, at the time Korea was often spelled in English with a "C" ("Corea") as it still is, for example, in French.

46. Hirobumi, *Fuku Meisho,* 15 April 1885, 8.

47. The controversial 1965 "normalization" treaty between Japan and South Korea that addressed the complicated colonial past, for example, contained the customary provision stating that, should any discrepancy of meaning arise, the English version

would be the legal text. See Secretariat of the United Nations, *Treaty Series: Treaties and International Agreements Registered or Filed and Recorded with the Secretariat of the United Nations,* vol. 583, nos. 8470–8473, 33–49.

48. *Nihon Gaikō Monjo,* vol. 28, no. 2, 366.

49. W. G. Beasley, *Japanese Imperialism 1894–1945* (Oxford: Oxford University Press, 1991), 58.

50. Akira Iriye, *China and Japan in a Global Setting* (Cambridge, Mass.: Harvard University Press, 1992), 30.

51. *Nihon Gaikō Monjo,* vol. 28, no. 2, 383.

52. Andre Schmid, "Constructing Independence: Nation and Identity in Korea, 1895–1910," Ph.D. diss., Columbia University, 1995, 206. See also Schmid, *Korea between Empires, 1895–1919* (New York: Columbia University Press, 2002).

53. *Nihon Gaikō Monjo,* vol. 38, no. 1, 489. More of this speech was quoted at the outset of this chapter.

54. Ibid., 488, 489. As Prime Minister in 1910, Yi Wanyong sealed the annexation treaty with Terauchi Masatake.

55. *Nihon Gaikō Monjo,* vol. 31, no. 1, 490.

56. Prasenjit Duara, *Rescuing History from the Nation* (Chicago: University of Chicago Press, 1995), 23.

57. *Nihon Gaikō Monjo,* vol. 38, no. 1, 491.

58. A myriad number of references can be shown to emphasize European and American fascination with the victories their "little yellow brothers" were having. Bearing in mind that "Bloomsday" was 16 June 1904, one I particularly like is from Joyce's *Ulysses:* "What's that, Mr. O'Rourke? Do you know what? The Russians, they'd only be an eight o'clock breakfast for the Japanese." James Joyce, *Ulysses* (New York: Vintage, 1986), 47.

59. *Nihon Gaikō Monjo,* vol. 38, no. 1, 450–452.

60. Kajima Morinosuke, *The Diplomacy of Japan, 1894–1922* (Tokyo: Kajima Institute of International Peace, 1976), vol. 2, 390–395.

61. John Dower, *War without Mercy* (New York: Pantheon, 1986), 147.

62. Hilary Conroy, *The Japanese Seizure of Korea, 1868–1910: A Study of Realism and Idealism in International Relations* (Philadelphia: University of Pennsylvania Press, 1960), 415–417.

63. Kurachi Tetsukichi, *Kankoku Heigō no Iki Satsu* (reprint; Tokyo: Gaimushō, 1950), collected at the Foreign Ministry Archives and quoted in Conroy, *The Japanese Seizure of Korea,* 417.

64. Conroy, *The Japanese Seizure of Korea,* 417.

65. Kurachi, quoted in Conroy, *The Japanese Seizure of Korea,* 416.

66. Conroy, *The Japanese Seizure of Korea,* 416.

67. Ibid., 417.

68. Ibid., 416.

69. Ariga Nagao, *Hogokokuron* (Tokyo: Waseda Daigaku Shuppan, 1906).

70. Ibid., 23, 159.

71. Ibid., 111–113.

72. Peter Duus, *The Abacus and the Sword: The Japanese Penetration of Korea* (Berkeley and Los Angeles: University of California Press, 1995), 423.

73. See Unno Fukuju, ed., *Nikkan Kyōyaku to Kankoku Heigō: Chōsen Shokuminchi Shihai no Gōhōsei o Tomonau* (Tokyo: Akashi Shoten, 1995), 381–395.

74. Recently, for example, see Moriyama Shigenori, *Nikkan Heigō* (Tokyo: Yoshikawa Kokubunkan, 1992).

75. Takahashi Sakuei, *Heiji Kokusaihōron* (Tokyo: Shinsui Shoten, 1903). Among his other representative works from the time, see *Senji Kokusaihōron* (A Treatise on International Law During Wartime) (Tokyo: n.p., 1906) and a two-volume series called *Kokusaihō Gaikōron* (Diplomacy and International Law) (Tokyo: n.p., 1911).

76. Takahashi, *Heiji Kokusaihōron*, 202–204. Professor Sasagawa Norikatsu of Tokyo's International Christian University has examined Takahashi's legal theories in relation to Japan's colonization of Korea. See, for example, Sasagawa, *Sekai* (July 1999): 236–247; also Sakamoto, "Kokusai Kyōchōshugi no Tenkai: Nikkan no Aratana Shinraishi Kankei no Yokochiku o Mezashite," in Sakanose et al., eds., *Heiwa Kenpō o Mamorihiromeru* (Tokyo: Shinkyō Shuppansha, 2001), 142–161.

77. Ariga, *Hogokokuron*, Preface, 1.

78. Ibid.

79. See E. H. Norman, *Japan's Emergence as a Modern State,* esp. 375; also John Dower, *War without Mercy,* 147.

80. Scholars such as Ariga and Takahashi taught classes at military academies, the Imperial Universities, and private colleges such as Waseda and Keio because the practical applications of their studies—taught to the military—often afforded more constant employment than educating law students in the more theoretical dimensions.

81. Ariga Nagao gained his reputation as a young man at age 29 with the publication of the first of his numerous books, *Kokkagaku* (Studies of the Nation) (1889), arguably derived from his education in Stats Wissenschaft (my thanks to Jim McClain for pointing this out to me). The book appeared to anticipate the promulgation of the Meiji constitution, and it was so successful that it immediately went into its second printing.

82. Dispatching Ariga to the frontlines followed European and American practice at the time, and it remains an undervalued element of wars fought to this day. In 1904, during the war with Russia, the Meiji government dispatched Ariga to Manchuria, where he lectured generals on their maneuvers there. See Ariga Nagao, *Nichirō Rikusen Kokusaihōron* (Tokyo: Genshinsha, 1911).

83. Ariga Nagao, *Nisshin Sen'eki Kokusaihōron* (Tokyo: Rikugun Daigakkō, 1896).

84. Ariga Nagao, *La Guerre Sino-Japonaise au Point de Vue du Droit International* (Paris: Libraire de la Cour d'Appel, 1896).

85. Ibid., 9.

86. Ibid., 173; *Nisshin Sen'eki,* 228.

87. Inoue Haruki, *Ryojun Gyakusatsu Jiken* (Tokyo: Chikuma Shobō, 1995). Inoue's book includes press releases as well as photos of piles of corpses taken by British and Japanese photographers.

88. John Westlake in Sakuye Takahashi, *Cases on International Law during the Chino-Japanese War* (Cambridge: Cambridge University Press, 1899), Introduction.

89. See W. Michael Reisman and Chris T. Antoniou, eds., *The Laws of War: A Comprehensive Collection of Primary Documents on International Laws Governing Armed Conflict* (New York: Vintage Press, 1994). The authors offer a matter-of-fact treatment of these laws, stressing how, in the late nineteenth century, "a range of popular organizations and movements sought to condemn war, to temper its severity when it occurred and, even more ambitiously, to create international dispute mechanisms that might obviate it entirely" (xviii–xix).

90. Reprinted in Endō Yukio and Ōkubo Toshiaki, eds., *Nihon Rekishi* Shirizu: *Nisshin/Nichiro Sensō* (Tokyo: Sekai Bunkasha, 1967), vol. 19, 54.

91. See for example, Ezra Vogel, *Japan as Number One: Lessons for America* (New York: Harper & Row, 1979); and Karl Van Wolfren, *The Enigma of Japanese Power: People and Politics in a Stateless Nation* (New York: Vintage, 1990).

92. Ariga, *Hogokokuron,* Preface, 4.

93. Ibid., 1.

94. Ibid., 3.

95. Ibid., 212.

96. Ibid., 57.

97. Ibid., 227.

98. Tachi Sakutarō, "Ariga Hakase no Hogokokuron," in *Gaikō Jihō,* no. 107 (October 1906): 93–95. See also Tanaka Shinichi, "Hogokoku Mondai: Ariga Nagao/Tachi Sakutarō no Hogokoku Ronsō," in *Shaken Kagaku Kenkyū* 28, no. 2 (1976): 126–163.

99. See Tachi Sakutarō and Hakaseronkō Iinkai, eds., *Tachi Hakase Gaikōshi Ronbunshū* (Tokyo: Nihon Hyōronshapan, 1946). Tachi was a member of Japan's delegation to the Washington Conference in 1921.

100. Tachi, "Ariga Hakase no Hogokokuron," 93.

101. Ibid., 94–95.

102. Ibid., 95.

103. Ariga Nagao, "Hogokokuron o Arawashitaru Riyū," in *Kokusaihō Gaikō Zasshi* 5, no. 2 (1906): 1; 5.

104. Francis Rey, "La Situation International de la Coreé," in *Revue Générale de Droit International Public,* no. 13 (Paris: Paul Fauchille, 1906), 40–58. *The Times* of London, however, intimated what many suspected around the world: "A simple straightforward document, it nevertheless contained internal evidence of difficulties in drafting" (*The Times* [London], 13 January 1906).

105. Rey, "La Situation International de la Coreé," 55; numerous scholars have cited this article to argue that the colonization of Korea was illegal. See the collected essays in Unno, *Nikkan Kyōyaku to Kankoku Heigō*; see also Unno Fukuju, *Kankoku Heigō* (Tokyo: Iwanami Shinsho, 1995). For a fascinating discussion of how a collective sense of injustice orders national memory see Mark J. Osiel, "Ever Again: Legal Remembrance of Administrative Massacre," in *University of Pennsylvania Law Review* 144, no. 2 (December 1995): 463–704.

106. Rey, "La Situation International de la Coreé," 58.

107. George Trumbull Ladd, *In Korea with Marquis Itō: A Narrative of Personal Experiences and a Critical Historical Inquiry* (New York: Charles Scribner's Sons, 1908), 277–278.

## CHAPTER 4    VOICES OF DISSENT

1. Pierre Bourdieu, *Language and Symbolic Power*, trans. Gino Raymond and Matthew Adamson (Cambridge, Mass.: Harvard University Press, 1991), 138.

2. In this vein, Michel Foucault usefully suggested to "analyze what occurs in the field of illegality to understand what we want to say when we talk of legality" (226). See "Le sujet et le pouvoir," in Daniel Defert and François Ewald, eds., *Michel Foucault —Dits et Écrits: 1954–1988*, vol. 4 (Paris: Gallimard, 1994), 222–243.

3. Klemens von Klemperer suggests that the "solitary witnessess" should be in "the center stage of resistance studies." See "'What Is the Law That Lies behind These Words?' Antigone's Question and the German Resistance against Hitler," in Michael Geyer and John W. Boyer, eds., *Resistance against the Third Reich, 1933–1990* (Chicago: University of Chicago Press, 1994), 141–150. James Scott's term "hidden transcripts" is eloquent and methodologically useful, but, unlike von Klemperer, Scott seems to require a certain number of people—almost a quorum of protesters—in order to qualify something as "resistance." See James B. Scott, *Domination and the Arts of Resistance: Hidden Transcripts* (New Haven, Conn.: Yale University Press, 1990).

4. Frederick Arthur McKenzie, *Korea's Fight For Freedom* (London: Fleming Revell, 1920), 161–162; also in McKenzie, *The Tragedy of Korea* (London: Hodder & Stoughton, 1908).

5. See *Chōsen Bōto To Batsuji*, collected in *Chosŏn Chuch'agun Saryŏngbu, Chosŏn Tongnip Undong*, vol. 1, 166.

6. See Cho Tonggŏl, *Kugyŏk Wang San Chŏnsŏ* (Seoul: Aseha Munwhasa, 1985). I am indebted to Choi Hyŏnggun for his help in obtaining this book. See also Sin Yongha, "Hŏ Wi ŭi Ŭibyŏng Undong," in *Narasarang* 27 (1977): n.p. Hŏ Wi's Thirty Demands are also translated and published in Peter Lee, ed., *Sourcebook of Korean Civilization*, vol. 2, *From the Seventeenth Century to the Modern Period* (New York: Columbia University Press, 1996), 2:406–407.

7. *TaeHan Maeil Sinbo,* 23 May 1908. For a compelling discussion of Japanese colonial press restrictions, see Andre Schmid, "Censorship and the *Hwangsŏng Sinmun,*" in Chang Yun-shik et al., *Korea between Tradition and Modernity: Selected Papers from the Fourth Pacific and Asian Conference on Korean Studies* (Vancouver: Institute of Asian Research, 2000), 158–171.

8. From the Residency General materials, *Bōtō ni Kansuru Hensatsu,* collected in *Han'guk Tongnip Undongsa Saryoso* (vols. 8 and 9).

9. Yu Insŏk, "Guko p'aldo yor up," quoted in Sin Yongha, *Han'guk Kundae Minjok Jui ŭi Hyŏngsong kwa Chongae,* chap. 5; also see Ch'oe Ikhyŏn's earlier description of the Japanese at the time of the Kanghwa Treaty (1876) in similar terms in *Kojon Kugyŏk ch'ongso* (Seoul: Minjok Munhwa Ch'ujinhoe 1977), 124–126.

10. See Pak Songsu, ed., *Han'guk Tongnip Undongsa Charyojip: Ŭibyong P'yŏn* (Songnam: Han'guk Chongsin Munhwa Yŏn'guwŏn), 1993, 11–79.

11. Cho Tonggŏl, *Kugyŏk Wang San Chŏnsŏ,* xv–xviii.

12. See Michael D. Shin, "Conceptions of Korea in *The Independent,*" unpublished master's thesis, University of California at Berkeley 1993. Shin discusses how Independence Movement thinkers were concerned with defining the political entity "Chosŏn" as a nation as understood by the West, thus displacing "Chosŏn" from its position in the Confucian scholar–upheld Chinese hierarchy of relations. The group is widely known for its promotion of *han'gul* (the Korean phonetic script), but Shin demonstrates that also by using English it became "possible to discuss the unity of Chosŏn as a nation" (15). On the heels of the Ulmi Movement, Hŏ Wi did not intend to challenge his thinking so drastically.

13. See Young L. Lew's useful piece, "Korean-Japanese Politics behind the Kabo-Ulmi Reform Movement, 1894–1896," *Journal of Korean Studies* 3 (1982): 39–81; see also Edward Baker, "Establishment of a Legal System under Japanese Rule," in Sang Hyun Song, ed., *Introduction to the Law and Legal System of Korea* (Seoul: Kyung Mun Sa, 1983).

14. Cho Tonggŏl, *Kugyŏk Wang San Chŏnsŏ,* xii; see also Cho Hangnae, *1900 Nyŏndae ŭi Aeguk Kyemong Undong Yŏng'gu* (Seoul: Asea Munhwasa, 1993).

15. Cho Tonggŏl, *Kugyŏk Wang San Chonso,* viii.

16. *Hwangsŏng Sinmun,* 1 July 1904. I am indebted to Yasuoka Akio of Hōsei University for allowing me to use these materials in their collection. This newspaper is also quoted in Sin Yongha, *Han'guk Kundae Minjok Jui ŭi Hyŏngsong kwa Chongae.*

17. *Hwangsŏng Sinmun,* 1 July 1904.

18. Andre Schmid, "Rediscovering Manchuria: Sin Ch'aeho and the Politics of Territorial History in Korea," *Journal of Asian Studies* 56, no. 1 (February 1997): 26–47; also Schmid, *Korea between Empires, 1895-1919* (New York: Columbia University Press, 2002). Also see Henry Em's discussion of the connection between Sin Ch'aeho's territorial thinking and the construction of the nation in Em, "Minjok as a Modern and

Democratic Construct: Sin Ch'aeho's Historiography," in Gi-Wook Shin and Michael Robinson, eds., *Colonial Modernity in Korea* (Cambridge, Mass.: Harvard University Press, 1999), 336–361.

19. *Hwangsŏng Sinmun,* 1 July 1904 quoting the *Nikkan Giteisho,* 23 February 1904.

20. *Nihon Gaikō Monjo,* vol. 37, no. 1, 339–340.

21. *Hwangsŏng Sinmun,* 1 July 1904.

22. Ibid.

23. Yi Inyŏng's manifesto is collected in *Nihon Gaikō Monjo,* vol. 41, 819, which dates the manifesto 25 September 1907. In the records of Yi's trial, the date given is 2 September 1907.

24. *TaeHan Maeil Sinbo,* 28 July 1909. The manifesto is reprinted in an article about Yi Inyŏng.

25. Ibid.

26. Kim, "Seoul e suh ŭi Sutibunsu ŭi Chin'il Oekong Hwangdong," vol. 46 (1988): 59–120. The most fulsome account of this incident in English is a chapter of Hyung June Moon, "The Korean Immigrants in America: The Quest of Identity in the For-mative Years, 1903–1918," Ph.D. diss., University of Nevada at Reno, 1976; see also Andrew C. Nahm, "Durham White Stevens and the Japanese Annexation of Korea," in *The United States and Korea* (Kalamazoo, Mich.: Center for Korean Studies, Western Michigan University, 1979), 110–136; and also Ronald Takaki, *Strangers from a Differ-ent Shore: A History of Asian Americans* (New York: Penguin Books, 1989), 283–284.

27. *San Francisco Chronicle,* 24 March 1908.

28. *San Francisco Chronicle,* 28 March 1908.

29. *Nihon Gaikō Monjo,* vol. 41, 837.

30. Kim Wonyong, *Chaemi Hanin Osipnyŏnsa* (Reedley, Calif.: Charles Ho Kim, 1959), 328–329.

31. Gaimushō [The Japanese Foreign Ministry], *Nihon Gaikō Nenpyō,* 252.

32. See Wayne Patterson, *The Korean Frontier in America: Immigration to Hawaii, 1896–1910* (Honolulu: University of Hawai'i Press, 1988).

33. *New York Times,* 24 March 1908.

34. *San Francisco Chronicle,* 24 March 1908.

35. Chang's sworn statement, in *San Francisco Chronicle,* 25 March 1908.

36. *San Francisco Chronicle,* 3 January 1909; *Kongnip Sinmun,* 6 January 1909.

37. *San Francisco Chronicle,* 28 March 1908.

38. See Owen Denny, *China and Korea* (Shanghai: Kelly and Walsh, 1888); Wil-liam Franklin Sands, *Undiplomatic Memories: At the Court of Korea* (London: Century Reprints, 1987); Martina Deuchler, *Confucian Gentlemen and Barbarian Envoys: The Opening of Korea, 1875–1885* (Seattle: University of Washington, 1977); and Fred Harrington, *God, Mammon, and the Japanese: Dr. Horace Allen and Korean-American Relations, 1884–1905* (Madison: University of Wisconsin Press, 1944).

39. In Unno Fukuju, *Nikkan Kyōyaku to Kankoku Heigō: Chōsen Shokuminchi Shihai no Gōhōsei o Tomonau* (Tokyo: Akashi Shoten, 1995), 385.

40. Bruce Cumings, "Archaeology, Descent, Emergence: Japan in British/American Hegemony, 1900–1950," in Masao Miyoshi and H. D. Harootunian, eds., *Japan in the World* (Durham, N.C.: Duke University Press, 1993), 106.

41. See, for example, George Kennan, "Korea: A Degenerate State," *The Outlook* (1905): n.p.; and Kennan, "What Japan Has Done in Korea?" *The Outlook* (1905): n.p.

42. Patterson, *The Korean Frontier in America*, 151.

43. *San Francisco Chronicle*, 21 March 1908.

44. Ibid.

45. After the shooting of Stevens, the *New York Times* published the manifesto, 25 March 1908; see also Koike to Hayashi, telegram no. 24, *Nihon Gaikō Monjo*, vol. 41, 819, which dates the proclamation 25 September 1907.

46. *Kongnip Sinmun*, 25 March 1908.

47. *San Francisco Chronicle*, 24 March 1908.

48. *Kongnip Sinmun*, 25 March 1908.

49. *San Francisco Chronicle*, 23 March 1908; see also Moon, "The Korean Immigrants in America," 333–335; *Kongnip Sinmun*, 25 March 1908.

50. *San Francisco Chronicle*, 23 March 1908; *New York Times*, 24 March 1908.

51. *San Francisco Chronicle*, 23 March 1908; *New York Times*, 24–27 March 1908.

52. *New York Times*, 25 March, 1908; 5 April 1908.

53. *New York Times*, 24 March 1908.

54. *San Francisco Chronicle*, 24 March 1908.

55. Ibid.

56. *Nihon Gaikō Monjo*, vol. 41, 875–877.

57. Ibid., 819.

58. See Judith Butler, *Excitable Speech: A Politics of the Performative* (New York: Routledge, 1997), 30–31.

59. Only several years before Leon Czglosz had shot President McKinley, an event that touched off a great furor in the press about assassination and immigrants. Several reporters alluded to the Czglosz affair in reference to the Korean men, generalizing about immigrants and making extreme theories about the potential assassin in each immigrant.

60. *San Francisco Chronicle*, 25 March 1908.

61. Ibid.

62. *New York Times*, 29 March 1908.

63. *New York Times*, 27 March 1908. In his linguistic analysis, Valentin Volosinov proposed that "reported speech is speech within speech; utterance within utterance. . . . A reported utterance, however, is not just a theme of speech: it has the capacity of entering on its own, so to speak, into speech, into its own syntactic makeup, as an integral unit of the construction. . . . However, once it becomes a constructional unit in the

author's speech, into which it has entered on its own, the reported utterance becomes a theme of that speech." Valentin Volosinov, *Marxism and the Philosophy of Language,* trans. Ladislav Matejka and I. R. Titunik (Cambridge, Mass.: Harvard University Press, 1986), 115.

64. *San Francisco Chronicle,* 25 March 1908.

65. Shiota Shobei, ed., *Zōho Kōtoku Shūsui no Nikki to Shokan* (Tokyo: Miraisha, 1965); F. G. Notehelfer, *Kōtoku Shūsui: Portrait of a Japanese Radical* (Cambridge, Mass.: Cambridge University Press, 1971), esp. chap. 3, 55–87.

66. The most famous of these critiques was Kōtoku's 1901 book, *Imperialism: The Monstrosity of the Twentieth Century* [Teikokushugi: Nijū Seiki no Kaibutsu]; collected in "Kōtoku Shūsui Zenshū Henshū Iinkai, *Kōtoku Shūsui Zenshū* (Tokyo: Meiji Bunken, 1970), vol. 3, 107–196.

67. Shiota, *Zōho Kōtoku Shūsui no Nikki to Shokan.*

68. Louise Young, *Japan's Total Empire: Manchuria and the Culture of Wartime Imperialism* (Berkeley and Los Angeles: University of California Press, 1998), 15.

69. Meiji Bunken, *Kōtoku Shūsui Zenshū,* vol. 4, 338–340.

70. Ibid., 270.

71. For a substantial discussion of how the thought of Kōtoku and his peers came out of the "peoples' rights movement," see Nakamura Fumio, *Daigyaku Jiken to Chishikijin* (Tokyo: San'ichi Shobō, 1982).

72. Kōtoku joined the staff of Kuoriwa Ruikō's paper in 1903, where he worked for a year until he and Sakai Toshihiko stormily quit when the paper refused to adopt an antiwar stance. Together with former *Yorozu* reporter Ishikawa Sanshiro and former *Ni Roku* reporter Nishikawa Kojiro, Kōtoku and Toshihiko started publishing the *Heimin Shinbun.* See Yamamoto Taketoshi, *"Yorozu Chōhō" no Hatten to Suitai* (Tokyo: Nihon Tosho Senta, 1984); also Matsuo Hiroshi, *Jian Ijihō to Tokkō Keisatsu* (Tokyo: Kyōikusha, 1979), 42–43.

73. Jacqueline Bhabha has examined how contemporary human rights groups assert the primacy (and morality) of human-level international relations, noting that "the commitment to universalism in the recognition of fundamental human rights was inextricably linked from the start with a challenge to doctrines of strong, national, territorially based sovereignty." See Bhabha, "Embodied Rights: Gender Persecution, State Sovereignty, and Refugees," in *Public Culture,* vol. 9 (1996): 3–32.

74. Carol Gluck juxtaposed late-Meiji advocates of civilization with Kōtoku Shūsui's condemnation of its failures to show how, "hailed or defamed, the existence of 'civilization' was itself no longer a question." See Gluck, *Japan's Modern Myths: Ideology in the Late Meiji Period* (Princeton, N.J.: Princeton University Press, 1985), 256.

75. Kōtoku Shūsui Zenshū Henshū Iinkai, *Kōtoku Shūsui Zenshū* (Tokyo: Meiji Bunken, 1970), vol. 4, 339.

76. *Yorozu Chōhō,* 28 August 1903; collected in Kōtoku Shūsui Zenshū Henshū Iinkai, *Kōtoku Shūsui Zenshū,* vol. 4, 338–340. I have translated *jinrui* both as "mankind"

and as "races" to capture the vocabulary of contemporary social Darwinism with which Kōtoku was well versed.

77. Kōtoku Shūsui Zenshū Henshū Iinkai, *Kōtoku Shūsui Zenshū,* vol. 4, 340.

78. A similar dispute arose in 1996, and the Japanese Foreign Ministry reprinted the complete, handwritten records of the early Meiji incident. Also included in the reprint is the exchange between Tokugawa and Yi representatives in 1693 discussing the islands. Gaimushō [The Japanese Foreign Ministry], ed., *Takeshima Mondai—"Takeshima Kōshō"* (Tokyo: MT Publishers, 1996).

79. Reprinted in the Gaimushō facsimile, *Takeshima Mondai,* 166. (I believe a secretary at the Foreign Ministry made a hurried mistake when transcribing this particular letter into the official record because Toda Takayoshi's surname is written as "Ishida" in this one instance, and in the other five pieces of correspondence he is "Toda.")

80. 6 May 1877; Mutō Tsunenori, in Gaimushō, *Takeshima Mondai,* 225.

81. Namiki Yorihisa, "Tarui Tōkichi no 'Ajia Shugi'—Higashi Ajia no 'Kindai' to 'Kokka,'" in Yoshie Akio, Yamauchi Masayuki, and Motomura Ryōji, eds., *Rekishi no Bunpō* (Tokyo: University of Tokyo Press, 1997), 232.

82. Tarui Funaki [Tōkichi], "Mujintō Tansenki," in *Ajia Kyōkai Hōkoku,* no. 5 (June 1883): 19. The July and August issues of the journal published the remaining parts of Tarui's diary.

83. Tanaka wrote that when he interviewed Taketomi Tokitoshi—the man who ran a school where Tarui taught in the early 1880s—Taketomi took credit for telling Tarui about the "uninhabited island." Taketomi apparently maintained that the island appeared in a text he studied, the *Tōgoku Tsūkan,* and that he had pointed out the reference to Tarui. Tanaka found the claim dubious and maintained that his Tokyo acquaintance Matsuzono was Tarui's source of information about the "uninhabited island." See Tanaka Sōgōrō, *Tōyō Shakaitōkō* (Tokyo: Ichigensha, 1930), 65–66; and, for more on Matsuzono, 46–48; also Namiki, "Tarui Tōkichi no 'Ajia Shugi,'" 236–238.

84. Tarui, "Mujintō Tansenki," 20; also quoted in Namiki, "Tarui Tōkichi no 'Ajia Shugi,'" 236–238. By pure coincidence Tarui lost his way on this voyage in the same waters that Admiral Yi's naval forces defeated Hideyoshi's ships in the 1590s.

85. Tarui, "Mujintō Tansenki," 21; Namiki, "Tarui Tōkichi no 'Ajia Shugi,'" 236. Two letters that Tarui wrote to his brother-in-law Kusunoki revealing his frustrations at not finding the island are reprinted in Tanaka Sōgōro's *Tōyō Shakaitōkō,* 198–200.

86. The Charter for the *Tōyō Shakaitōkō* is found in Tanaka, *Tōyō Shakaitōkō,* 3–5; see also *Meiji Bunka Zenshu,* vol. 2, 434–435.

87. Cited in John Dower, *Origins of the Modern Japanese State: Selected Writings of E. H. Norman* (New York: Pantheon, 1975), 288, n. 31.

88. Ibid., 288, n. 31.

89. Tanaka, *Tōyō Shakaitōkō,* 3–4.

90. Ibid., 51–52.

91. Takeuchi Yoshimi, "Ajia Shugi no Tenbo" [Introductory Essay], in Takeuchi Yoshimi, ed., *Ajia Shugi: Gendai Nihon Shisō Taikei*, vol. 9 (Tokyo: Chikuma Shobō, 1963), 36.

92. Tanaka, *Tōyō Shakaitōkō*, 34.

93. Kuzuo Yoshihisa, *Tōa Senkaku Shishi Kiden* (Tokyo: Kokuryūkai, 1933); the section on Tarui Tōkichi is reproduced also in Takeuchi Yoshimi, ed., *Ajia Shugi: Gendai Nihon Shisō Taikei*, 32–34. Takeuchi is credited with the postwar "discovery" of Tarui.

94. See Han Sang'il, *Nikkan Kindaishi no Kūkan* (Tokyo: Nihon Keizai Hyoronsha, 1984), 31; also Namiki Yorihisa, "Tarui Tokichi no 'Ajia Shugi'—Higashi Ajia no 'Kindai' to 'Kokka,'" in Yoshie Akio, Yamauchi Masayuki, and Motomura Ryōji, eds., *Rekishi no Bunpō* (Tokyo: University of Tokyo Press, 1997), 225–239.

95. See Harold F. Cook, *Korea's 1884 Incident: Its Background and Kim Ok-Kyun's Elusive Dream* (Seoul: Royal Asiatic Society, 1972).

96. Tarui Tōkichi, *Daitō Gappōron: Saipan Daitō Gappōron* (Tokyo: Choryo Shorin, 1975). The text is a reprint of the 1910 edition, which included the 1893 copy and the copy that Tarui reissued to celebrate the annexation of Korea. In 1963, Takeuchi Yoshimi published a modern Japanese translation in *Ajia Shugi: Gendai Nihon Shisō Taikei*. I reference both.

97. Takeuchi, *Ajia Shugi: Gendai Nihon Shisō Taikei*, 117.

98. The line comes from Book 13, Verse 3 of the *Analects*.

99. Tarui Tōkichi, *Daitō Gappōron*, 6; Takeuchi, *Ajia Shugi: Gendai Nihon Shisō Taikei*, 109.

100. See the United Nations High Commission for Refugees' Web site, which is updated daily: www.unhcr.ch.

**CHAPTER 5   *MISSION LÉGISLATRICE***

1. For related examples of British, French, and American patterns see Timothy Mitchell, *Colonising Egypt* (New York: Cambridge University Press, 1988); Bernard Cohn, *Colonialism and Its Forms of Knowledge: The British in India* (Princeton, N.J.: Princeton University Press, 1996); David Prochaska, *Making Algeria French: Colonial Bone* (Chicago: University of Chicago Press, 1990); and Sally Engle Merry, *Colonizing Hawai'i: The Cultural Power of Law* (Princeton, N.J.: Princeton University Press, 1998).

2. See Chulwoo Lee, "Modernity, Legality, and Power in Korea under Japanese Rule," in Gi-Wook Shin and Michael Robinson, eds., *Colonial Modernity in Korea* (Cambridge, Mass.: Harvard University Press, 1999), 21–51. Lee makes the necessary point that while much historiography points out the one-sidedness of Japan's "modernization" of Korea's legal system, "it does not take issue with the modernization of the legal form itself" (35).

3. See two studies that examine this "gaze" in different and thoughtful ways. See

Anne McClintock, *Imperial Leather: Race, Gender, and Sexuality in the Colonial Context* (New York: Routledge, 1995); see also Ann Laura Stoler, *Race and the Education of Desire: Foucault's "History of Sexuality" and the Colonial Order of Things* (Durham, N.C.: Duke University Press, 1995).

4. Photographs of this ilk were particularly popular. See, for example, Felix Beatto's shots reprinted in Tsuyoshi Ozawa, *Bakumatsu: Shashin no Jidai* (Tokyo: Chikuma Shobō, 1993).

5. Discussed in chap. 4.

6. One of the most famous English-language travel writers of the day, Isabella Bird Bishop (1831–1904), drew attention to such customs in her *Korea and Her Neighbors: A Narrative of Travel with an Account of the Recent Vicissitudes and Present Condition of the Country* (London: Kegan Paul, 1897). It is useful to bear in mind that she, like many other Euro-American travelers and political observers, often arrived in Korea via Japan, and they naturally made comparisons. See Bishop's 1878 account, *Unbeaten Tracks in Japan* (reprinted most recently in 2001).

7. Edward J. Baker pointed to this partial feature of Japanese colonial rule in his "The Role of Legal Reforms in the Japanese Annexation and Rule of Korea, 1905–1919," in *Harvard Law School: Studies in East Asian Law: Korea,* reprinted from *Studies on Korea in Transition,* Harvard Occasional Papers, no. 9 (Cambridge, Mass.: Harvard University Press, 1979). See also Lee, "Modernity, Legality, and Power," 31–33.

8. Quoted in chap. 1.

9. In late July 1907, Resident General Itō Hirobumi and Prime Minister Yi Wanyong signed an agreement transferring all judicial power in Korea to Japanese control. See *Nihon Gaikō Monjo,* vol. 40, 492–493.

10. *The Times* (London), 29 July 1907.

11. The Shufeldt Treaty, 1882, quoted in Resident General of Korea, *Annual Report on the Reforms and Progress in Korea, 1907–1910* (Seoul: Resident General of Japan, 1908–1910), 28.

12. The 1899 Korean Court Organization Law had changed the name of the Korean High Court to the Court of Cassation, which followed the route the Meiji government had adopted for its own reorganization in Japan in the 1880s. The term "cassation" is not in practical use in English, but it refers to the High Court of Appeals.

13. For example, Tsumaki Yorinaka, working for the German firm of Ende-Boeckmann, took charge of the massive "Court of Cassation" in Tokyo, across from the Imperial Palace that he completed only a decade before the Japanese regime in Seoul built its own there in a different style. Like most other young architects in the early Meiji period, Tsumaki first studied with Josiah Conder and then went on for further training at Cornell University and in Berlin. See Dallas Finn, *Meiji Revisited: The Sites of Victorian Japan* (New York: Weatherhill, 1995).

14. Gwendolyn Wright's study of French colonial architecture addresses the interplay of political power and structural display. See Wright, *The Politics of Design in*

*French Colonial Urbanism* (Chicago: University of Chicago Press, 1991). For a topical analysis of Daniel Burnham's vision of the U.S. colonial presence in the Philippines, see Thomas S. Hines, *Burnham of Chicago: Architect and Planner* (Chicago: University of Chicago Press, 1979), 197–216. See also Ron Robin, *Enclaves of America: The Rhetoric of American Political Architecture Abroad, 1900–1965* (Princeton, N.J.: Princeton University Press, 1992).

15. Deleuze discusses the meaning of a city's organization of people and things as "assemblages." See Giles Deleuze and Félix Guattari, *What Is Philosophy?* (New York: Columbia University Press, 1994), 186; see also John Rajchman, *Constructions* (Cambridge, Mass.: MIT Press, 1998).

16. See report by H.I.J.M.'s Residency General, in Resident General of Korea, *Annual Report on Reforms and Progress in Korea 1908–1909* (Seoul: Resident General of Japan, December 1909).

17. This particular photograph is also included in a recent, nostalgic book depicting "Lifestyles and Customs in the Yi Dynasty." See *Sajin u ro Ponun Chosŏn Sidae: Senghwal kwa P'ungsŏk* (Seoul: Sumundang, 1993), 202. The widely differing uses of colonial archive materials offers a glimpse of competing claims to the era.

18. The title of Ōkubo Yasuo's book is, among others, *Nihon Kindaihō no Chichi—Bowasonado* (Tokyo: Iwanami Shinsho, 1977). His legacy endures most recently at Hosei University in downtown Tokyo, where the university just completed its new skyscraper called "Boissonade Tower."

19. "Notice individuelle de G. Boissonade demandée par le Ministere de l'Instruction publique, c. 1870"; cited in Yasuo Okubo, "Gustave Boissonade, père français du droit japonais modèrne (1825–1910)," in *Revue Historique de Droit Français et Etranger,* series 4 (1981): 49.

20. Ōkubo Yasuo, *Nihon Kindaihō no Chichi—Bowasonado,* 77.

21. In reprint, Kikkawa Tsuneo, ed., *Notes des Correspondances avec Monsieur Boissonade* (Tokyo: Hosei University, 1978), 32.

22. Ibid., 43.

23. Ibid.

24. For elaboration on nativist responses to the barbarians' terms, see H. D. Harootunian, *Things Seen and Unseen* (Chicago: University of Chicago Press, 1987). See also F. C. Jones, *Extraterritoriality in Japan and the Diplomatic Relations Resulting in Its Abolition, 1853–1899* (New Haven, Conn.: Yale University Press, 1931), 47.

25. Gustave Boissonade, *Projet de Code de Procédure Criminelle Pour L'Empire du Japon Accompagné d'un Commentaire* (Paris: Ernest Thorin, 1882), xvi.

26. Boissonade, *Commentaire,* xii–xiii. It is fair to suggest that there is a similar tone in present discussions—pro and con—of the Bush administration's push for military tribunals following the September 11, 2001 attacks. For example, Yale law professor and human rights theorist Harold Koh has suggested that instead of establishing new tribunals—a move he does not support—the United States should hold trials in exist-

ing U.S. federal courts: "Why not show that American courts can give universal justice?" Harold Hongji Koh, *New York Times,* 23 November, 2001. Also quoted in Aryeh Neier, "The Military Tribunals on Trial," *New York Review of Books,* 14 February, 2002, 14.

27. Roland Barthes described language as a horizon on which distinctive styles manifest vertically, and Boissonade thus assumed he blended Japan into this line in a nondistinctive fashion. See Roland Barthes, *Writing Degree Zero* (New York: Farrar, Strauss, and Giroux, 1990).

28. Boissonade, *Commentaire,* xiii.

29. *Annual Report for 1907 on Reforms and Progress in Korea,* 27.

30. Bernard S. Cohn, *Colonialism and Its Forms of Knowledge: The British in India* (Princeton, N.J.: Princeton University Press, 1996), 63–65.

31. *Annual Report for 1907 on Reforms and Progress in Korea,* 22–25; 28.

32. I am grateful to Professor Igarashi Akio of Rikkyo University and librarians there for providing space in which to read the collected volumes of the *Hōritsu Shinbun.*

33. See Kiyomizu Takashi, "Takagi Masutarō," *Hōgaku Semina* (November 1972): n.p.; and also Saeki Shigeto, "Ko Takagi Masutarō," in *Gendai Bengoshi Taikan,* vol. 1 (Tokyo: n.p., 1932).

34. *Hōritsu Shinbun,* 25 May 1908.

35. *Hōritsu Shinbun,* 10 June 1908; see also 20 December 1907; 27 December 1907; 29 February 1908.

36. See Tokutomi Kenjirō, *Omoide no Ki* (Tokyo: Minyusha, 1901); see also Tokutomi Kenjirō, *Footprints in the Snow* (Rutland, Vt.: Charles Tuttle and Sons, 1970).

37. See title published by Hosei University, Hōsei Daigaku Daigakushi Shiryōiinkai, ed., *Hōritsugaku no Yoake to Hōsei Daigaku* (Tokyo: Hōsei Daigaku Shuppankyoku, 1993), 317–321.

38. Articles about Ume and his aims for reforming Korea appeared in almost every issue of the *Hōritsu Shinbun* during the time between Ume's arrival in Seoul and his death there in 1910. The Japanese colonial regime published Ume's work in 1912, *Kanshu Chosa Hokokusho.* See Lee's "Modernity, Legality, and Power" for a concise explanation of how Ume's survey impacted the reordering of civil codes under colonial rule, esp. 25–31.

39. *Hōritsu Shinbun,* 15 June 1906.

40. *Hōritsu Shinbun,* 15 May 1905; 25 May 1905.

41. Discussions of the development of the electric chair began appearing in this newspaper at the time, and there were even occasional photographs of American-made devices complete with engineering details.

42. *Hōritsu Shinbun,* 15 May 1905.

43. Ibid.

44. For discussion of Fukuzawa's particular views of Korea in the 1880s, see Kine-

fuchi Nobuo, *Fukuzawa Yukichi to Chōsen: Jiji Shinbun Shasetsu o Chūshin shi* (Tokyo: Sairyūsha, 1997).

45. Quoted in Rachel G. Fuchs, *Poor and Pregnant in Paris: Strategies for Survival in the Nineteenth Century* (New Brunswick, N.J.: Rutgers University Press, 1992), 38.

46. See Jan Goldstein, *Console and Classify: The French Psychiatric Profession in the Late Nineteenth Century* (New York: Cambridge University Press, 1990); see also Daniel Pick, *Faces of Degeneration: A European Disorder, c. 1848–c. 1918* (New York: Cambridge University Press, 1993), 126–128; Susan Thorne, "'The Conversion of Englishmen and the Conversion of the World Inseparable': Missionary Imperialism and the Language of Class in Early Industrial Britain," in Frederick Cooper and Ann Laura Stoler, eds., *Tensions of Empire: Colonial Cultures in a Bourgeois World* (Berkeley and Los Angeles: University of California Press, 1997), 238–262.

47. Katherine Fischer Taylor, *In the Theater of Criminal Justice: The Palais de Justice in Second Empire Paris* (Princeton, N.J.: Princeton University Press, 1993), 65.

48. The death penalty remains a glaring contradiction to these beliefs. Legal executions have, however, moved indoors in so-called civilized states, displaying the death only to a select few.

49. *Hōritsu Shinbun*, 15 July 1906.

50. Umemori Naoyuki, "The Discovery of the Productive Body: Studies on the Genealogy of Modern Space and Subjectivity in Tokugawa Japan," unpublished paper, University of Chicago, 1993, 29–32; Daniel Botsman, "Punishment and Profit: Nakai Riken's Critique of Tokugawa Justice," paper presented at the annual meeting of the Association of Asian Studies, Chicago, March 1997.

51. For a discussion of the extension of new police systems throughout the Japanese countryside at the time, see Obinata Sumio, *Kindai Nihon to Keisatsu to Chiiki Shakai* (Tokyo: Chikuma Shobo, 2000).

52. A wonderful (but very dark) photograph of the inaugural meeting of this organization appears in *Hōritsu Shinbun*, 10 November 1907. Japanese and Koreans in equal numbers flank long tables covered with white tablecloths, name cards, and bottles of beer.

53. The *Hōritsu Shinbun* printed the fullest version of Kuratomi's essay and referenced the segments that the other papers had published as well. *Hōritsu Shinbun*, 5 August 1909; also the *Tōyō Jihō* and the *Osaka Mainichi*.

54. *Hōritsu Shinbun*, 5 August 1909.

55. Yoshimi Yoshiaki, ed., *Jūgun Ianfu Shiryōshu* (Tokyo: Ōtsuki Shoten, 1992), 36.

56. Yoshimi, *Jūgun Ianfu Shiryōshu*, 33–36. Current examples endure. China, for example, has gone to great lengths recently to display a response to human rights criticisms—the boon, of course, being WTO membership. One such measure has included publicly executing traffickers of Chinese women and girls. Traffickers of female refugees from North Korea along the Tumen River, however, have discovered a "giant loophole" in the law.

57. The three-tiered system operated as follows: at first, district and local courts try a case. District courts heard minor offenses or civil suits under 200 yen. The right to appeal to a local court existed. A case that started in a local court proceeded to a regional appellate court, but cases that had progressed from district to local courts went directly to the main court of appeal and Supreme Court.

58. In comparing the organization of the judiciaries in Taiwan and Korea, Edward I-te Chen has explained that in Taiwan, "speedy and efficient intimidation of the indigenous population seemed to be the overriding concern of the Japanese rulers. In Korea, even before the annexation, Japan's dominant position in the peninsula enabled it to remodel the court system after the pattern of Japanese courts." Although Koreans served on the bench and as prosecutors if they met the qualifications, Chen explained that "no corresponding treatment was ever accorded to Taiwanese, and no more than three Taiwanese ever served on the bench of courts in Taiwan." Unequal and hierarchical scales of power defined colonizing machinations, and the Japanese regime held Korean judges to subordinate positions. Nonetheless, Itō and his juridical missionaries intended to incorporate Koreans into Japan's idea of a legitimate Korea. Chen, "The Attempt to Integrate the Empire: Legal Perspectives," in Raymond H. Myers and Mark R. Peattie, eds., *The Japanese Colonial Empire, 1895–1945* (Princeton, N.J.: Princeton University Press, 1984), 268.

59. Edward J. Baker, "The Role of Legal Reforms in the Japanese Annexation," 32; Lee, "Modernity, Legality, and Power," 31–34.

60. Baker, "The Role of Legal Reforms in the Japanese Annexation," 32.

61. Henry Chung, *The Case for Korea: A Collection of Evidence on the Japanese Domination of the Korean Independence Movement* (New York: Fleming H. Revell, 1921), 74.

62. *Hōritsu Shinbun*, 20 July 1909.

63. Ibid.

64. Frederick McKenzie, *Korea's Fight for Freedom* (New York: Fleming H. Revell, 1920), 183–184.

65. It is also the period that bears much examination for issues of collaboration, a point that Carter Eckert makes strongly in *Offspring of Empire: The Koch'ang Kims and the Colonial Origins of Korean Capitalism, 1876–1945* (Seattle: University of Washington Press, 1991); see also Hildi Kang, *Under the Black Umbrella: Voices from Colonial Korea, 1910–1945* (Ithaca, N.Y.: Cornell University Press, 2001).

66. For elaboration on the 1920s, see Shin and Robinson, *Colonial Modernity in Korea;* see also Michael Robinson, *Cultural Nationalism in Colonial Korea, 1920–1925* (Seattle: University of Washington Press, 1989). Disturbing perhaps to historians only, in 1998 Japanese Prime Minister Obuchi Keizō and South Korean President Kim Dae-jung launched a new era of "cultural policy and exchange."

67. Yoshino Sakuzō, *Chūō Kōron* (September 1919), reprinted in Matsuo Takamichi et al., eds., *Yoshino Sakuzō Senshū*, vol. 9 (Tokyo: Iwanami Shoten, 1995), 115.

68. Even Yoshino used the less-than-sympathetic term *"sōjō"* (riot) to describe the Korean Independence Movement.

69. There are strong parallels to post-1945 apologist explanations for the war being the result of a "few militarists" leading the unknowing Japanese on a wild path of destruction. The "single, biggest improvement" according to the post-1945 logic holds that Japan, with no legal military after the war, necessarily became a peaceful state.

70. Chalmers Johnson, *Blowback: The Costs and Consequences of American Empire* (New York: Metropolitan Books, 2000). Johnson's prescience for the post–September 11 world is chilling to say the least.

71. Edward Baker has made it clear that by 1912, the Japanese Governor General had worked in a "loophole" of its own, whereby only the repressive elements of the new codes—the Ordinance of Civil Matters rather than the Civil Code, and the Ordinance on Penal Matters and not the Criminal Code—were in effect for Koreans. See Baker, "The Role of Legal Reforms in the Japanese Annexation."

72. *Kankoku Heigō ni Kansuru Sengen,* 29 August 1910; Gaimushō [The Japanese Foreign Ministry], *Nihon Gaikō Nenpyō,* 341.

73. Komura to O'Brien, collected in *Ilbon Oemusong T'uksu Chosa Munso* (Seoul: Koryŏ Sorim, 1989), 721–735. I have quoted the official translation (729).

74. Materials on the "Korean Conspiracy Case" are archived at the American Presbyterian Board of Foreign Missions in Philadelphia (Board of Foreign Missions, Presbyterian Church in the United States of America, *The Korean Conspiracy Case. Japanese Colonial Government 1912; Selected Correspondence, Reports and Miscellaneous Papers,* 1912 [The Presbyterian Historical Society, Philadelphia]). The Governor General's translators rendered all correspondence with the Japanese regime into Japanese, and Koryŏ Publishers in Seoul reprinted this compilation in 1986.

75. My thanks to Han Sŭk-Jŭng for this information. The expression "6-25" *(yuk-i-o)* refers to the date the Korean War began.

76. *Japan Weekly Mail,* 29 February 1912.

77. Yamamoto Shirō, ed., *Terauchi Masatake Nikki, 1900–1919* (Kyoto: Dōmeisha, 1970), 525.

78. Ibid., 527.

79. Letter no. 13, Board of Foreign Missions, Presbyterian Church in the United States of America, *The Korean Conspiracy Case.*

80. *Japan Weekly Chronicle,* 13 June 1912.

81. Miscellaneous materials, Board of Foreign Missions, Presbyterian Church in the United States of America, *The Korean Conspiracy Case.*

82. While not as violent an outcome, I cannot help but notice the similarity between this event and the U.S. government's official position concerning the three American nuns and one layworker killed in El Salvador on 2 December 1980. In order to morally justify the enormous monies (roughly $7 billion) the United States government funneled into El Salvador throughout the 1980s to suppress left-wing fighters

and politicians from gaining power, the State Department officially maintained that the El Salvadoran regime had no connection in the women's rapes and executions. Even despite recent testimony from the killers that they acted on "orders from above," the State Department continues to question the men's "veracity." See *New York Times*, 3 April 1998.

83. Charles W. Eliot to Arthur Judson Brown, 4 September 1912, quoted in manuscript edition of Brown, November 1912 (Board of Foreign Missions, Presbyterian Church in the United States of America, *The Korean Conspiracy Case*), emphasis mine; see also, Brown, *The Mastery of the Far East: The Story of Korea's Transformation and Rise to Supremacy in the Orient* (New York: Charles Scribner's Sons, 1919), 571–573.

84. "The Korean Situation," Representatives of Missions Boards in Washington, 29 July 1912 (Board of Foreign Missions, Presbyterian Church in the United States of America, *The Korean Conspiracy Case*).

85. James Brown Scott, as trustee and secretary of the Carnegie Endowment for International Peace and editor of its "Classics of International Law" series, sponsored the Carnegie Endowment's 1936 reprint of Henry Wheaton's *Elements of International Law* that I have quoted from throughout. At the time, Scott was also president of the American Society of International Law.

86. "Confidential Conference on the Situation in Korea" (Board of Foreign Missions, Presbyterian Church in the United States of America, *The Korean Conspiracy Case*).

87. Ibid.

88. Arthur Judson Brown, 20 November 1912 (Board of Foreign Missions, Presbyterian Church in the United States of America, *The Korean Conspiracy Case*).

89. Arthur Judson Brown, edited manuscript, 1 (Board of Foreign Missions, Presbyterian Church in the United States of America, *The Korean Conspiracy Case*).

90. Ibid.

91. Arthur Judson Brown, edited manuscript, 15 (Board of Foreign Missions, Presbyterian Church in the United States of America, *The Korean Conspiracy Case*).

92. *Japan Weekly Chronicle*, 27 March 1913.

93. *Nihon Gaikō Monjo*, Taishō 2, no.1, 297–311.

94. The transcripts of the proceedings are reprinted in both Japanese and Korean in Kuksa P'yŏnch'an Wiwŏnhoe, eds., *Han Minjok Tongnip Undongsa Charyojip: Paekoin Sagun* (Seoul: Sisamunhwasa, 1986).

95. Kuksa P'yŏnch'an Wiwŏnhoe, *Han Minjok Tongnip Undongsa Charyojip: Paekoin Sagun*, 407.

96. Ibid., 413.

97. *Japan Weekly Chronicle*, 5 December 1912.

98. Kuksa P'yŏnch'an Wiwŏnhoe, *Han Minjok Tongnip Undongsa Charyojip: Paekoin Sagun*, 419.

99. Ch'oe Cheku's testimony, in Kuksa P'yŏnch'an Wiwŏnhoe, *Han Minjok Tongnip Undongsa Charyojip: Paekoin Sagun*, 431; Pak Choh'yŏng's testimony, in Kuksa P'yŏnch'an Wiwŏnhoe, *Han Minjok Tongnip Undongsa Charyojip: Paekoin Sagun*, 442.

100. Yi Pyŏngje's testimony, in Kuksa P'yŏnch'an Wiwŏnhoe, *Han Minjok Tongnip Undongsa Charyojip: Paekoin Sagun*, 575–576.

101. *The Report on Reforms and Progresses, 1912–1913*, 46–47.

## CODA

1. Several of the best English-language ones include Leo T. S. Ching, *Becoming Japanese: Colonial Taiwan and the Politics of Identity Formation* (Berkeley and Los Angeles: University of California Press, 2001); Stefan Tanaka, *Japan's Orient: Rendering Pasts into History* (Berkeley: University of California Press, 1993); Barbara Brooks, *Japan's Imperial Diplomacy: Consuls, Treaty Ports, and War with China* (Honolulu: University of Hawai'i Press, 2000); and Louise Young, *Japan's Total Empire: Manchuria and the Culture of Wartime Imperialism* (Berkeley: University of California Press, 1998).

2. Nitobe Inazō's career included professorships at the Sapporo Agricultural College, Kyoto Imperial University, Tokyo Imperial University, and Takushoku University; visiting lectureships and/or emeriti honors from Waseda University, the University of California at Berkeley, Stanford University, Columbia University, the University of Minnesota, Haverford College, Brown University, the University of Virginia, the University of Illinois, the University of Geneva, and the University of British Columbia among others; and he also served as headmaster of the First Higher School of Tokyo and founder of the Tokyo Women's College. Nitobe gained his international fame early with the 1900 publication of *Bushidō: The Soul of Japan* (Nitobe Inazō, *Bushidō: The Soul of Japan* [Philadelphia: Reeds and Biddle, 1900]). Most libraries have copies of the tenth and revised edition published in 1905 by George Putnam's Sons of New York.

3. Nitobe Inazō's written material is catalogued in a work of twenty-two volumes: Nitobe Inazō Zenshū Henshū Iinkai, eds., *Nitobe Inazō Zenshū* (Tokyo: Kyōbunkan, 1960–1982). In addition, there is a five-volume set of his English writings and select translations of his famous Japanese pieces in Shigeru Nambara, ed., *The Works of Inazō Nitobe* (Tokyo: University of Tokyo Press, 1972).

4. See Paul Barclay, "Japanese and American Colonial Projects: Anthropological Typification in Taiwan and the Philippines," Ph.D. diss., University of Minnesota, 1999.

5. In 1927 when Nitobe returned from his duties in Geneva at the League of Nations, his former student and intellectual inheritor Yanaihara Tadao asked Nitobe to publish the lecture notes from his colonial policy courses at the University of Tokyo. Yanaihara and other former students had themselves become teachers of colonial policy courses at public and private universities throughout the country, and they wanted Nitobe to compile materials that they could use as a textbook for their respective courses. Nitobe refused and suggested that Yanaihara coauthor a book with him. Yanai-

hara declined his teacher's offer, maintaining that only Nitobe himself could fully retell his thinking. Nonetheless, Yanaihara and the others published a collection of essays derived from their class notes. The essays were reprinted following Nitobe's death and continue to inform most of the scholarship on Nitobe's ideas about colonization. Yanaihara's vignette as well as the colonial essays are reprinted together in Nitobe Inazō Zenshū Henshū Iinkai, eds., *Nitobe Inazō Zenshū*, vol. 4, 7–10; 17–167.

6. Adams made sure that the work his exotic student did under him was included in the Studies of Historical and Political Science that he edited for Hopkins Press. See Nitobe Inazō (Ota Yūzō), *The Intercourse between the U.S. and Japan* (Baltimore: Johns Hopkins Press, 1891).

7. Letter to Miyabe Kingo, 13 November 1885, on display at the Youth Center in Sapporo, Japan.

8. Nitobe, quoted in Nambara, *The Works of Inazō Nitobe*, vol. 4, 120.

9. Quoted in Nitobe Inazō Zenshū Iinkai, *Nitobe Inazō Zenshū*, vol. 4, 7–10.

10. In 1905, Nitobe received a second doctoral degree in colonial policy from Kyoto University, a degree that Goto urged him to obtain in order to gain a full faculty post at one of the country's imperial universities. He had received his first Ph.D. abroad (Halle), but Goto did not want the Ministry of Education to have any reason to oppose his plan. Unfortunately no dissertation appears to remain. Tanaka Shinichi has argued that Nitobe would not have been required to write one because of his previous schooling and experience. See Tanaka Shinichi, "Nitobe Inazō to Chōsen," in *Kikan Sansenri*, no. 34 (1983): n.p.

11. Dipesh Chakrabarty has described this problem in a critique of John Stuart Mill's proclamations about who was ready for "History" as such and when: "Mill's historicist argument thus consigned Indians, Africans, and other 'rude' nations to an imaginary waiting room of history." Chakrabarty, *Provincializing Europe: Postcolonial Thought and Historical Difference* (Princeton, N.J.: Princeton University Press, 2000), 8.

12. Nitobe Inazō Zenshū Henshū Iinkai, *Nitobe Inazō Zenshū*, vol. 5, 78–82.

13. Ibid., 79; see Isabella L. Bird Bishop, *Korea and Her Neighbors: A Narrative of Travel with an Account of the Recent Vicissitudes and Present Condition*, 2 vols. (London: Kegan Paul, 1897); George Trumbull Ladd, *In Korea with Marquis Itō: A Narrative of Personal Experiences and a Critical Historical Inquiry* (New York: Charles Scribner's Sons, 1908); and George Kennan, "Korea: A Degenerate State" and "What Japan Has Done in Korea?" *The Outlook* (1905).

14. Nitobe Inazō Zenshū Henshū Iinkai, *Nitobe Inazō Zenshū*, vol. 5, 81.

15. Ibid., 82.

16. Nitobe Inazō, "Kōchō Ensetsu," 13 September 1910, quoted in Tanaka Shinichi, "Nitobe to Chōsen," 93. In the wake of World War II, one of Japan's largest publishing houses excised this speech in a reprint essay about Nitobe. Hokkaido University economist Tanaka Shinichi's careful reading of the different editions of Yanaihara Tadao's *Our Nation's People of Merit* [Ware no Sonkei Suru Jinbutsu] reveals that Iwanami Pub-

lishers allowed the speech's inclusion in printings between 1940 and 1944 but deleted it when publication resumed again in 1948.

17. Nitobe Inazō, quoted in Tanaka Shinichi, "Nitobe to Chōsen," 93.

18. Ibid., 93–94.

19. Ibid.

20. Nitobe Inazō, "Shokumin Naru Meiji ni Tsukite," *Hōgakkai Zasshi,* vol. 29, no. 2 (1911); also Nitobe Inazō Zenshū Iinkai, *Nitobe Inazō Zenshū,* vol. 4, 346–353.

21. Ibid., 349–350.

22. Ibid., 353.

23. Nitobe Inazō Zenshū Iinkai, *Nitobe Inazō Zenshū,* vol. 4, 350; linguist Yanabu Akira has discussed how the Doeff-Haruma dictionary dealt with the Dutch word (and European concept) *"natur."* See Yanabu Akira, *Honyaku no Shisō: "Shizen" to NATURE* (Tokyo: Chikuma Gakui Bunko, 1995). Of note, Itō Hirobumi carried a copy of Hori's dictionary abroad with him on his clandestine escape to England in the early 1860s. See Itō Hirobumi, *Marquis Itō's Experience,* trans. Teizō Kuramata (Nagasaki: Gwaiko-kugo Kyojusho, 1904).

24. Nitobe Inazō Zenshū Iinkai, *Nitobe Inazō Zenshū,* vol. 4, 346–347.

25. Kusano Fumio, ed., *Takushoku Daigaku Hachijūnenshi* (Tokyo: Takushoku Dai-gaku Sōritsu Hachijūshūnen Kinen Jigyō Jimukyoku, 1980), 66 (see also the sixtieth anniversary issue). On 18 April 1897, Fukushima Yasumasa, Mizuno Jun, Ōkura Kiha-chirō, Yokoyama Magoichirō, and Nagata Tadaichi gathered at the *Momijikan* in Tokyo's Shiba Park and established the Taiwan Association *(Taiwankai).* Two days ear-lier, a notice in the *Asahi Shinbun* paper announced that the organizers hoped "mili-tary men, politicians, scholars, businessmen, and newspaper reporters" who had spent time in Taiwan and who wished to relive "the memories they had in common and also share in the warmth of friendship" would join them. During the following year, some of the men called for sharpening the group's aims to focus more specifically on Japa-nese government policy relating to Taiwan. Almost a year later, on 2 April 1898, Mizuno, Ōkura, and almost sixty other men interested in discussing Japan's policies in Taiwan (including historian Taguchi Ukichi) met to form an offshoot organization, the Taiwan Society *(Taiwan Kyōkai).* The men agreed to establish a provisional office in Kojimachi, and in July the Society chose Katsura Tarō, former Governor General of Tai-wan (among other political accomplishments), as its first president.

26. *Takushoku Daigaku Hachijūnenshi,* 67.

27. Ibid., 83–84. See also *Hosei Daigaku, Hōritsuko no Yoake to Hōsei Daigaku* (n.p.: n.d.).

28. Kanai was a proponent of social economic plans and an organizer of the *Sha-kai Seisaku Gakkai.* Earlier in 1900, he and five fellow faculty members from Tokyo University and another from Gakushuin signed an open letter in the Tokyo *Asahi Shin-bun* demanding war against Russia in protest of Russia's advances into Manchuria. The same seven men loudly protested the terms to which Katsura agreed in the peace

treaty with Russia in 1905. See Yasuoka Akio, *Nihon Kindaishi* (Tokyo: Geirin Shobō, 1996), 315. Legal scholar Takahashi Sakuei (whose work was discussed with Ariga Nagao's) was a fellow signatory.

29. See Michael A. Schneider, "Colonial Policy Studies in a Period of Transition: Nitobe Inazō, Ōkawa Shūmei, and Tōgō Minoru at Takushoku University," in *Takushoku Daigaku Hyakunenshi Kenkyu*, no. 3 (n.d.): n.p.; also Schneider, *The Future of the Japanese Colonial Empire, 1914–1931*, Ph.D. diss., University of Chicago, 1996.

30. *Takushoku Daigaku Hachijūnenshi,* 156.

31. Ibid., 117.

32. See Peter Duus's discussion of *Haikara* ("High-collar") colonialists in *The Abacus and the Sword: The Japanese Penetration of Korea* (Berkeley and Los Angeles: University of California Press, 1995): 245–363.

33. *Takushoku Daigaku Hachijūnenshi,* 120.

34. Unfortunately, the CBS radio archives do not have a recording of these broadcasts. Nitobe himself, however, published the unabridged transcripts as "Japan and the Peace Pact: With Special Reference to Japan's Reaction to Mr. Stimson's Note Regarding the Pact." Trinity College in Hartford, Connecticut has a copy in its library.

35. Mary Nitobe in Takagi Yasaka, *The Works of Inazō Nitobe* (Tokyo: University of Tokyo Press, 1969), vol. 4, 5. For clear articulation of anti-Nitobe sentiment in the United States at the time, see Raymond Leslie Buell, "An Open Letter to Dr. Inazō Nitobe," in *The New Republic,* May 1932. See also Nitobe, "Manshū de no Dekigoto no Kyōjun," *Zenshū* 4 (12 January 1932): 393–394; and "Shin Kokka no Tanjō," *Zenshū* 4 (19 February 1932): 421–422.

36. Nitobe in Takagi, *The Works of Inazō Nitobe,* 238; Ienaga Saburo made a parallel observation about how Japan's "internationalist" foreign minister, Shidehara Kijūrō, was "explicitly expansionist" when it came to Japan's Manchuria policy. See Saburo Ienaga, *The Pacific War, 1931–1945* (New York: Pantheon, 1977), 10.

37. Nitobe in Takagi, *The Works of Inazō Nitobe,* 238.

38. Ibid.

39. Ibid., 252.

40. Ibid., 249.

41. Ibid., 247.

42. Ibid., 252. Of related interest, see Armin Rappaport, *Henry Stimson and Japan, 1931–1933* (Chicago: University of Chicago Press, 1963).

43. Nitobe, "The Manchurian Question" (lecture delivered 21 September 1932), in Takagi, ed., *The Works of Inazō Nitobe,* vol. 4, 221–233.

44. Nitobe, in Takagi, *The Works of Inazō Nitobe,* 226–227.

45. George Trumbull Ladd, *In Korea with Marquis Itō,* 278.

46. Norma Field, *From My Grandmother's Bedside: Sketches of Postwar Tokyo* (Berkeley: University of California Press, 1997), 93.

47. Akira Iriye has most clearly articulated and sustained this method of remem-

bering Nitobe, from his *Pacific Estrangement: Japanese and American Expansion, 1897–1911* (Cambridge, Mass.: Harvard University Press, 1972) to his more recent *China and Japan in a Global Setting* (Cambridge, Mass.: Harvard University Press, 1992) and *Cultural Internationalism and World Order* (Baltimore: Johns Hopkins University Press, 1997). Ian Nish has followed this pattern as well in his *Japanese Foreign Policy, 1869–1942: Kasumigaseki to Miyakezaka* (London: Routledge and Kegan Paul, 1977). Nish's widely followed chronology of "the Powers versus Japan, 1853–1894; Japan among the Powers, 1894–1934; Japan versus the Powers, 1934–1945" counts Nitobe squarely in the "among" category. See also Ian Nish, *Japan's Struggle with Internationalism: Japan, China, and the League of Nations, 1931–1933* (London: Kegan Paul, 1993). Both these scholars' publications have clearly shaped much Japanese scholarship as well. For more nuanced interpretations in Japanese scholarship, see, for example, Tanaka Shinichi's "Nitobe to Chōsen"; and Kang Sangjung, *Orientarizumu no Kanata e: Kindai Bunka Hihan* (Tokyo: Iwanami Shoten, 1996).

48. For a similar argument, see Tomoko Akami's *Internationalizing the Pacific: The U.S., Japan, and the Institute of Pacific Relations in War and Peace, 1919–1945* (New York: Routledge, 2002).

49. Melvyn Leffler's essay, "The Cold War: What Do 'We Now Know'?" elucidates the influence of containment theory ideas during the past half-century. Leffler, *American Historical Review* 104, no. 2 (1999): 501–524.

50. Yoshimi Yoshiaki, ed., *Jūgun Ianfu Shiryōshū* (Tokyo: Ōtsuki Shoten, 1992), 36.

51. Yoshimi has suggested, for example, that Japan's 1932 ratification of the International Labor Organization's (ILO) "Forced Labor Convention" makes the enforced labor that the comfort women performed a violation of an international standard. Whether or not defense lawyers would demonstrate that the ILO's conventions were not recognized by the League of Nations is another matter. Japan's withdrawal from the League also makes such a code nonbinding.

52. For discussion of rape as a war crime in an international context, see Julie Peters and Andrea Wolper, eds., *Women's Rights, Human Rights: International Feminist Perspectives* (New York: Routledge, 1995).

53. Sidney B. Fay, *The Origins of the World War* (New York: Macmillan, 1939), vii.

54. See Kai Bird and Lawrence Lifschultz's excellent compendium of materials, *Hiroshima's Shadow: Writings on the Denial of History at the Smithsonian* (Stony Creek, N.Y.: Pamphleteer's Press, 1998); see also Lisa Yoneyama, "For Transformative Knowledge and Postnationalist Public Spheres: The Smithsonian *Enola Gay* Controversy," in Takashi Fujitani, Geoffrey M. White, and Lisa Yoneyama, eds., *Perilous Memories: The Asia-Pacific War(s)* (Durham, N.C.: Duke University Press, 2001), 323–346.

# Bibliography

## ARCHIVED COLLECTIONS

Board of Foreign Missions, Presbyterian Church in the United States of America. *The Korean Conspiracy Case. Japanese Colonial Government 1912; Selected Correspondence, Reports and Miscellaneous Papers,* 1912. The Presbyterian Historical Society, Philadelphia.

Capron, Horace. Papers, 1872. Yale University Library, Manuscripts and Archives.

## NEWSPAPERS AND JOURNALS

*Asahi Shinbun*
*Chosŏn Ilbo*
*Dong'A Ilbo*
*Gaikō Jihō*
*Harper's Weekly*
*Hōchi Shinbun*
*Hokkaidō Mainichi Shinbun*
*Hōritsu Shinbun*
*Hwangsŏng Sinmun*
*Japan Weekly Chronicle*
*Japan Weekly Mail*
*Kokka Gakkai Zasshi*
*Kokusaihō Gaikō Zasshi*
*Kokusaihō Zasshi*
*Kongnip Sinmun*
*Mainichi Shinbun*
*New York Times*

*New York Tribune*
*Ōsaka Mainichi Shinbun*
*Outlook*
*Revue Générale de Droit International Public*
*San Francisco Chronicle*
*Seoul Press*
*Shigaku Zasshi*
*Shokumin Kōhō*
*Shokumin Kyōkai Hōkoku*
*South China Daily Mail*
*TaeHan Maeil Sinbo*
*Taiwan Kyōkai Kaihō*
*Le Temps*
*The Times*
*Tokyo Puck*
*Yorozu Chōhō*

## BOOKS AND JOURNALS

Ajia Keizai Kenkyūjo Tosho Shiryōbu, ed. *Kyū Shokuminchi Kankei Kikan Kankōbutsu Sōgō Mokuroku (Chōsen hen)*. Vol. 2. Tokyo: Ajia Keizai Kenkyūjo, 1974.

Akami, Tomoko. *Internationalizing the Pacific: The U.S., Japan, and the Institute of Pacific Relations in War and Peace, 1919–1945*. New York: Routledge, 2002.

Anderson, Benedict. *Imagined Communities: Reflections on the Origins and Spread of Nationalism*. Rev. ed. London: Verso, 1991.

Arahata Kanson. *Hantaisei o Ikite*. Tokyo: Shingensha, 1969.

Arakawa Sobe. *Gairaigo Gaisetsu*. Tokyo: Sanshodō, 1945.

———. *Gairaigo Jitten*. Tokyo: Kadokawa Shoten, 1967.

Ariga Nagao. *La Guerre Sino-Japonaise au Point de vue de Droit International*. Paris: Libraire de la Cour d'Appel, 1896.

———. *Hogokokuron*. Tokyo: Waseda Daigaku Shuppan, 1906.

———. "Hogokokuron o Arawashitan Riyo." In *Kokusaiho Gaiko Zasshi* 5, no. 2 (1906).

———. *Kokkagaku*. Tokyo: n.p., 1889.

———. *Nichirō Rikusen Kokusaihōron*. Tokyo: Genshinsha, 1911.

———. *Nippon Kodaihō Yakugi*. Tokyo: Hakubunkan, 1908.

———. *Nisshin Sen'eki Kokusaihōron*. Tokyo: Rikugun Daigakkō, 1896.

———. *Saikin Sanjūnen Gaikōshi*. 2 vols. Tokyo: Waseda Daigaku Shuppanbu, 1910.

———. *Senji Jūyō Jyōyakushū*. Tokyo: Kaigun Daigakkō, 1910.

Armstrong, Charles. *The North Korean Revolution, 1945–1950*. Ithaca, N.Y.: Cornell University Press, 2002.

Asaishi Seietsu. *Nitobe Inazō no Sekai.* Tokyo: Kyōbunsha, 1995.

Asami Noboru. "Japanese Colonial Government." Ph.D. diss., Columbia University, 1924.

Asukai Masamichi. *Kōtoku Shūsui: Chokusetsu Kōdōron no Genryū.* Tokyo: Chuko Shinsho, 1969.

Asukai Masamichi, ed. *Kōtoku Shūsuishū. Kindai Nihon Shisō Taikei.* Vol. 13. Tokyo: Chikuma Shobō, 1975.

Baker, Edward. "The Role of Legal Reforms in the Japanese Annexation and Rule of Korea, 1905–1919." In *Harvard Law School: Studies in East Asian Law—Korea,* reprinted from *Studies on Korea in Transition,* Harvard Occasional Papers, no. 9. Cambridge, Mass.: Harvard University Press, 1979.

Baker, Keith Michael. *Condorcet: From Natural Philosophy to Social Mathematics.* Chicago: University of Chicago Press, 1982.

Bakumatsu/Meiji Shoki ni Okeru Seiyō Bunmei no Yunyū ni Kan Suru Kenkyūkai, eds. *Yōgaku Jishi.* Tokyo: Bunka Shobō, 1993.

Baldwin, Frank P., Jr. "The March First Movement: Korean Challenge and Japanese Response." Ph.D. diss., Columbia University, 1969.

Banno Junji. *Kindai Nihon no Gaikō to Seiji.* Tokyo: Kyūbun Shuppan, 1985.

Barclay, Paul. "Japanese and American Colonial Projects: Anthropological Typification in Taiwan and the Philippines." Ph.D. diss., University of Minnesota, 1999.

Barshay, Andrew. *State and Intellectual in Imperial Japan: The Public Man in Crisis.* Berkeley and Los Angeles: University of California Press, 1988.

Barthes, Roland. *Writing Degree Zero.* New York: Farrar, Strauss, and Giroux, 1990.

Beasley, W. G. *Japanese Imperialism 1894–1945.* Oxford: Oxford Clarendon Series, 1991.

Beasley, W. G., and E. G. Pulleybank, eds. *Historians of China and Japan.* London: Oxford University Press, 1961.

Bentham, Jeremy. *An Introduction to the Principles of Morals and Legislation.* New York: Hafner Press, 1948.

Bhabha, Jacqueline. "Embodied Rights: Gender Persecution, State Sovereignty, and Refugees." *Public Culture* 9 (1996): 3–32.

Bigelow, Poultney. *Japan and Her Colonies.* London: Edward Arnold and Co., 1923.

Bird, Kai, and Lawrence Lifschultz, eds. *Hiroshima's Shadow: Writings on the Denial of History at the Smithsonian.* Stony Creek, N.Y.: Pamphleteer's Press, 1998.

Bishop, Isabella L. Bird. *Korea and Her Neighbors: A Narrative of Travel with an Account of the Recent Vicissitudes and Present Condition of the Country.* 2 vols. London: Kegan Paul, 1897.

———. *Unbeaten Tracks in Japan.* N.p.: Indypublish.com, 2002.

Bix, Herbert. "The Showa Emperor's 'Monologue' and the Problem of War Responsibility." *Journal of Japanese Studies* 18, no. 2 (1992).

Boissonade, Gustave. *Projet de Code de Procédure Criminelle pour L'Empire du Japon Accompagné d'un Commentaire.* Paris: Ernest Thorin, 1882.

Boling, David Alan. "Mass Rape, Enforced Prostitution, and the Japanese Imperial Army." *Columbia Journal of Transnational Law* 32 (1995).

Botsman, Daniel. "Punishment and Profit: Nakai Riken's Critique of Tokugawa Justice." Paper presented at the Annual Meeting of the Association for Asian Studies, Chicago, March 1997.

Bourdieu, Pierre. *Language and Symbolic Power.* Trans. Gino Raymond and Matthew Adamson. Cambridge, Mass.: Harvard University Press, 1991.

Brierly, J. L. *The Law of Nations: An Introduction to the International Law of Peace.* London: Oxford University Press, 1928.

Brooks, Barbara. *Japan's Imperial Diplomacy: Consuls, Treaty Ports, and War with China.* Honolulu: University of Hawai'i Press, 2000.

Brown, Arthur Judson. *The Mastery of the Far East: The Story of Korea's Transformation and Rise to Supremacy in the Orient.* New York: Charles Scribner's Sons, 1919.

Buell, Raymond Leslie. "An Open Letter to Dr. Inazo Nitobe." *The New Republic,* May 1932.

Bureau of Aboriginal Affairs, ed. *Report on the Control of the Aborigines in Formosa.* Taihoku: Government of Formosa, 1911.

Butler, Judith. *Excitable Speech: A Politics of the Performative.* New York: Routledge, 1997.

Calvet, Louis-Jean. *La Guerre des Langues et les Politiques Lingustiques.* Paris: Payot, 1987.

Chakrabarty, Dipesh. *Provincializing Europe: Postcolonial Thought and Historical Difference.* Princeton, N.J.: Princeton University Press, 2000.

Chandra, Vipan. "An Outline of the Ilchin-hoe (Advancement Society) of Korea." *Occasional Papers on Korea,* no. 2, March 1974.

Chang Yun-shik et al. *Korea between Tradition and Modernity: Selected Papers from the Fourth Pacific and Asian Conference on Korean Studies.* Vancouver: Institute of Asian Research, 2000.

Chatterjee, Partha. *Nationalist Thought and the Colonial World: A Derivative Discourse.* Minneapolis: University of Minnesota Press, 1993.

Chevalier, Louis. *La Formation de la population Parisienne au XIXe siècle.* Paris: Presses Universitaires de France, 1950.

Chibaken Bijutsukan, ed. *Serizawa Keisuke ten: Sono kōzō no subete.* Chiba: Chibaken Bijutsukan, 1973.

Ching, Leo T. S. *Becoming Japanese: Colonial Taiwan and the Politics of Identity Formation.* Berkeley and Los Angeles: University of California Press, 2001.

Cho Hangnae. *1900 Nyŏndae ŭi Aeguk Kyemong Undong Yŏng'gu.* Seoul: Asea Munhwasa, 1993.

Chōsen Sōtokuf, ed. *Chōsen no Hogo oyobi Heigō.* 1918. Reprint. Tokyo: Ryukei Shobo, 1995.

———. *Chōsen Sōtokufu tōkei nenpō.* Seoul: n.p., 1912–1943.

Cho Tonggŏl. *Kugyŏk Wang San Chŏnsŏ.* Seoul: Asea Munhwasa, 1985.

Christy, Alan. "The Making of Imperial Subjects in Okinawa." *Positions: East Asia Cultures Critique* 1, no. 3 (1993).

Chung, Henry. *The Case for Korea: A Collection of Evidence on the Japanese Domination of the Korean Independence Movement.* New York: Fleming H. Revell, 1921.

Cohn, Bernard. *Colonialism and Its Forms of Knowledge: The British in India.* Princeton, N.J.: Princeton University Press, 1996.

Committee on Intellectual Co-operation, ed. *Minutes of the Committee on Intellectual Co-operation.* Geneva: League of Nations, 1922–1926.

*Compte-Rendu du Congrès International Colonial: Exposition Internationale de Bruxelles.* Brussels: Commissariat du Gouvernement, 1897.

*Congressional Record of Foreign Relations, 1922.* Washington, D.C.: Government Printing Office, 1938, vol. 2, 591.

Conklin, Alice. "Colonialism and Human Rights, A Contradiction in Terms? The Case of France in West Africa, 1895–1914." *American Historical Review* 103, no. 2 (1998): 419–442.

Conroy, Hilary. *The Japanese Seizure of Korea, 1868–1910: A Study of Realism and Idealism in International Relations.* Philadelphia: University of Pennsylvania Press, 1960.

Cook, Harold F. *Korea's 1884 Incident: Its Background and Kim Ok-Kyun's Elusive Dream.* Seoul: Royal Asiatic Society, 1972.

Cooper, Frederick, and Ann Laura Stoler, eds. *Tensions of Empire: Colonial Cultures in a Bourgeois World.* Berkeley and Los Angeles: University of California Press, 1997.

*Correspondence Relating to the War with Spain and Conditions Growing Out of the Same.* Vol. 2. Washington, D.C.: Center of Military History, U.S. Army, 1993.

Cortazzi, Hugh. *Isles of Gold: Antique Maps of Japan.* New York: Weatherhill, 1983.

Covell, Ralph. *W.A.P. Martin, Pioneer of Progress in China.* Washington, D.C.: Christian College Consortium, 1978.

Crossley, Pamela Kyle. *Orphan Warriors: Three Manchu Generations at the End of the Qing World.* Princeton, N.J.: Princeton University Press, 1990.

Cumings, Bruce. "Archaeology, Descent, Emergence: Japan in British/American Hegemony, 1900–1950." In *Japan in the World,* ed. Masao Miyoshi and H. D. Harootunian. Durham, N.C.: Duke University Press, 1993, 79–111.

———. "Occurrence at Nogun-ri Bridge: An Inquiry into the History and Memory of a Civil War." In *Critical Asian Studies* 33, no. 4 (December 2001).

———. *Parallax.* Durham, N.C.: Duke University Press, 1999.

Dai Nippon Shosantō, ed. *Honryū Nashyonarizumu no Shōgen.* Tokyo: Hara Shobō, 1981.

Daitōjuku Jōyon Resshi Ikoshū Hensan Iinkai, ed. *Daitōjuku Jūyon Resshi Ikoshū.* Tokyo: Daitōjuku Shuppanbu, 1978.

Dana, Richard Henry, ed. *Elements of International Law: With a Sketch of the History of the Science.* 8th ed. Boston: Little, Brown, 1866.

de Becker, J. E. *Elements of Japanese Law.* Tokyo: Asiatic Society of Japan, 1916.

Defert, Daniel, and François Ewald, eds. *Michel Foucault—Dits et Écrits: 1954–1988.* 4 vols. Paris: Gallimard, 1994.

de Gobineau, Joseph Arthur. *Essai Sur L'Inégalité des Races Humaines.* Paris: 1853–1854.

Deleuze, Giles, and Félix Guattari. *What Is Philosophy?* New York: Columbia University Press, 1994.

Denny, Owen. *China and Korea.* Shanghai: Kelly and Walsh, 1888.

Der Derian, James. *On Diplomacy.* Oxford: Basil Blackwell, 1991.

Deuchler, Martina. *Confucian Gentlemen and Barbarian Envoys: The Opening of Korea, 1875–1885.* Seattle: University of Washington Press, 1977.

Dikötter, Frank. *The Discourse of Race in Modern China.* London: C. Hurst, 1992.

Dower, John. *War without Mercy: Race and Power in the Second World War.* New York: Pantheon Books, 1985.

Dower, John, ed. *Origins of the Modern Japanese State: Selected Writings of E. H. Norman.* New York: Pantheon Books, 1975.

Duara, Prasenjit. "Bifurcating Linear History: Nations and Histories in China and India." *Positions: East Asia Cultures Critique,* vol. 1, no. 3 (1993).

———. "The Regime of Authenticity: Timelessness, Gender, and National History in Modern China." *History and Theory, Studies in the Philosophy of History* 37, no. 3 (1998).

———. *Rescuing History from the Nation.* Chicago: University of Chicago Press, 1995.

———. "Transnationalism and the Predicament of Sovereignty: China, 1900–1945." *American Historical Review* 102, no. 4 (1997).

Dudden, Arthur. *The American Pacific: From the Old China Trade to the Present.* New York: Oxford University Press, 1992.

Duus, Peter. *The Abacus and the Sword: The Japanese Penetration of Korea.* Berkeley and Los Angeles: University of California Press, 1995.

Eckert, Carter. *Offspring of Empire: The Koch'ang Kims and the Colonial Origins of Korean Capitalism, 1876–1945* (Seattle: University of Washington Press, 1991).

Eizawa Kōji. *Nihon no Fashizumu.* Tokyo: Kyōikusha, 1977.

Em, Henry. "Yi Sang's 'Wings' Read as an Anti-Colonial Allegory." *Muae—A Journal of Transcultural Production,* no. 1 (1995).

Endō Yukio and Ōkubo Toshiaki. *Nihon Rekishi Shirizu: Nisshin/Nichiro Sensō.* Tokyo: Sekai Bunkasha, 1967.

"Executive Committee on International Public Hearing concerning Post War Compensation of Japan." In *War Victimization and Japan: International Public Hearing Report.* Tokyo: Toho Shuppansha, 1993.

Fairbank, John King. *The Chinese World Order.* Cambridge, Mass.: Harvard University Press, 1968.

Fanon, Frantz. *Black Skin, White Masks.* New York: Grove Press, 1991.

Fay, Sidney B. *The Origins of the World War.* New York: Macmillan, 1939.

Field, Norma. *From My Grandmother's Bedside: Sketches of Postwar Tokyo.* Berkeley and Los Angeles: University of California Press, 1997.

————. "War and Apology: Japan, Asia, the Fiftieth, and After." *Positions: East Asia Cultures Critique* 5, no. 1, special issue: "The Comfort Women: Colonialism, War, and Sex" (1997).

Finn, Dallas. *Meiji Revisited: The Sites of Victorian Japan.* New York: Weatherhill, 1995.

Foreign Office, ed. *Treaties and Conventions between the Empire of Japan and Other Powers.* N.p.: Z. P. Maruya, 1899.

Foster, Anne, and Julian Go, eds. *The American Colonial State in the Philippines: Global Perspectives.* Durham, N.C.: Duke University Press, 2003.

Foucault, Michel. *The Archaeology of Knowledge and the Discourse on Language.* New York: Pantheon, 1972.

————. *Surveiller et Punir: Naissance de la Prison.* Paris: Gallimard, 1975.

Fuchs, Rachel G. *Poor and Pregnant in Paris: Strategies for Survival in the Nineteenth Century.* New Brunswick, N.J.: Rutgers University Press, 1992.

Fujita Hisakazu. *Sensō Hanzai to wa nani ka.* Tokyo: Iwanami Shinsho, 1999.

Fujitani, Takashi. *Splendid Monarchy: Power and Pageantry in Modern Japan.* Berkeley and Los Angeles: University of California Press, 1996.

Fujitani, Takashi, Geoffrey M. White, and Lisa Yoneyama, eds. *Perilous Memories: The Asia-Pacific War(s).* Durham, N.C.: Duke University Press, 2001.

Fukuda Tosaku. *Kankoku Heigō Kinenshi.* Tokyo: Dai Nippon Jitsugyō Kyōkai, 1911.

Fukuzawa Yukichi. *Bunmeiron no Gairyaku.* Tokyo: Iwanami Bunko, 1995.

Furuya Testuo. *Nichirō Sensō.* Tokyo: Chūkō Shinsho, 1966.

Furuya Tetsuo, ed. *Kindai Nihon no Ajia Ninshiki.* Kyoto: Kyōto Daigaku, 1994.

Gaimushō [The Japanese Foreign Ministry], ed. *Bankoku Shokumin Kaigi Ikken.* N.p.: 1897.

————. *Nihon Gaikō Monjo.* Tokyo: Nihon Kokusai Renmei Kyōkai, 1933–.

————. *Nihon Gaikō Nenpyō oyobi Juyō Monjo.* 2 vols. Tokyo: Gaimushō, 1955.

————. *Takeshima Mondai—"Takeshima Kōshō."* Tokyo: MT Publishers, 1996.

Gakueikai. *Sapporo Nogakkō.* 1898. Reprint. Sapporo: Hokkaido Daigaku Toshoken-kokai, 1975.

Gallagher, John, and Ronald Robinson. "The Imperialism of Free Trade." *Economic Review,* 2d series, no. 6 (1953).

Genyōsha, ed. *Genyōsha Shashi.* Tokyo: Genyosha, 1917.

George, Henry. *The Land Question: What It Involves, and How Alone It Can be Settled.* New York: John Lovell, 1883.

Geyer, Michael, and John W. Boyer, eds. *Resistance against the Third Reich, 1933–1990.* Chicago: University of Chicago Press, 1994.

Gluck, Carol. *Japan's Modern Myths: Ideology in the Late Meiji Period.* Princeton, N.J.: Princeton University Press, 1985.

Goldstein, Jan. *Console and Classify: The French Psychiatric Profession in the Late Nineteenth Century.* New York: Cambridge University Press, 1990.

Goodman, Grant. *Japan: The Dutch Experience.* London: Athlone Press, 1986.

Gordon, Andrew. *Labor and Imperial Democracy in Prewar Japan.* Berkeley and Los Angeles: University of California Press, 1992.

Gordon, Andrew, ed. *Postwar Japan as History.* Berkeley and Los Angeles: University of California Press, 1993.

Gordon, Colin. *Michel Foucault: Power/Knowledge: Selected Interviews and Other Writings, 1972–1977.* New York: Pantheon, 1980.

Gotō Shinpei. *Formosa: Its Present Financial and Economic Position.* London: Waterlow and Sons, 1902.

———. *Nihon Shokumin Seisaku Ippan: Nihon Bōchō ron.* Tokyo: n.p., 1944.

Government General of Chōsen. *Annual Report on Reforms and Progress in Chōsen (Korea), 1910.* Seoul: Government General of Chōsen, 1911–1945.

Guizot, François. *General History of Civilization in Europe.* New York: D. Appleton, 1840.

Gulick, Sidney Lewis. *The White Peril in the Far East—An Interpretation of the Significance of the Russo-Japanese War.* New York: Fleming H. Revell, 1905.

Gurahikku Tokubetsu Soken, ed. *Nippon no Chōsen.* Tokyo: Yūrakusho, 1911.

Habermas, Jürgen. *The Structural Transformation of the Public Sphere: An Inquiry into a Category of Bourgeois Society.* Cambridge, Mass.: MIT Press, 1992.

Hacking, Ian. *The Taming of Chance.* London: Cambridge University Press, 1990.

Hagihara Nobutoshi. *Mutsu Munemitsu.* Tokyo: Asahi Shinbunsha, 1997.

Ham Dongju. "Meiji Discourse on Asia: A Study of Asianism." Ph.D. diss., University of Chicago, 1993.

Han San'il. *Nikkan Kindai no Kūmon.* Tokyo: Nihon Keizai Hyōronsha, 1984.

Han Sŭk-Jŭng. *Manchu'guk Kunguk ŭi Chehesŭk.* Busan: Busan Donga Taehakkyo, 1998.

———. "Puppet Sovereignty: The State Effect of Manchukuo from 1932 to 1936." Ph.D. diss., University of Chicago, 1995.

Hane, Mikiso. *Reflections on the Way to the Gallows: Rebel Women in Prewar Japan.* Berkeley and Los Angeles: University of California Press, 1993.

Han'guk Minjok Undongsa Yŏn'guhoe, ed. *Ŭibyŏng Chŏngjaeng Yŏn'gu.* Seoul: Chisik San'ŏpsa, 1990.

Harada Tamaki. "Jūkyū seiki no Chōsen ni okeru Taigaiteki Ishiski." *Chōsenshi Kenkyūkai Ronbunshū* 21 (March 1984).

Hardt, Michael, and Antonio Negri. *Empire.* Durham, N.C.: Duke University Press, 2000.

Harootunian, H. D. *Things Seen and Unseen.* Chicago: University of Chicago Press, 1987.

Harrington, Fred Harvey. *God, Mammon, and the Japanese: Dr. Horace Allen and Korean-American Relations, 1884–1905.* Madison: University of Wisconsin Press, 1944.

Harvey, David. *The Condition of Postmodernity.* Cambridge: Blackwell, 1990.

Hasegawa Michiko. *Kara Gokoro: Nihon Seishin no Gyakusetsu.* Tokyo: Chūōkoron Shinsha, 1986.

Hatada Takashi. *Nihonjin no Chōsenkan.* Tokyo: Keisō Shobō, 1969.

Hatsuse Ryūhei. *Dentōteki na Uyoku: Uchida Ryōhei no Kenkyū.* Fukuoka: Kyūshū Daigaku, 1980.

Havens, Thomas. *Nishi Amane and Modern Japanese Thought.* Princeton, N.J.: Princeton University Press, 1970.

Hevia, James. *Cherishing Men from Afar: Qing Guest Ritual and the Macartney Embassy of 1793.* Durham, N.C.: Duke University Press, 1995.

Hines, Thomas S. *Burnham of Chicago: Architect and Planner.* Chicago: University of Chicago Press, 1979.

Hirai Kagemura. *Tōyama Mitsuru to Genyōsha Monogatari.* Tokyo: Kobunsha, 1914.

Hirano Kenichiro, ed. *Kindai Nihon to Ajia: Bunka Kōryū to Masatsu.* Tokyo: Tokyo Daigaku Shuppan, 1984.

Hirano, Kyoko. *Mr. Smith Goes to Tokyo: Japanese Cinema under the American Occupation, 1942–1952.* Washington, D.C.: Smithsonian Institution Press, 1992.

Hirota Masaki, ed. *Sabetsu no Shosō: Nihon Kindai Shisō Taikei.* Vol. 22. Tokyo: Iwanami Shoten, 1990.

Hishida Seiji. *The International Position of Japan as a Great Power.* New York: Columbia University Press, 1905.

Hobsbawm, Eric, and Terence Ranger, eds. *The Invention of Tradition.* Cambridge: Cambridge University Press, 1983.

Hokkaidō Daigaku Toshokenkokai. *Sapporo Nogakkō Nenpyō.* 6 vols., 1877–1881. Sapporo: n.p., 1976.

Holls, F. W. *The Peace Conference at The Hague.* New York: n.p., 1900.

Hori Tatsunosuke. *Eiwa Taigi Shūchin Jisho.* Edo: n.p., 1867.

Hōsei Daigaku Daigakushi Shiryōiinkai, ed. *Hōritsugaku no Yoake to Hōsei Daigaku.* Tokyo: Hōsei Daigaku Shuppankyoku, 1993.

Houchins, Chang-su. *Artifacts of Diplomacy: Smithsonian Collections from Commodore Matthew Perry's Japan Expedition (1853–1854).* Washington, D.C.: Smithsonian Institution Press, 1995.

Howell, David. *Capitalism from Within: Economy, Society and the State in a Japanese Fishery.* Berkeley and Los Angeles: University of California Press, 1995.

Howland, Douglas. *Borders of Chinese Civilization: Geography and History at Empire's End.* Durham, N.C.: Duke University Press, 1996.

———. *Translating the West: Language and Political Reason in Nineteenth-Century Japan.* Honolulu: University of Hawai'i Press, 2001.

Hulbert, Homer. *History of Korea.* Seoul: Methodist Publishing House, 1905.

———. *The Passing of Korea.* New York: Doubleday Page, 1906.

Hull, William Isaac. *The Two Hague Conferences and Their Contributions to International Law.* Boston: Ginn, 1908.

Ienaga Saburo. *The Pacific War, 1931–1945.* New York: Pantheon, 1977.

*Ilbon Oemusong T'uksu Chosa Munso.* Seoul: Koryŏ Sorim, 1989.

Inoue Haruki. *Ryojun Gyakusatsu Jiken.* Tokyo: Chikuma Shobō, 1995.

Inoue Tetsujirō, ed. *Tetsugaku Jii.* Tokyo: n.p., 1881.

Institut Colonial International, ed. *Compte-Rendu de La Session Tenue A La Haye.* Paris: Armand Colin, 1895.

International Law Commission, ed. *International Law on the Eve of the Twenty-First Century: Views From the International Law Commission.* New York: United Nations, 1997.

Iriye, Akira. *China and Japan in a Global Setting.* Cambridge, Mass.: Harvard University Press, 1992.

———. *Cultural Internationalism and World Order.* Baltimore: Johns Hopkins University Press, 1997.

———. *Pacific Estrangement: Japanese and American Expansion, 1897–1911.* Cambridge, Mass.: Harvard University Press, 1972.

Ishii Ryōsuke, ed. *Japanese Legislation in the Meiji Era.* Trans. William J. Chambliss. Tokyo: Pan-Pacific Press, 1958.

Ishiwatari Zensaku. *Sekai Eikyū Heiwaron.* Tokyo: Hakubunken, 1919.

Itō Hirobumi. *Commentaries on the Constitution of the Empire of Japan.* Trans. Itō Miyoji. Tokyo: Igirisu Horitsu Gakko, 1889.

———. *Fuku Meisho.* Tokyo: Gaimushō, 1885.

———. "The Future of Japan—with Special Reference to the Chinese Problem." *Leslie's Monthly Magazine* 58, no. 6 (October 1904).

———. *Marquis Itō's Experience.* Trans. Teizō Kuramata. Nagasaki: Gwaikokugo Kyojusho, 1904.

———. *Report of Count Itō Hirobumi, Ambassador Extraordinary to His Imperial Majesty the Emperor of Japan of His Mission to the Court of China, Eighteenth Year of Meiji Itō Tokuha Zenken Taishi, Fuku Meisho.* Tokyo: Gaimushō, 1885.

Itō Hirobumi and Hiratsuka Atsushi, eds. Hisho Ruisan: *Chōsen Kōshō Shiryō.* Rev. ed. 3 vols. Tokyo: Hara Shobō, 1969.

———. *Hōsei Kankei Shiryo.* Rev. ed. 3 vols. Tokyo: Hara Shobō, 1968.

Itō Hirobumi Kankei Monjo Kenkyūkai, ed. *Itō Hirobumi Kankei Monjo.* Tokyo: Hanawa Shobō, 1974.

Itoya Toshio. *Kanno Suga: Heiminsha no Fujin no Kakumeikashō*. Tokyo: Iwanami Shinsho, 1974.

Japanese Association of the Pacific Northwest, ed. *Japanese Immigration: An Exposition of Its Real Status*. Seattle: Japanese Association of the Northwest, 1907.

JDA, ed. *2001 Defense of Japan: Toward a More Vigorous and Professional SDF in the Twenty-First Century*. Tokyo: Urban Connections/Defense Agency, 2001.

Johnson, Chalmers. *Blowback: The Costs and Consequences of American Empire*. New York: Metropolitan Books, 2000.

Jones, F. C. *Extraterritoriality in Japan and the Diplomatic Relations Resulting in Its Abolition, 1853–1899*. New Haven, Conn.: Yale University Press, 1931.

Joyce, James. *Ulysses*. New York: Vintage, 1986.

Jyosefu Hiko Kinenkai Waseda Daigaku, ed. *Jyosefu Hiko Kaigai Shinbun*. Tokyo: Waseda Daigaku Shuppanbu, 1977.

Kajima Morinosuke. *The Diplomacy of Japan, 1894–1922*. 3 vols. Tokyo: Kajima Institute of International Peace, 1976.

Kaneko Akio et al., eds. *Disukuru no Teikoku: Meiji 30 nendai no Bunka Kenkyu*. Tokyo: Shinyosha, 2000.

Kang, Etsuko Hae-Jin. *Diplomacy and Ideology in Japanese-Korean Relations*. New York: St. Martin's Press, 1997.

Kang, Hildi. *Under the Black Umbrella: Voices from Colonial Korea, 1910–1945*. Ithaca, N.Y.: Cornell University Press, 2001.

Kang Sangjung. *Orientarizumu no Kanata e: Kindai Bunka Hihan*. Tokyo: Iwanami Shoten, 1996.

Kashima Kaima. *Itō Hirobumi wa Naze Korosareta ka*. Tokyo: Sanichi Shinsho, 1995.

Katō Shōichi and Maruyama Masao, eds. *Honyaku no Shisō: Nihon Kindai Shisō Taikei*. Vol. 15. Tokyo: Iwanami Shoten, 1991.

Kawaguchi Hisao. *Bakumatsu/Meiji Kaigai Taiken Shishū*. Tokyo: Daitō Bunka Daigaku Tōyō Kenkyūjo, 1984.

Kawakami Kiyoshi. *Asia at the Door: A Study of the Japanese Question in Continental United States, Hawaii, and Canada*. New York: Fleming H. Revell, 1914.

Kawamura Minato. *Sakubun no Naka no Dai Nippon Teikoku*. Tokyo: Iwanami Shoten, 2000.

Keijō Teikoku Daigaku, ed. *Keijō Teikoku Daigaku*. Seoul: Chōsen Insatsu Kabushikigaisha, 1927.

Keene, Donald. *The Japanese Discovery of Europe, 1720–1830*. Stanford, Calif.: Stanford University Press, 1969.

Kendō Shirosuke. *I Okyu Hishi*. Seoul: Chōsen Shinbunsha, 1926.

Kennan, George. "Korea: A Degenerate State." *The Outlook* (1905).

———. "What Japan Has Done in Korea?" *The Outlook* (1905).

Ketelaar, James Edward. *Of Heretics and Martyrs in Meiji Japan: Buddhism and Its Persecution*. Princeton, N.J.: Princeton University Press, 1990.

Kida Junichirō. *Nihongo Daihaku Butsukan: Akuma no Bunji to Tatakatta Hitobito.* Tokyo: Jyasuto Shisutemu, 1994.

Kikkawa Tsuneo, ed. *Notes des Correspondances avec Monsieur Boissonade.* Tokyo: Hosei University, 1978.

Kim Chŏngmyŏng. *Nikkan Gaikō Shiryō Shusei.* 10 vols. Tokyo: Gannando Shoten, 1962–1967.

Kim Gi'ung, ed. *Kan-Nichi Kōryō Nisennen.* Seoul: Yulhwado, 1984.

Kim, Key-hiuk. *The Last Phase of the East Asian World Order: Korea, Japan, and the Chinese Empire, 1860–1882.* Berkeley and Los Angeles: University of California Press, 1980.

Kim Wonyong. *Chaemi Hanin Osipnyŏnsa.* Reedley, Calif.: Charles Ho Kim, 1959.

Kinefuchi Nobuo. *Fukuzawa Yukichi to Chōsen: Jiji Shinbun Shasetsu o Chūshin shi.* Tokyo: Sairyūsha, 1997.

———. *Kaigai no Shinbun ni Miru Nikkan Heigō.* Tokyo: Sairyūsha, 1995.

Kiyomizu Takashi. "Takagi Masutarō." In *Hōgaku Semina* (November 1972).

Kobori Keiichi. *Sakoku no Shisō.* Tokyo: Chūō Koronsha, 1974.

Kodama Koichi and Kodama Sato. *Meiji no Yokohama: Eigo/Kurisutokyō bungaku.* Tokyo: Kasamon, 1979.

Kojima Kazuhito. *Inō Tadataka.* Tokyo: Sanseidō, 1978.

Kokkai Bangi Chōsakai, ed. *Nihon Gaikō Hakunenshi.* Tokyo: Nihon Kokkai Nenkan Hensatsukai, 1984.

Komori Tokuji. *Akashi Genjirō.* 2 vols. Tokyo: Hara Shobō, 1968.

Kōtoku Shūsui Zenshū Henshū Iinkai. *Kōtoku Shūsui Zenshū.* Tokyo: Meiji Bunken, 1970.

Kuboi Norio. *Zusetsu Chōsen to Nihon no Rekishi: Hikari to Kage.* Tokyo: Akashi Shoten, 1994.

Kuksa P'yŏnch'an Wiwŏnhoe, eds. *Han Minjŏk Tongnip Undongsa Charyojip: Paekoin Sagun.* 2 vols. Seoul: Sisamunhwasa, 1986.

———. *Tongmun Hwigo.* 4 vols. Seoul: Kuksa P'yŏnch'an Wiwŏnhoe, 1978.

Kurakichi Tetsukichi. *Kankoku Heigō no Iki Satsu.* Tokyo: Gaimushō, 1950.

Kuroda Kinichi. *Nihon Shokumin Shisōshi.* Tokyo: Kōbundō, 1942.

Kurokawa Mayori. *Yokobunji Hyakujin Isshū.* Tokyo: Bunnendō, 1873.

Kusano Fumio, ed. *Takushoku Daigaku Hachijūshunenshi.* Tokyo: Takushoku Daigaku Sōritsu Hachijūshūnen Kinen Jigyō Jimukyoku, 1980.

Kuzuo Yoshihisa. *Tōa Senkaku Shishi Kiden.* Tokyo: Kokuryūkai, 1933.

Kyōkasho ni Shinjitsu to Jiyū o Renkokai, ed. *"Kokumin no Rekishi" no Tettei Hihan.* Tokyo: Ōtsuki Shoten, 2000.

Kyōto Daigaku Bungakubu Kokugogaku Kokubungaku Kenkyūshitsu, ed. *Maema Kyosaku Chosakushū.* 2 vols. Kyōto: Kyōto Daigaku Kokubun Gakkai, 1974.

Ladd, George Trumbull. "The Annexation of Korea: An Essay in 'Benevolent Assimilation.'" *Yale Review* 1 (1911–1912).

————. *In Korea with Marquis Itō: A Narrative of Personal Experiences and a Critical Historical Inquiry*. New York: Charles Scribner's Sons, 1908.

Lee, Chong-sik. *Japan and Korea: The Political Dimension*. Stanford, Calif.: Hoover Institution Press, 1985.

Lee, Peter, ed. *Sourcebook of Korean Civilization*. Vol. 2, *From the Seventeenth Century to the Modern Period*. New York: Columbia University Press, 1996.

Lee, Tae-Jin, ed. *Japanese Occupation of the Dae-Han Empire*. Seoul: Kachi, 1995.

Leffler, Melvyn. "The Cold War: What Do 'We Now Know'?" *American Historical Review* 104, no. 2 (1999): 501–524.

Lensen, George Alexander. *The Russian Push toward Japan, 1697–1875*. Princeton, N.J.: Princeton University Press, 1959.

Lew, Young L. "Korean-Japanese Politics behind the Kabo-Ulmi Reform Movement, 1894–1896." *Journal of Korean Studies* 3 (1982): 39–81.

Linenbaugh, Peter, and Michael Rediker. *The Many-Headed Hydra: Sailors, Slaves, Commoners, and the Hidden History of the Revolutionary Atlantic*. Boston: Beacon Press, 2000.

Liu, Lydia. *Translingual Practice: Literature, National Culture, and Translated Modernity: China, 1900–1937*. Stanford, Calif.: Stanford University Press, 1995.

Liu, Lydia, ed. *Tokens of Exchange: The Problem of Translation in Global Circulations*. Durham, N.C.: Duke University Press, 1999.

Lockwood, John. *Topical Brief of Swinton's Outlines of History: A Suggestive Analysis*. New York: Ivison, Blakemore, Taylor, 1877.

Martin, William. *The Awakening of China*. New York: Doubleday, Page, 1907.

————. *A Cycle of Cathay or China, South and North*. New York: Fleming H. Revell, 1897.

Marx, Karl. *Capital: A Critique of Political Economy*. Vol. 1. New York: Penguin, 1990.

Masini, Frederico. *The Formation of a Modern Chinese Lexicon and Its Evolution toward a National Language, 1848–1898*. New York: E. J. Brill, 1996.

Matsuda Hisao. *Ajia no Rekishi*. Tokyo: Iwanami Shoten, 1992.

Matsuo Hiroshi. *Jian Ijihō to Tokkō Keisatsu*. Tokyo: Kyōikusha, 1979.

Matsuo Takamichi, ed. *Yoshino Sakuzoshū, Kindai Nihon Shisō Taikei*. Vol. 17. Tokyo: Chikuma Shobō, 1976.

Matsuo Takamichi et al., eds. *Yoshino Sakuzō Senshū*. Vol. 9. Tokyo: Iwanami Shoten, 1995.

Matsushita Yoshio. *Hansen Undōshi*. Tokyo: Gengensha, 1954.

Matsu'ura Rei. *Meiji no Kaishu to Ajia*. Tokyo: Iwanami Shoten, 1987.

Mayo, Marlene. "The Korean Crisis of 1873 and Early Meiji Foreign Policy." *Journal of Asian Studies* 31, no. 4 (1972): 793–819.

McClain, James, and Osamu Wakita, eds. *Osaka: The Merchants' Capital of Early Modern Japan*. Ithaca, N.Y.: Cornell University Press, 1999.

McClintock, Anne. *Imperial Leather: Race, Gender, and Sexuality in the Colonial Context.* New York: Routledge, 1995.

McKenzie, Frederick Arthur. *Korea's Fight for Freedom.* New York: Fleming Revell, 1920.

———. *The Tragedy of Korea.* London: Hodder and Stoughton, 1908.

———. *The Unveiled East.* New York: E. P. Dutton, 1907.

Meiji Bunken, ed. *Kōtoku Shūsui Zenshū.* Tokyo: Meiji Bunkensha, 1968.

Meiji Kinenkai, ed. *Takushoku Hakurankai.* Tokyo, 1912.

Mérignhac, A. *La Conférence Internationale de la Paix.* Paris: Librairie Nouvelle de Droit et de Jurisprudence, 1900.

Merry, Sally Engle. *Colonizing Hawai'i: The Cultural Power of Law.* Princeton, N.J.: Princeton University Press, 1998.

Mitchell, Timothy. *Colonising Egypt.* New York: Cambridge University Press, 1988.

Miwa Kimitada. *Shiga Shigetaka (1863–1927): A Meiji Japanist's View of Action and International Relations.* Tokyo: Sophia University Press, 1978.

Miyanaga Kiyoshi. *Nihonshi no naka no Furansugo: Bakumatsu Meiji no Nichifu Bunka Kōryū.* Tokyo: Hakusuisha, 2000.

Miyazaki Toten. *My Thirty Years' Dream.* Trans. Etō Shinkichi and Marius Jansen. Princeton, N.J.: Princeton University Press, 1982.

Miyoshi, Masao, and H. D. Harootunian, eds. *Japan in the World.* Durham, N.C.: Duke University Press, 1993.

Momma Takashi. *Ajia Eiga ni Miru Nihon.* Vols. 1 and 2. Tokyo: Shakai Hyōronsha, 1996.

Moon, Hyung June. "The Korean Immigrants in America: The Quest of Identity in the Formative Years, 1903–1918." Ph.D. diss., University of Nevada at Reno, 1976.

Mori Hajime. *Takuboku no Shisō to Eibungaku.* Tokyo: Yōyōsha, 1982.

Moriyama Shigenori. *Kindai Nikkan Kankeishi Kenkyū.* Tokyo: Tokyo Daigaku Shuppankai, 1987.

———. *Nikkan Heigō.* Tokyo: Yoshikawa Kokubunkan, 1992.

Morris-Suzuki, Tessa. "Becoming Japanese: Imperial Expansion and Identity Crises in the Early Twentieth Century." Paper presented at the Annual Meeting of the Association of Asian Studies, Honolulu, 1996.

———. *The Technological Transformation of Japan: From the Seventeenth to the Twenty-First Century.* New York: Cambridge University Press, 1994.

———. *Time, Space, Nation.* Armonk, N.Y.: M. E. Sharpe, 1997.

Müller, Frederich Max. *Lectures on the Science of Language.* London: Longman, Green, Longman, and Roberts, 1861–1864.

Muramatsu Sadataka. *Nitobe Inazō: Sekai Heiwa ni Tsukushita Kyōikusha.* Tokyo: Shueisha, 1998.

Mutsu Munemitsu. *Kenkenroku.* Tokyo: n.p., 1895.

Mutsu Munemitsu. *Kenkenroku: A Diplomatic Record of the Sino-Japanese War, 1894–1895.* Trans. Gordon Mark Berger. Tokyo: University of Tokyo Press, 1982.

Myers, Raymond H., and Mark R. Peattie, eds. *The Japanese Colonial Empire, 1895–1945.* Princeton, N.J.: Princeton University Press, 1984.

Nagamine Hideki. *Yuroppa no Bunmei Gairyaku.* Tokyo: n.p., 1877.

Nagata Akifumi. *Seodoa Ruzuberuto to Kankoku.* Tokyo: Miraisha, 1992.

Nahm, Andrew. *The United States and Korea.* Kalamazoo, Mich.: Center for Korean Studies, Western Michigan University, 1979.

Naikaku Kanpōkyoku. *Hōrei Zensho.* Tokyo: Harushobō, 1974.

Najita, Tetsuo. "Ambiguous Encounters: Ogata Koan and International Studies in Late Tokugawa Osaka." In James McClain and Osamu Wakita, *Osaka: The Merchants' Capital of Early Modern Japan.* Ithaca, N.Y.: Cornell University Press, 1999.

———. *Visions of Virtue in Tokugawa Japan: The Kaitokudo Merchant Academy of Osaka.* Chicago: University of Chicago Press, 1987.

Nakae Chōmin. *Sansuijin Keirin Mondō.* Tokyo: Iwanami Bunko, 1995.

Nakamura, et al. *Kamiyūbetsu Tondenhei Monogatari.* Hokkaido: Kamiyubetsu City Office, 1998.

Nakamura Fumio. *Daigyaku Jiken to Chishikijin.* Tokyo: San'ichi Shobō, 1982.

Nakamura Takafusa. *Shōwashi.* 2 vols. Tokyo: Tōyō Keizai Shinposha, 1995.

Nakanishi Susumu and Yamamoto Shichihei. *Kanji Bunka o Kangaeru.* Tokyo: Daishūkan, 1991.

Nakao Hiroshi. *Chōsen no Tsushinshi no Kiseki.* Tokyo: Meiseki Shoten, 1993.

Nakatsuka Akira. *Kindai Nihon no Chōsen Ninshiki.* Tokyo: Kenbun Shuppan, 1993.

Nambara, Shigeru, ed. *The Works of Inazō Nitobe.* Tokyo: University of Tokyo Press, 1972.

Narita Ryūichi, ed. *Kindai no Bunkashi Kindaishi no Seiritsu 1870–1910 nendai.* Tokyo: Iwanami Shoten, 2001.

Netherlands Ministry of Foreign Affairs. *Conference de la Paix de la Haye 1899.* Amsterdam: n.p., 1899.

Nihon no Sensō Sekinin Shiryō Senta, ed. *Sensō Sekinin Kenkyū.* Tokyo: Nihon no Sensō Sekinin Shiryō Senta, 1993–.

Ninagawa Akira. "Kokusaihōjō ni iwayuru Bunmeikoku to Yabankoku." *Kokusaihō Zasshi* 2, no. 1 (1903).

Nish, Ian. *Japanese Foreign Policy, 1869–1942: Kasumigaseki to Miyakezaka.* London: Routledge and Kegan Paul, 1977.

———. *Japan's Struggle with Internationalism: Japan, China, and the League of Nations, 1931–1933.* London: Kegan Paul, 1993.

———. *The Origins of the Russo-Japanese War.* London and New York: Longman, 1985.

Nishi Amane. "Yōji wo motte Kokugo o Kaku Suru Ron." *Meiroku Zasshi,* no. 1 (1874).

Nishida Kitaro. *Sunshin Nikki.* Tokyo: Kobundo, 1948.

Nishikawa Nagao. *Chikyū Jidai no Minzoku = Bunka Riron: Datsu "Kokumin Bunka" no tame ni.* Tokyo: Shinyōsha, 1995.

Nishio Kanji. *Kokumin no Rekishi.* Tokyo: Sankei Shinbun, 1999.

Nishioka Tsutomu. *Nikkan Gokai no Shin'en.* Tokyo: Aki Shobō, 1992.

Nishiyama Takehiko and I. Tamijun, eds. *Kankoku no Kenchiku to Geijutsu.* Tokyo: Kankoku no Kenchiku to Geijutsu Kenkōkai, 1988.

Nitobe, Inazō. *Bushido: The Soul of Japan.* Philadelphia: Reeds and Biddle, 1900.

———. *The Imperial Agricultural College of Sapporo, Japan.* Sapporo: Imperial Agricultural College, 1893.

———. *The Intercourse between the U.S. and Japan.* Baltimore: Johns Hopkins Press, 1891.

———. "Shokumin Naru Meiji ni Tsukite." *Hōgakkai Zasshi* 29, no. 2 (1911).

Nitobe Inazō Zenshū Henshū Iinkai, eds. *Nitobe Inazō Zenshū.* 22 vols. Tokyo: Kyōbunkan, 1960–1982.

Nitobe Kensuke and Nitobe Akira. *Towadashi, Sanbongihara Kaitaku to Nitobe Sandai no Rekishi Gaidobukku.* Towadashi: Taiso Tokeikai, 1998.

Noda Masa'aki. *Sensō to Zaiseki.* Tokyo: Iwanami Shoten, 1998.

Norman, E. H. "The Genyosha: A Study in the Origins of Japanese Imperialism." *Pacific Affairs* 17, no. 3 (1944): 261–284.

———. *Soldier and Peasant in Japan: The Origins of Conscription.* New York: Institute of Pacific Relations, 1943.

Notehelfer, F. G. *Kōtoku Shūsui: Portrait of a Japanese Radical.* Cambridge: Cambridge University Press, 1971.

Obinata Sumio. *Kindai Nihon no Keisatsu to Chiiki Shakai.* Tokyo: Chikuma Shobō, 2000.

Ōe Shinobu. *Nihon Shokuminchi Tanbō.* Tokyo: Shinyōsenshō, 1999.

Oguma Eiji. *"Nihonjin" no Kyōkai: Okinawa, Ainu, Taiwan, Chōsen Shokuminchi Shihai Kara Fukki Undō Made.* Tokyo: Shinyōsha, 1998.

———. *Tanitsu Minzoku Shinwa no Kigen: Nihonjin Jigazō no Keifu.* Tokyo: Shinyōsha, 1995.

Ōkawa Nobuyoshi. *Dai Saigō Zenshū.* Tokyo: Heibonsha, 1926.

Ōkubo Toshiaki. *Meiji no Shisō to Bunka.* Tokyo: Yoshikawa Kokubunkan, 1988.

———. *Nishi Amane Zenshū.* Vol. 2. Tokyo: Shuko Shobō, 1961.

Ōkubo Toshiaki, ed. *Iwakura Shisetsu no Kenkyū.* Tokyo: n.p., 1976.

Ōkubo Yasuo. "Gustave Boissonade, père français du droit japonais modèrne (1825–1910)." *Revue Historique de Droit Français et Etranger,* series 4 (1981).

———. *Nihon Kindaihō no Chichi—Bowasonado.* Tokyo: Iwanami Shinsho, 1977.

Onojima Sachiko. "Kankoku Heigō ni Kansuru Hitotsu Kōsai: Kankoku Kōtaishi I Un no Nihon Ryūgaku." *Hokudai Shigaku,* no. 28 (1988).

Osatake Takeki. *Ishinshi Gyōsetsu.* Tokyo: Gakushika Shoin, 1935.

———. *Kinsei Nihon no Kokusai Kannen no Hattatsu.* Tokyo: Kyōritsusha, 1932.

———. *Kokusaihō Yori Mitaru Bakumatsu Gaikō Monogatari.* Tokyo: Bunka Seikatsu Kenkyukai, 1926.

———. *Konan Jiken.* Tokyo: Iwanami Shinsho, 1951.

Osiel, Mark. "Ever Again: Legal Remembrance of Administrative Massacre." *University of Pennsylvania Law Review* 144, no. 2 (1995).

Ōta Yuzo. *"Taiheiyō no Hashi" toshite Nitobe Inazō.* Tokyo: Misuzu Shobo, 1986.

Ōtsuki Fumihiko. *Mitsukuri Rinshōkun den.* Tokyo: Maruzen, 1907.

Otsuki Nyoden. *The Infiltration of European Civilization in Japan during the Eighteenth Century* [Shinsen Yōgaku Nenpyō]. Trans. Carel Krieger. Leiden: E. J. Brill, 1940.

Ozawa Tsuyoshi. *Bakumatsu: Shashin no Jidai.* Tokyo: Chikuma Shobō, 1993.

Pai Hyung Il. *Constructing "Korean" Origins: A Critical Review of Archaeology, History, and Racial Myth in Korean State-Formation Theories.* Cambridge, Mass.: Harvard University Press, 2000.

Pak Songsu, ed. *Han'guk Tongnip Undongsa Charyojip: Ŭibyong P'yŏn.* Songnam: Han'guk Chongsin Munhwa Yŏn'guwŏn, 1993.

Pak Yŏngsŏk, ed. *Han Minjok Tongnip Undongsa.* 3 vols. Seoul: P'yŏn'chan Palhaeng, 1987.

Park Young-jae. "Ideology and Action in Mutsu Munemitsu." Ph.D. diss., University of Chicago, 1982.

Patterson, Wayne. *The Korean Frontier in America: Immigration to Hawaii, 1896–1910.* Honolulu: University of Hawai'i Press, 1988.

Perels, F. *Manuel de Droit Maritime Internationale.* Paris: Librairie Guillaumin, 1884.

Peters, Julie, and Andrea Wolper, eds. *Women's Rights, Human Rights: International Feminist Perspectives.* New York: Routledge, 1995.

Pick, Daniel. *Faces of Degeneration: A European Disorder, c. 1848–c. 1918.* New York: Cambridge University Press, 1993.

Porter, Robert P. *The Full Recognition: Being a Detailed Account of the Economic Progress of the Japanese Empire to 1911.* London: Oxford University Press, 1911.

Postone, Moishe. *Time, Labour, and Social Domination: A Reinterpretation of Marx's Critical Theory.* New York: Cambridge University Press, 1993.

Prochaska, David. *Making Algeria French: Colonial Bone.* Chicago: University of Chicago Press, 1990.

*Questions Diplomatiques et Coloniales—Revue de Politique Extérieure.* Paris: n.p., 1895.

Raddeker, Hélène Bowen. "'Death as Life': Political Metaphor in the Testimonial Prison Literature of Kanno Suga." In *Bulletin of Concerned Asian Scholars* 29, no. 4 (October–December 1997).

Rajchman, John. *Constructions.* Cambridge, Mass.: MIT Press, 1998.

Rappaport, Armin. *Henry Stimson and Japan, 1931–1933.* Chicago: University of Chicago Press, 1963.

Reisman, W. Michael, and Chris Antoniou, eds. *The Laws of War: A Comprehensive*

Collection of Primary Documents on International Laws Governing Armed Conflict. New York: Vintage Press, 1994.

Renault, Louis. Cours de Droit International Public 1907–1908. Paris: A. Grujon, 1908.

Resident General of Korea. Annual Report on the Reforms and Progress in Korea, 1907–1910. Seoul: Resident General of Japan, 1908–1910.

Rey, Francis. "La Situation International de la Coreé." Revue Générale de Droit Intenational Public, no. 13. Paris: Paul Fauchille, 1906.

Ri Yoonsuk. "Kokugo" to iu Shisō: Kindai Nihon no Gengo Ninshiki. Tokyo: Iwanami Shoten, 1999.

Rimer, J. Thomas. Culture and Identity: Japanese Intellectuals during the Interwar Years. Princeton, N.J.: Princeton University Press, 1990.

Robin, Ron. Enclaves of America: The Rhetoric of American Political Architecture Abroad, 1900–1965. Princeton, N.J.: Princeton University Press, 1992.

Robinson, Michael. Cultural Nationalism in Korea, 1920–1925. Seattle: University of Washington Press, 1988.

Robinson, Ronald, and John Gallagher. "The Imperialism of Free Trade." Economic History Review, no. 6 (1953).

Rossetti, Carlo. Corea e Coreani, Impressioni e Ricerche Sull' Impero del Gran Han. Bergamo: Instituto Italiano D'Arti Grafiche, 1904.

Saburo Ienaga. The Pacific War, 1931–1945. New York: Pantheon, 1977.

Saeki Shigeto. "Ko Takagi Masutarō." In Gendai Bengoshi Taikan, vol. 1. Tokyo: n.p., 1932.

Said, Edward. Orientalism. New York: Random House, 1978.

Saint-Yves, G. A L'Assaut de L'Asie—La Conquête Européene en Asie. Tours: Maison Alfred Mame et Fils, 1901.

Saitō Tōru. Bakamatsu/Meiji Shokigōi no Kenkyū. Tokyo: Sakurasha, 1986.

Sakanose, et al. Heiwa Kenpō o Mamorihiromeru. Tokyo: Shinkyō Shuppansha, 2001.

Sands, William Franklin. Undiplomatic Memories: At the Court of Korea. London: Century Reprints, 1987.

Saneto Keishu. Kindai Nitchu Kōshōshiwa. Tokyo: Shunshusha, 1973.

Sapporo Kyōiku Iinkai, eds. Nitobe Inazō. Sapporo: Hokkaido Shinbunsha, 1985.

Schmid, Andre. "Constructing Independence: Nation and Identity in Korea, 1895–1910." Ph.D. diss., Columbia University, 1995.

———. Korea between Empires, 1895–1919. New York: Columbia University Press, 2002.

———. "Rediscovering Manchuria: Sin Ch'aeho and the Politics of Territorial History in Korea." Journal of Asian Studies 56, no. 1 (February 1997): 26–47

Schneider, Michael. The Future of the Japanese Colonial Empire, 1914–1931. Ph.D. diss., University of Chicago, 1996.

Schumpeter, Joseph. Imperialism/Social Classes. Trans. Heinz Norden. New York: Meridian, 1955.

Schwab, Raymond. *The Oriental Renaissance*. New York: Columbia University Press, 1986.

Scott, James B. *Domination and the Arts of Resistance: Hidden Transcripts*. New Haven, Conn.: Yale University Press, 1990.

Scott, James Brown. *The Classics of International Law: Elements of International Law by Henry Wheaton (A Literal Reproduction of the 1866 Edition of Richard Henry Dana, Jr., edited by George Grafton Wilson)*. Oxford: Clarendon Press, 1936.

Secretariat of the United Nations. *Treaty Series: Treaties and International Agreements Registered or Filed and Recorded with the Secretariat of the United Nations*. Vol. 583, nos. 8470–8473, n.d.

Shapiro, Ann-Louise. *Breaking the Codes: Female Criminality in Fin-de-Siècle Paris*. Stanford, Calif.: Stanford University Press, 1996.

Shaw, William, ed. *Human Rights in Korea: Historical and Policy Perspectives*. Cambridge, Mass.: Harvard Council on East Asian Studies, 1991.

Shibahara Takuji, Ikai Takaaki, and Ikeda Masahiro, eds. *Taigaikan: Nihon Kindai Shisō Taikei*. Vol. 12, *Nihon Kindai Shisō Taikei*. Tokyo: Iwanami Shoten, 1991.

Shiga Fujiaki, ed. *Shiga Shigetaka Zenshū*. Tokyo: Shiga Shigetaka Zenshū Kenkōkai, 1927.

Shiga Shigetaka. *History of Nations—Specially Adapted for Japanese Students*. Tokyo: Maruzen Shosha, 1888.

Shigeno Yasutsugu. *Bankoku Kōhō*. Kagoshima: n.p., 1869.

———. *Nippon Bushidō*. Tokyo: Daishūdō, 1909.

Shimizu Isao. *Nihon Kindai Manga no Tanjō*. Tokyo: Yamakawa Shuppan, 2001.

Shimizu Unosuke, ed. *Kanno Sugako Zenshū*. 3 vols. Tokyo: Fumiosha, 1984.

Shimizu Yoshiaki. *Japan: The Shaping of Daimyo Culture, 1185–1868*. Washington, D.C.: National Gallery of Art, 1988.

Shin, Gi-Wook, and Michael Robinson, eds. *Colonial Modernity in Korea*. Cambridge, Mass.: Harvard University Press, 1999.

Shin, Michael D. "Conceptions of Korea in *The Independent*." Master's thesis, University of California at Berkeley, 1993.

Shinohara Hatsue. "The Rise of a New International Law in America." *Japanese Journal of American Studies,* no. 5 (1993–1994).

Shiota Shobei, ed. *Zōho Kōtoku Shūsui no Nikki to Shokan*. Tokyo: Miraisha, 1965.

Shiratori Kurakichi. "Ni Kan Ainu Sankokugo no Sūshi ni Tsuite." *Shigaku Zasshi,* nos. 230–232 (1909).

Siegel, James T. *A New Criminal Type in Jakarta: Counter-Revolution Today*. Durham, N.C.: Duke University Press, 1998.

Sievers, Sharon L. *Flowers in Salt: The Beginnings of Feminist Consciousness in Japan*. Stanford, Calif.: Stanford University Press, 1983.

Sin Yongha. *Han'guk Minjok Tongnip Undongsa Yŏn'gu*. Seoul: Ulyoo Munhwasa, 1985.

———. "Hŏ Wi ŭi Ŭibyŏng Undong." *Narasarang* 27 (1977).

Sōgō Masaaki. *Yōgaku no Keifu—Edo kara Meiji e.* Tokyo: Kenkyūsha, 1984.

Sōgō Masaaki and Hida Yoshifumi, eds. *Meiji no Kotoba Jiten.* Tokyo: Tōkyōdō, 1989.

Song, Sang Hyun, ed. *Introduction to the Law and Legal System of Korea.* Seoul: Kyung Mun Sa, 1983.

Son Sungchŭl and Yu Jech'un. *Kunseh Han-Il Oegyo Pisa.* Kangwondo: Kangwŏn Tae-hakkyo, 1988.

Spurr, David. *The Rhetoric of Empire: Colonial Discourse in Journalism, Travel Writing, and Imperial Administration.* Durham, N.C.: Duke University Press, 1993.

Stern, John Peter. *The Japanese Interpretation of the "Law of Nations," 1854–1874.* Princeton, N.J.: Princeton University Press, 1979.

Stocking, George. *Victorian Anthropology.* New York: Free Press, 1987.

Sugimoto Tsutomu. *Edo no Honyakukatachi.* Tokyo: Waseda University Press, 1995.

Stoler, Ann Laura. *Race and the Education of Desire: Foucault's "History of Sexuality" and the Colonial Order of Things.* Durham, N.C.: Duke University Press, 1995.

Suzuki Shuji. *Kango to Nihonjin.* Tokyo: Misuzu Shobo, 1978.

Swinton, William. *Outlines of the World's History, Ancient, Medieval, and Modern— With Special Relation to the History of Civilization and the Progress of Mankind.* New York: Ivison, Blakeman, Taylor, 1874.

Taboulet, George. *La Geste Française en Indochine.* Paris: Librairie d'Amerique et d'Orient, 1956.

Tachi Sakutarō. "Ariga Hakase no Hogokokuron." *Gaikō Jihō,* no. 107 (October 1906): 93–95.

Tachi Sakutarō and Hakaseronkō Iinkai, eds. *Tachi Hakase Gaikōshi Ronbunshū.* Tokyo: Nihon Hyōronshapan, 1946.

Taguchi Ukichi. *Nihon Kaika Kōshi.* Tokyo: n.p., 1874.

Takagi Yasaka. *The Works of Inazō Nitobe.* Tokyo: University of Tokyo Press, 1969.

Takahashi Hidenao. *Nisshin Sensō e no Michi.* Tokyo: Tokyo Sogensha, 1996.

Takahashi Sakuei (Sakuye). *Cases on International Law during the Chino-Japanese War.* Cambridge: Cambridge University Press, 1899.

———. *Heiji Kokusaihōron.* Tokyo: Shinsui Shoten, 1903.

———. *Kokusaihō Gaikōron.* Tokyo: n.p., 1911.

———. *Senji Kokusaihōron.* Tokyo: n.p., 1906.

Takahashi Tetsuya. *Sengo Sekininron.* Tokyo: Kodansha, 1999.

Takaki, Ronald. *Strangers from a Different Shore: A History of Asian Americans.* New York: Penguin Books, 1989.

Takao Hiroshi. *Chōsen Tsūshinshi no Kiseki: Zōho/Zen Kindai no Nihon to Chōsen.* Tokyo: Akashi Shoten, 1993.

Takasaki Jikido, ed. *Higashi Ajia no Bukkyō.* Tokyo: Iwanami Shoten, 1988.

Takasaki Sōji. *"Bōgen" no Genkei.* Tokyo: Mokuseisha, 1996.

Takekuni Tomohiko. *Aru Nikkan Rekishi no Tabi.* Tokyo: Asahi Shinbunsha, 1999.

Taketomi Tomio and Hayashi Eidai. *Ikyo no Yama: Mitsui Sannoko Kyōsei Rōdō no Kiroku*. Fukuoka: Kaijimasha, 2000.

Takeuchi Yoshimi. *Hōhō toshite no Asia: Waga Senzen, Senchu, Sengo 1935–1976*. Tokyo: Sojusha, 1978.

Takeuchi Yoshimi, ed. *Ajia Shugi: Gendai Nihon Shisō Taikei*. Vol. 9. Tokyo: Chikuma Shobō, 1963.

Takushoku Daigaku, eds. *Takushoku Daigaku Yōran*. Tokyo: Takushoku Daigaku, 1919.

Takushoku Daigaku Rokujūnenshi Hensaniinkai, eds. *Takushoku Daigaku Rokujūnenshi*. Tokyo: Takushoku Daigaku, 1960.

Takushoku Daigaku Sōritsu Hachijūshūnen Kinen Jigyō Jimukyoku, eds. *Takushoku Daigaku Hachijūnenshi*. Tokyo: Takushoku Daigaku, 1980.

Tamaki, Norio. *Yukichi Fukuzawa 1835–1901: The Spirit of Enterprise in Modern Japan*. New York: Palgrave, 2001.

Tanaka Shinichi. "Bunka to Keizai." *Hokkaidō Daigaku Keizai Kenkyū* 48, no. 3 (1999).

———. "Hogokoku Mondai: Ariga Nagao/Tachi Sakutarō no Hogokoku Ronsō." *Shaken Kagaku Kenkyū* 28, no. 2 (1976).

———. "Nitobe Inazō to Chōsen." *Kikan Sansenri*, no. 34 (1983).

———. "No no Jikai." *Hokkaidō Daigaku Keizai Kenkyū* 47, no. 4 (1998).

Tanaka Sōgōrō. *Kōtoku Shūsui—Hitotsu Kakumeika no Shisō to Shōgai*. Tokyo: Rironsha, 1955.

———. *Tōyō Shakaitōko*. Tokyo: Ichigensha, 1930.

Tanaka, Stefan. *Japan's Orient, Rendering Pasts into History*. Berkeley: University of California Press, 1993.

Tarui Tōkichi. *Daitō Gappōron*. Reprint ed., includes both 1893 and 1910 versions. Tokyo: Choryo Shorin, 1975.

———. "Mujintō Tansenki." *Ajia Kyōkai Hōkoku*, no. 5 (1883).

Taylor, Katherine Fischer. *In the Theater of Criminal Justice: The Palais de Justice in Second Empire Paris*. Princeton, N.J.: Princeton University Press, 1993.

Taylor, Talbot. *Mutual Misunderstanding: Scepticism and the Theorizing of Language and Interpretation*. Durham, N.C.: Duke University Press, 1992.

*Terauchi Chōsen Sōtokufu Bōsatsu Misui Hikoku Jiken*. 4 vols. Seoul: Koryŏ, 1986.

Terauchi Masatake. "Reforms and Progress in Korea." In Angus Hamilton, Herbert A. Austin, and Masatake Terauchi, eds., *Korea: Its History, Its People, and Its Commerce*. Boston and Tokyo: J. B. Millet, 1910.

Toby, Ronald. *State and Diplomacy in Early Modern Japan: Asia in the Development of the Tokugawa Bakufu*. Stanford, Calif.: Stanford University Press, 1991.

Todorov, Tzvetan. *Les Morales de L'Histoire*. Paris: Hachette, 1991.

Tōkanfu. *Kankoku Heigō Tenmatsusho*. Seoul: Kankoku Tokanfu, 1910.

Tokutomi Kenjirō. *Footprints in the Snow*. Rutland, Vt.: Charles Tuttle and Sons, 1970.

———. *Omoide no Ki*. Tokyo: Minyusha, 1901.

Tōkyō Joshi Daigaku Nitobe Inazō Kenkyūkai, ed. *Nitobe Inazō Kenkyū.* Tokyo: Shun-jyūsha, 1969.

Tōkyō Kokuritsu Hakubutsukan. *Chōsen Tsushinshi: Kinsei 200 nen no Nikan Bunka Kōryū.* Tokyo: Kodansha, 1985.

Tønnesson, Stein, and Hans Antlöv, eds. *Asian Forms of the Nation.* Surrey, UK: Curzon Press, 1996.

Totsuka Etsutarō. "1905 nen 'Kankoku Hogo Jōyaku' no Mukō to Jyūgun Ianfu/Kyōsei Renkō Mondai no Yukue." *Hōgaku Seminaa* 10 (1993).

Towadashi Kyōiku Kenshu Senta, ed. *Nitobe Inazō: Kokoro no Furusato to Towadashi.* Towadashi: Towada Kyōiku Kenshū Senta, 1985.

Tōyō Kyōkai, ed. *Tōyō Kyōkai Chōsabu Gakujutsu Hokoku.* Tokyo: Tōyō Kyōkai, 1909.

Trouillot, Michel-Rolph. *Silencing the Past: Power and the Production of History.* Boston: Beacon Press, 1995.

Tsutsumi Kokushishi. *Bankoku Kōhō Yakugi.* Tokyo: n.p., 1868.

Tyama Seiji. *Nihon Minzokuha no Undō: Minzokuha Bungaku no Keifu.* Tokyo: Kofusha Shoten, 1969.

Tytler, Alexander Fraser. *Universal History from the Creation of the World to the Beginning of the Eighteenth Century.* Boston: Benjamin B. Mussey, 1844.

Uchiyama Nagaichiaki. *Bannen no Inazō.* Morioka: Iwate Nipposha, 1983.

Umemori Naoyuki. "The Discovery of the Productive Body: Studies on the Genealogy of Modern Space and Subjectivity in Tokugawa Japan." Unpublished paper, University of Chicago, 1993.

Umeno Masanobu and Sawada Tatsuo, eds. *Sensōron/Bōsōron.* Tokyo: Kyōiku Shiryō Shuppankai, 1999.

United States Naval War College. *International Law Situations with Solutions and Notes.* Washington, D.C.: Government Printing Office, 1902–1908.

Unno Fukuju. *Kankoku Heigō.* Tokyo: Iwanami Shinsho, 1995.

Unno Fukuju, ed. *Nikkan Kyōyaku to Kankoku Heigō: Chōsen Shokuminchi Shihai no Gōhōsei o Tomonau.* Tokyo: Akashi Shoten, 1995.

Utsumi Akio, ed. *Shikeidai kara Mieta Futatsu no Kuni: Kankoku/Chōsenjin BC kyū Senzai no Shōgen; Mun Taebok, Hon Chanmuk.* Tokyo: Nashi no Kisha, 1992.

Utsumi Aiko and Takahashi Tetsuya, eds. *Senban Saiban to Seibōryoku.* Tokyo: Rokufu Shuppan, 2000.

Van Wolferen, Karl. *The Enigma of Japanese Power: People and Politics in a Stateless Nation.* New York: Vintage, 1990.

Viola, Herman J. *Diplomats in Buckskins: A History of Indian Delegations in Washington City.* Bluffton, S.C.: Rivilo Books, 1995.

Virgin, Louise. *Japan at the Dawn of the Modern Age: Woodblock Prints from the Meiji Era, 1868–1912.* Boston: MFA Publications, 2001.

Virilio, Paul. *War and Cinema: The Logistics of Perception.* New York: Verso, 1992.

Vlastos, Steven, ed. *Mirrors of Modernity: Invented Traditions of Modern Japan.* Berkeley and Los Angeles: University of California Press, 1998.

Vogel, Ezra. *Japan as Number One: Lessons for America.* New York: Harper and Row, 1979.

Volosinov, Valentin. *Marxism and the Philosophy of Language.* Trans. Ladislav Matejka and I. R. Titunik. Cambridge, Mass.: Harvard University Press, 1986.

Wada Haruki. *Hoppō Ryōchi Mondai: Rekishi to Mirai.* Tokyo: Asahi Shinbunsha, 1999.

———. "Nikkan Jōyaku o Kangaeru." *Seikyu* 16 (1993).

Wada Haruki and Ishizaka Koichi. *Nihon wa Shokuminchi Shihai o dō Kangaete Kitaka.* Tokyo: Nashi no Kisha, 1996.

Walker, Brett. *The Conquest of Ainu Lands: Ecology and Culture in Japanese Expansion, 1590–1800.* Berkeley and Los Angeles: University of California Press, 2001.

———. "Reappraising the *Sakoku* Paradigm: The Ezo Trade and the Extension of Tokugawa Political Space Into Hokkaido." *Journal of Asian History* 30, no. 2 (1996).

Waquet, Françoise. *Le Latin ou L'Empire d'Un Signe, XVIe–XXx Siecle.* Paris: Albin Michel, 1998.

Watanabe Ichirō. *Inō Tadataka Aruita Nihon.* Tokyo: Chikuma Shinsho, 1999.

Watanabe Ichirō, ed. *Tadataka to Inōzu.* Tokyo: Gendai Shokan, 1998.

Watanabe Kogorō. *Yōgaku Jishi.* Tokyo: Bunka Shobō Hakabunsha, 1993.

Wheaton, Henry. *Elements of International Law: With a Sketch of the History of the Science.* Philadelphia: n.p., 1836.

Wigmore, John Henry, ed. *Law and Justice in Tokugawa Japan.* Vols. 1–10. Tokyo: University of Tokyo Press, 1969.

Wilson, George Grafton, ed. *Henry Wheaton, Elements of International Law.* New York: Carnegie Endowment for International Peace, 1936.

Winbush, Raymond A., ed. *Should America Pay? Slavery and the Raging Debate on Reparations.* New York: Amistad Books, 2003.

Wolfe, Patrick. "History and Imperialism: A Century of Theory, from Marx to Postcolonialism." *American Historical Review* 102, no. 2 (1997): 388–420.

Wright, Gwendolyn. *The Politics of Design in French Colonial Urbanism.* Chicago: University of Chicago Press, 1991.

Yamabe Kentarō. *Nikkan Heigō Kōshi.* Tokyo: Iwanami Shinsho, 1995.

Yamada Akira, ed. *Gaikō Shiryō: Kindai Nihon no Bōchō to Shinryaku.* Tokyo: Shin Nihon Shuppansha, 1997.

Yamamoto Shirō, ed. *Terauchi Masatake Nikki, 1900–1918.* Kyoto: Dōmeisha, 1970.

Yamamoto Taketoshi. *"Yorozu Chōhō" no Hatten to Suitai.* Tokyo: Nihon Tosho Senta, 1984.

Yamamuro Shin'ichi. *Shisō Kadai Toshite no Ajia.* Tokyo: Iwanami Shoten, 2001.

Yanabu Akira. *Honyakugo Seiritsu Jijō.* Tokyo: Iwanami Shinsho, 1995.

———. *Honyaku no Shisō: Shizen to NATURE.* Tokyo: Chikuma Gakuei Bunko, 1995.

Yasuda Toshiaki. *"Kokugo" to "Hōgen" no Aida Gengo Kochiku no Seijigaku.* Tokyo: Jinbun Shoin, 1999.

———. *Shokuminchi no naka no Gengogaku.* Tokyo: Sangensha, 1997.

———. *Teikoku Nihon no Gengo Hensei.* Yokohama: Yoshoku Shobo, 1997.

Yasuoka Akio. *Nihon Kindaishi.* Tokyo: Geirin Shobō, 1996.

Yi Kyuhoon, ed. *Sajin u ro Ponun Dongnip Undong.* Vol. 1. Seoul: Sumundang, 1992.

Yoshida Yoshishige, ed. *Eiga Denrai: Shinematogurafu to "Meiji no Nihon."* Tokyo: Iwanami Shoten, 1995.

Yoshie Akio, Yamauchi Masayuki, and Motomura Ryōji, eds. *Rekishi no Bunpō.* Tokyo: University of Tokyo Press, 1997.

Yoshimi Shunya. *Hakurankai no Seijigaku: Manazashi no Kindai.* Tokyo: Chūō Koron, 1992.

Yoshimi Yoshiaki, ed., *Jūgun Ianfu Shiryōshu.* Tokyo: Ōtsuki Shoten, 1992.

Yoshioka Yoshinori. *Nihon no Shinryaku to Bōchō.* Tokyo: Shin Nihon Shuppansha, 1995.

Young, Louise. *Japan's Total Empire: Manchuria and the Culture of Wartime Imperialism.* Berkeley and Los Angeles: University of California Press, 1998.

Young, Marilyn. *Rhetoric of Empire: American China Policy, 1895–1901.* Cambridge, Mass.: Harvard University Press.

Young, Robert. *Colonial Desire: Hybridity in Theory, Culture, and Race.* London: Routledge, 1995.

Yūhō Kyōkai, ed. *Nihon Tōjika no Chōsen ni okeru Chōsengō Kyōiku.* Tokyo: Yūhō Kyōkai, 1966.

Yun Gyöng'no. "105." In *Sagun khwa Sinminhoe Yŏn'gu.* Seoul: Ilsasa, 1990.

Yuza Shōgo and Kondō Norihiko. *Ishikawa Takuboku Nyūmon.* Kyoto: Shibunkaku Shuppan, 1992.

# Index

# Studies of the Weatherhead East Asian Institute, Columbia University

## SELECTED TITLES

*Divorce in Japan: Family, Gender, and the State, 1600–2000*, by Harald Fuess. Stanford, Calif.: Stanford University Press, 2004

*The Communist Takeover of Hangzhou: The Transformation of City and Cadre, 1949–1954*, by James Gao. Honolulu: University of Hawai'i Press, 2004

*Gutenberg in Shanghai: Chinese Print Capitalism, 1876–1937*, by Christopher A. Reed. Vancouver: University of British Columbia Press, 2004

*The North Korean Revolution: 1945–1950*, by Charles Armstrong. Ithaca, N.Y.: Cornell University Press, 2002

*Taxation without Representation in Rural China*, by Thomas P. Bernstein and Xiaobo Lü. Modern China Series, Cambridge: Cambridge University Press, 2003

*Korea Between Empires, 1895–1919*, by Andre Schmid. New York: Columbia University Press, 2002

*Limits to Power: Asymmetric Dependence and Japan's Foreign Aid*, by Akitoshi Miyashita. Lanham, MD: Lexington Books, 2003

*The Dawn that Never Comes: Shimazaki Toson and Japanese Nationalism*, by Michael Bourdaghs. New York: Columbia University Press, 2003

*Spanning Japan's Modern Century: The Memoirs of Hugh Borton*, by Hugh Borton. Lanham, MD: Lexington Books, Inc., 2002

*Consumer Politics in Postwar Japan: Institutional Boundaries of Citizen Activism*, by Patricia Maclachlan. New York: Columbia University Press, 2001

*Abortion before Birth Control: The Politics of Reproduction in Postwar Japan*, by Tiana Norgren. Princeton, N.J.: Princeton University Press, 2001

*Japan's Imperial Diplomacy: Consuls, Treaty Ports, and War in China, 1895–1938*, by Barbara Brooks. Honolulu: University of Hawai'i Press, 2000

*Japan's Budget Politics: Balancing Domestic and International Interests,* by Takaaki Suzuki. Boulder, CO: Lynne Rienner Publishers, 2000

*Assembled in Japan: Electrical Goods and the Making of the Japanese Consumer,* by Simon Partner. Berkeley: University of California Press, 1999

*Civilization and Monsters: Spirits of Modernity in Meiji Japan,* by Gerald Figal. Durham, N.C.: Duke University Press, 1999

*The Logic of Japanese Politics: Leaders, Institutions, and the Limits of Change,* by Gerald L. Curtis. New York: Columbia University Press, 1999.

*Trans-Pacific Racisms and the U.S. Occupation of Japan,* by Yukiko Koshiro. New York: Columbia University Press, 1999

*Bicycle Citizens: The Political World of the Japanese Housewife,* by Robin LeBlanc. Berkeley: University of California Press, 1999

*Alignment despite Antagonism: The United States, Japan, and Korea,* by Victor Cha. Stanford, Calif.: Stanford University Press, 1999

*Chaos and Order in the Works of Natsume Sōseki,* by Angela Yiu. Honolulu: University of Hawai'i Press, 1998

# About the Author

Alexis Dudden received her B.A. in East Asian Studies from Columbia University and holds a master's and doctorate in history from the University of Chicago. She has studied at Rikkyo University and Keio University in Tokyo and Yonsei University in Seoul. She is currently Sue and Eugene Mercy Assistant Professor of History at Connecticut College.

**PRODUCTION NOTES**

Dudden  Japan's Colonization of Korea

Interior design by the University of Hawai'i Press Design &
Production Department

Cover design by Adrianne Onderdonk Dudden

Composition by Josie Herr
Text set in Minion with display in Gill Sans

Printing and binding by The Maple-Vail Book Manufacturing Group
Printed on 60# Sebago Eggshell